WHAT THE CRITICS SAY

"A hallelujah of a book... that leaves you searching for superlatives."
— *Books in Canada*

"A masterly performance... that deserves to be read by anyone interested in North American history."   — *Jazz Journal* (UK)

"An amazingly comprehensive and highly readable portrait of the Montreal jazz community as it struggled to survive and nourish itself as part of the city's nightlife subculture.... Essential reading."   — *University of Toronto Quarterly*

"This impressive work is a resource of the utmost importance for understanding what led up to one of the greatest of all summer jazz events, the Montreal International Jazz Festival."   — *Jazz Hot* (France)

"It is not only jazz enthusiasts who should read this book for it makes an important contribution to the social history of Montreal, providing new perspectives on, for example, the history of the city's black community [and] Mayor Drapeau's campaign against organized crime and vice.... A particularly gripping chapter on free jazz enriches our understanding of the turbulent political agitation of the sixties and seventies."   — *Centre for Quebec Studies, University of Leicester* (UK)

"The tale is so rich and varied that most readers will quickly find themselves pulled in by the narrative flow.... [The book] might serve as a model for future books about the jazz history of other cities."   — *Cadence* (USA)

"Gilmore shows a genuine love and respect for the music and its creators, but he is also a disciplined researcher who doesn't let enthusiasm interfere with honest, balanced portrayals."   — *Ottawa Citizen*

"Essential reading for anyone interested in music in general and in Montreal in particular."   — *La Presse* (Montreal)

"Club Marc
Oct 6

SWINGING IN PARADISE

THE STORY OF JAZZ IN MONTREAL

JOHN GILMORE

Ellipse Editions

ELLIPSE EDITIONS

First published in Montreal in 1988 by Véhicule Press.
Second printing 1989 Véhicule Press.
Second edition 2011 Ellipse Editions.

Ellipse Editions is an imprint of John Gilmore.

Original 1988 cover and title page design by JW Stewart, used with the permission of
Véhicule Press.

Legal deposit: Library and Archives Canada, and Bibliothèque et Archives nationales du
Québec, 2011.

ISBN: 978-0-9867866-0-0

Research for this book, and its first publication, were funded in part by The Canada
Council for the Arts.

A French translation of this book, *Une histoire du jazz à Montréal*, is published by Lux
Éditeur, Montreal. www.luxediteur.com

Library and Archives Canada Cataloguing in Publication

Gilmore, John, 1951-
    Swinging in paradise : the story of jazz
in Montréal / John Gilmore. -- 2nd ed.

Includes bibliographical references and index.
ISBN 978-0-9867866-0-0

    1. Jazz music–Quebec (Province)–Montréal–History
and criticism. I. Title.

ML3509.C3G48 2011   781.6509714'28   C2011-900015-6

To Harry Stafford

... the delicious past shines through the somber present
— Charles Baudelaire

CONTENTS

ACKNOWLEDGEMENTS

This book could never have been completed without the encouragement, cooperation, and assistance of a great many individuals, organizations, and institutions to whom I am deeply grateful.

Andrew Homzy nurtured my interest in jazz history during the years I studied under him at Concordia University. He introduced me to Herb Johnson, who graciously welcomed me into his home and confidence and filled my head with vivid accounts of his long career in music. It was during the course of many hours of conversation with Mr. Johnson that I first appreciated the richness and scope of Montreal's jazz history. Josh Freed suggested writing a book on the subject. Simon Dardick of Véhicule Press, Andrew Homzy, and Suzanne Perron were quick to support the project, and the Canada Council helped fund a major portion of the research through a grant under its Explorations program.

Countless musicians and their relatives and friends gave freely of their time and memories in interviews and telephone conversations, in correspondence, and in detailed responses to written questionnaires. Many of these people allowed me to borrow and reproduce photographs and other memorabilia from their private collections, and some of these documents are reproduced here. Though the musicians have been the primary source for this book, they are too many to thank here individually. Those whose careers fall within the boundaries I have drawn for this history are documented in *Who's Who of Jazz in Montreal*, a companion reference volume, and I trust they will accept mention in that book, and this work as a whole, as an expression of my deep appreciation for their assistance, confidence, and hospitality. The faith and interest expressed on many occasions by Mark "Wilkie" Wilkinson has been especially encouraging. I also benefitted from interviews with musicians whose careers fall outside the scope of the companion volume, including: Raoul Duguay, Larry Edwards (Victoria), Tristan Honsinger (Italy), Mathieu Léger, and Bill Middell.

Special recognition is due the late Alex Robertson, a researcher and collector who lived in Pointe Claire, Quebec. Over a period of almost five years, Mr. Robertson sent me a steady stream of notes garnered from his painstaking, methodical scanning of microfilms of English Montreal newspapers from the early years of jazz. His research turned up advertisements and occasional reports documenting the first appearances in Montreal of American jazz musicians, black vaudeville performers, and "hot" dance bands; names and engagements of early Montreal musicians and bands; and locations of nightclubs. As well, he tirelessly gave of his time to help interpret the documentation we uncovered; to track down elusive facts on early jazz in reference books; and to provide information from his independent discographical research. It is no exaggeration to say that the fabric of the first two chapters of this book would be significantly thinner, and many important details would never have come to light, had it not been for Mr. Robertson's diligence and generosity.

Little informed writing on jazz has been published in Canada. I extracted many important facts from Len Dobbin's detailed columns in *Coda* and benefited from numerous conversations with him. As well, I freely mined two pioneering works of Canadian jazz scholarship: Jack Litchfield's *The Canadian Jazz Discography: 1916-1980*, and Mark Miller's *Jazz in Canada: Fourteen Lives*. Both authors provided helpful supplementary information, contacts, and insight, and Mr. Litchfield played recordings from his private collection for me. The *Encyclopedia of Music in Canada*, edited by Helmut Kallmann, Gilles Potvin, and Kenneth Winters, was a valuable source of information and background. Among the many foreign books on jazz which I have consulted, two stand out for the freshness of their thinking: James Lincoln Collier's *The Making of Jazz: A Comprehensive History*, and Leroy Ostransky's *Jazz City: The Impact of Our Cities on the Development of Jazz*; the latter, in particular, stimulated me to examine the social and political context in which jazz has been made in Montreal.

Countless other people provided information, background, contacts, guidance, or help. They include: Carlton Baird; Rita Beauséjour-Griffith and Claude Landry, Musicians' Guild of Montreal; Diana Beldham (Hamilton, Ont.); Eve Berliner; James Betts (Toronto); Dr. Maurice Bourne; John Bradley; Ross Brethour (Aurora, Ont.); Pierre Brousseau; Vivian Robbins Chavis (North Buxton, Ont.); John Chilton (England); Thryphenia Collins; George Cottle; Peter Danson; Mary Ellen Davis; Graeme Decarie; Roy Dohn; Francine Drouin, Protestant School Board of Greater Montreal; Yvon Dufresne; Isabel Duncan; Francine Dupuis; Yvan Ethier; Bill Falconer; Tom Ford; Louise Forestier; Morris Garber (Bayside, N.Y.); Arnold Gibb; Paul Grosney (Toronto); Marie-Claude Hansenne; Thomas Hardie; Karl Gert zur Heide (West Germany); Sharon Henstridge (Toronto); Lou Hooper, Jr.; Margaret Hooper; Tessy Hubbard; Emmie "Jackie" Jackson; Carl Johnson, Associate Curator, The

Whiteman Collection, Williams College, Williamstown, Mass.; Bert Joss; Frank Kappler; Jocelyne Kéroack; Jim Kidd (Toronto); Irving Kravitz; Henry J. Langdon; Tex Lecor; Gene Lees (Ojai, Calif.); Suzanne Léonard; Ruby Leslie; Jacques Levier; Nathan Levine; Ginette Lycke; John Lymberger; Daniel J. McConville (New York City); Nancy Marrelli and Josée Martel, Concordia University Archives; Eddie Miller; Walter de Mohrenschildt; Wally Newman; Jim Nichols; Rod North (St. Catherines, Ont.); Gene De Novi (Toronto); May Oliver; Adrien Paradis, Jr.; Judith Penn; J. Lyman Potts (Toronto); Pat Reardon; Jeanne L. Roberts (Detroit); Kenny Rockhead; Willa Rouder (New York City); Dianne Rudd (Vanier, Ont.); Jack Sadler; Evelyn Sealey; Marguerite Sealey (Brantford, Ont.); Winnie Sealey; Cécile Sherer; Joe Showler (Toronto); Alan Stevens (England); Daisy Peterson Sweeney; Ron Sweetman (Ottawa); Mae Sutton (Niagara Falls, Ont.); Florence Thomas; Marie Thomas; Millard J. Thomas (New York City); Stanley Thomas.

I also received documents, information, and services from: Bibliothèque nationale du Québec; Canadian Pacific Corporate Archives and Library; La Cinémathèque québécoise; Concordia University Library; Gazette library; Lachine City Library and Museum; McGill University Library; Montreal City Library; National Film Board Archives; National Library of Canada (Ottawa); Notman Photographic Archives; La Presse library; and Public Archives Canada (Ottawa).

A dozen people read all or some of the manuscript in earlier drafts and provided helpful comments, suggestions, and clarifications: Josh Freed; Judy Herault, Johnny Holmes; Stephen Homer; Andrew Homzy; Jim Kidd; Gene Lees; Jack Litchfield; Irving Lustigman; Jack Rider; Alex Robertson; and Brian Young. Scott Mitchell's editing and suggestions enhanced the final manuscript.

Finally, I will not attempt the impossible task of thanking individually and adequately the many people whose interest, encouragement, and personal support helped sustain me through this work. Among them are my family and closest friends, to whom I owe a special thanks. An extra measure of gratitude is warmly given to my mother, Grace Gilmore.

PREFACE

For almost half a century, more jazz was made in Montreal than any-where else in Canada. This book is both a portrait of that creative era and an attempt to explain its birth, vitality, and demise. Musicians who play jazz have been strongly individualistic by nature, but they have traditionally made their music in groups and among their peers. The history of jazz is both the history of individuals and the history of communities. In Montreal, the making of jazz has been profoundly influenced by political, social, and economic factors, many of them unique to the city and to the predominantly francophone province of Quebec in which it is situated. An awareness of these social conditions can deepen our understanding of the city's jazz history and enhance our appreciation of individual accomplishment. Accordingly, this book is as much about the social environment in which musicians lived, worked, and created—about how they were affected by it and how they felt about it—as it is about the lives and the music of individual musicians.

The story begins with the first strains of black music in Montreal; it ends with the first experiments in freeing up jazz and fusing it with other musics. Between, we watch a jazz community form, grow, thrive, and then disintegrate. A common theme links each stage in the life of this community: the need to work. Jazz has rarely enjoyed the government subsidy and private sponsorship which have nurtured other performing arts; instead, it has been left to fend for itself in the entertainment marketplace. As a result, professional musicians have had to concern themselves first with earning a living, and only later with creating jazz. It is no accident that the cities which have historically been centres of intense jazz activity have been those cities in which large numbers of musicians could find steady work. Montreal was no exception. The stability, spirit, and creative output of the city's jazz community during the era documented in this book were directly linked to the capacity of the city's entertainment industry to provide steady employment for musicians.

The musicians whose lives are chronicled in this book were rarely employed to play jazz. They worked, for the most part, at entertaining people with popular music in vaudeville theatres, dance halls, and nightclubs. They made their best jazz on their own time, out of the spotlight and largely ignored by society. For as long as Montreal provided work, the musicians stayed, interacted, and created. When work dwindled, the musicians dispersed—some to the television and recording studios, some to other trades or other kinds of music, and some to settle in other cities. In this way, and for reasons which had as much to do with changes in society as in music, an era of intense jazz activity in Montreal came to a bitter close. Even as this was happening, a younger generation was opening new doors for jazz with musical and social experiments which broke radically with the traditions of the stricken community.

I have pieced together Montreal's jazz history principally from the memories of the musicians who made it. Unless otherwise noted, all of the direct quotations in this book are from interviews I conducted from 1981 to 1986. Where possible I have checked the musicians' memories against one another and supplemented and corroborated their oral accounts with written and photographic documentation. However, before Len Dobbin began writing detailed reports on the Montreal jazz scene for the Toronto-based *Coda* magazine in 1959, there was no chronicler of the city's jazz community; press coverage was sporadic and often poorly informed. To complicate matters, Montreal newspapers prior to 1966 have not been indexed, making a systematic search for accounts of jazz and nightlife in the city practically impossible. I have, therefore, drawn most of my written sources on Montreal jazz prior to 1959 from clippings, contracts, correspondence, and other memorabilia found in musicians' scrapbooks. For the social and political history of the city and province, and for developments in jazz beyond Montreal, I have relied on published sources. I did not witness any of the events described in this book.

Writing history, in particular the history of a marginal community, is as much an act of imagination as it is an act of scholarship. Where reliable written documents are few and memories are coaxed from years of seclusion, the boundary between history and legend blurs. Much of jazz history may never attain the status of undisputed fact. This is particularly true in Canada where researchers have started late in tapping original oral sources, where the press had done such a lamentable job of reporting and criticizing jazz, and where the music itself has been only sporadically recorded. Tragically, many important sources and documents of early Canadian jazz have already been lost. I have rescued what I could in the course of my research, but readers ought to keep in mind that the history I have written has to some extent been determined by who was alive to talk to me, and the availability of documentation.

Writing history is also a process of selection and omission. The musicians I have chosen to write about and quote are representative, I feel, of significant developments, activities, and experiences in the history of the Montreal jazz community. My judgement in these matters has been influenced by the opinions of their peers and, unavoidably, by the availability of both the musicians themselves and reliable information about them. I have also felt a responsibility to bring to public attention musicians whose lives and contributions have hitherto gone largely unrecognized. For these reasons I have devoted less space to the three most famous jazz musicians Montreal has produced—Paul Bley, Maynard Ferguson, and Oscar Peterson—than to other, lesser-known figures. The careers of Bley, Ferguson, and Peterson have already been widely written about and will, it is hoped, be the subject of further, in-depth study. My concern in this book has been to place these musicians in the broader context of the history of Montreal's jazz community. I have also devoted less attention than they merit to Brian Barley, Wray Downes, Sonny Greenwich, Guy Nadon, Claude Ranger, Herbie Spanier, and Nelson Symonds; their careers have been well documented in Mark Miller's commendable book *Jazz in Canada: Fourteen Lives*. Clearly, then, the space devoted to musicians is not a reflection on the relative merits of their musicianship.

As the broad outline of Montreal's jazz history became apparent to me during the early stages of my research, I elected to focus on the lives and activities of professional, instrumental musicians who worked mainly before the public. I have, with only a few exceptions, excluded amateur and semiprofessional musicians, not because some among them were not capable of making good jazz, but because their part-time commitment to music and their economic independence of the entertainment industry distanced them from the jazz community and its concerns. I have completely excluded singers. Despite their intimate working relationship with musicians and their frequent use of jazz-style phrasing and techniques, few, if any, Montreal singers during the period under study regarded themselves as jazz musicians, participated in jam sessions, or improvised at any length. As well I have not emphasized the activities of musicians in Montreal's radio, television, and recording studios. The studios provided steady employment for jazz musicians relatively late in this story, and then only to select members of the community. The bands that made jazz in the studios rarely performed in public, and the circumstances under which studio musicians worked bore little resemblance to the world of the larger, nightclub-based jazz community. Accordingly I have treated the advent of the studio musician and studio jazz not as an integral part of Montreal's jazz history but as both a symptom of, and a factor in, the fragmentation of jazz in Montreal. Each of these subjects—nonprofessional musicians (particularly during the big-band era), singers, and studio jazz—merits further study in its own right, and no slight is intended against any individual by the boundaries I have drawn for this book.

I have also largely ignored the jazz made in Montreal by nonresident musicians. Leading jazz musicians and bands from the United States performed regularly in Montreal, in theatres and concert venues for the most part, but eventually in a few clubs. In relegating their work to the background I am not suggesting it was without value or significance; on the contrary, their music and presence was a source of continual inspiration to resident musicians. However, these visitors rarely stayed in the city more than a few days at a time, and their story is not the history of Montreal's jazz community.

Finally, while I listened to numerous recordings of Montreal musicians in the course of my research, I have not discussed recorded music here in any detail. I am concerned with the broad strokes of a community's history and the context in which jazz was made, not with analysis of the styles of individual musicians. Montreal's legacy of recorded jazz is inconsistent and misleading, and any attempt to allocate places in history on the basis of recorded output would be naive. Some of the city's pivotal musicians and bands were simply never recorded; others were recorded in groupings or under circumstances which did no justice to their skill or reputation. Thus, Montreal's legacy of recordings tell us less about the jazz made in the city than about the values of the society in which it was being made, and about the tastes, ambitions, and prejudices of those who controlled the means of recording. I have heard no evidence to suggest that any of the records made by Montrealers during the period under study—with the possible exception of the records of Willie Eckstein and Oscar Peterson—had a significant impact upon other professional musicians in the city, or upon the jazz community as a whole. An analysis of the music on some of these records would make a fascinating study, but that, too, is beyond the scope of this book.

What remains is a survey of the history of jazz in Montreal in its social context: how the musicians lived and worked; why they came and went; where and how they created; and how their lives and their music were affected by politics, corruption and organized crime, union battles, racism, and changes in social mores and tastes. I hope I have demonstrated that jazz is not made in isolation and that individual endeavor is shaped and tempered by social environment. The history of jazz in Montreal is pitted with frustration, wasted talent, and tragedy—but it is also brimming with humanity, idealism, and plain hard work. That jazz has survived decades of ignorance and exploitation in North America should be cause for reflection; that musicians in cities such as Montreal have created such life-affirming and expressive music in spite of the obstacles that have been placed in their path should be cause for celebration. This book is one man's toast to a great tradition.

John Gilmore
Montreal, 1987

CHAPTER ONE

Pre-History to 1925

In the autumn of 1916, while troop trains loaded in Montreal for the war in Europe, a shy, bespectacled, twenty-six-year-old Englishman shook hands with his mentor and boarded a Pullman car warming at Windsor station. His destination: Chicago; his destiny: Canadian recording history.

Reginald Thomas Broughton was a professional piano player, though he could scarcely read a note of music. His mentor and musical idol was Willie Eckstein,[1] a classically trained pianist less than two years Broughton's senior who was being touted by his employers at Montreal's Strand theatre as "The World's Foremost Motion Picture Interpreter." It was an opinion shared by enthusiastic Montreal audiences: they had been flocking to the St. Catherine Street theatre for some four years to hear the diminutive and exuberant pianist perform—even when the films themselves were hardly worth the price of admission. When Eckstein took a day off, it was his protégé Broughton who, sporting the stage name Harry Thomas, slipped behind the piano and attempted to disguise the master's absence.

The two men, though dissimilar in temperament and musical training, shared a fondness for two pleasures—liquor and improvisation. Both pianists could spontaneously weave snippets of melody from popular songs and classical masterpieces into an engaging and often humourous musical commentary on the events silently unfolding on the theatre screen. They also shared a fondness for a challenging style of solo piano playing known as ragtime, which had swept North America and Europe a couple of decades earlier after emerging from the pens of formally trained black pianists in the southern and midwestern United States. Together, the pair had composed two rags of their own, titling them "Delirious Rag" and "Perpetual Rag." Eckstein had written them down; Thomas had committed their precise syncopations and complex melodic lines to memory. Now the protégé was setting off for Chicago, probably with no more than a youthful desire to seek his fortune south of the border; perhaps, but only remotely so, with a letter of invitation from a manufacturer of piano rolls.

The circumstances surrounding Thomas's journey are probably lost to history forever, like so much of the fabric of North America's popular music history. All we know for certain is that a few months later the Q.R.S. Company sent out to music stores its piano roll issue of "Honolulu, America Loves You," a pop song which Thomas had recorded directly onto a master paper roll at the company's studio in Chicago that autumn of 1916. The melody was easily recognizable, but Thomas had coloured the music with ragtime and embellished the performance with improvised passages which were all his own.

A few weeks later he was in New York City, where he recorded "Delirious Rag" and "Perpetual Rag" onto piano rolls for Metro-Art and Universal. He made the four-hundred-kilometre overnight train journey from Montreal to New York at least once more before the year was over, to cut his first gramophone record for the Victor Talking Machine Company. One side of the heavy, brittle 78 r.p.m. disc featured "Delirious Rag." For the other side, Thomas concocted "A Classical Spasm," a ragtime interpretation of melodies by two Polish composers, one of them the widely loved Ignace Jan Paderewski.

If Thomas was pleased with his journeys to the United States and the approximately fifteen minutes of issued recordings that resulted,[2] he was probably unaware of their historical significance. Though Thomas was a white musician who didn't play anything that we would comfortably call jazz more than seventy years later, he was nevertheless the first musician living in Canada to record music played in a style which had

(left) Harry Thomas's solo recording of "Delirious Rag," recorded at Victor's studio in New York City in 1916. Victor issued the record in the United States, but, as this label shows, the record was also manufactured in Montreal by the Berliner Gramophone Company for sale across Canada. *Courtesy of Jack Litchfield. John Gilmore Jazz History Collection, Concordia University Archives.*
(right) Harry Thomas. *Alex Robertson Collection, Concordia University Archives.*

been created by black Americans. This was ragtime, a direct predecessor of jazz.[3] Nor could Thomas have known that less than three months after he recorded for Victor, five young white musicians from New Orleans would walk into the same company's studio in New York City and turn the world upside down with a record of their own.

The Original Dixieland Jazz Band (ODJB) arrived in New York City just weeks after Thomas returned to Montreal and a full-time job accompanying silent films at the Regent theatre. Like Thomas, the ODJB had travelled first to Chicago, but their home was far to the south, in New Orleans, the city regarded as the birthplace of jazz. An ambitious band of "hot" dance musicians, the ODJB had been hired to play at a prestigious restaurant and ballroom in Manhattan, where they quickly became the talk of the town. On 26 February 1917 they recorded two tunes at Victors studio in New York. Jazz historian James Lincoln Collier has written that even as the ODJB was recording, "jazz...was an obscure folk music played mainly by a few hundred blacks and a handful of whites in New Orleans, and rarely heard elsewhere."[4] Then, on 7 March, Victor released the record. It was, in Collier's words, "the single most significant event in the history of jazz."[5]

Within weeks, the United States was caught up in a "jazz" craze. The ODJB's first record to go on sale—"Livery Stable Blues" and "Dixie Jass Band One-Step" (now known as "Original Dixieland One-Step")[6]—sold over one million copies and triggered a musical and social tidal wave which swept across the country. Within a year its impact was being felt in Canada and Europe as well. Seemingly overnight, "jazz" became part of the vocabulary of white North Americans. The word, and the music, seemed to express as nothing else could the rebelliousness and the longing for escape and pleasure of a war-weary youth. North America erupted into a frenzy of intemperate music and daring new styles of social dancing with names like the Turkey Trot, the Grizzly Bear, and the Bunny Hug. The Establishment pleaded for a return to sanity, but youthful enthusiasm could not be dampened and the entertainment industry boomed. Songwriters and publishing houses began churning out music incorporating the new sounds. Dance halls sprang up across the continent; everywhere, musicians, especially white musicians, were in demand. Countless young whites devoured the ODJB's rash of records, learned the music note by note, and quickly formed their own jazz bands. Even established dance orchestras succumbed to the craze and began injecting ragged rhythms and the whinnying sounds associated with the ODJB's brand of jazz into their repertoires. And yet, unknown to the vast majority of whites who lived through what author F. Scott Fitzgerald labelled "The Jazz Age," the jazz that fueled the frenzy was but a crude imitation—promulgated first by the ODJB—of the rich and strikingly expressive music then being played by black musicians in New Orleans and elsewhere in the United States. But until improvised black music came to be widely recorded by black musicians themselves, beginning in 1923, white North American musicians and audiences remained largely ignorant about the origins of the new music they had embraced.[7]

Even as Harry Thomas and the ODJB were making history separately in the Victor studios, one of the most significant internal migrations in American history was reaching its peak. This was the movement of blacks from the South to the industrial cities of the North, and especially to Chicago, then the transportation hub of the United States. Between 1916 and 1918, one of every twenty blacks in the South—a total of more than 400,000 people—migrated northward in search of work and a better life. A few of them spilled across the border into Canada, slipping through a net of new immigration controls introduced by the federal government to restrict the entry of certain racial groups, especially Asians and blacks.[8]

One side effect of this mass movement of blacks in search of work was the flow of black music, and especially the blues, from south to north[9]—a musical migration that would, in a relatively short time, profoundly alter the character of music played around the world. Black musicians were caught up in the fever of migration as much as were black sharecroppers and stevedores. Joe "King" Oliver and Sidney Bechet were two influential black jazz musicians from New Orleans who arrived in Chicago in 1918—and many more would follow. The Mississippi riverboats bore the musicians north to St. Louis and Chicago, but the diaspora from the South was wider and the routes more complex than legend would have us believe. Besides, black musicians in other parts of the United States—the Southwest and the cities of the Northeast in particular—had already developed indigenous musical styles by the beginning of the 1920s which were enriching the black American musical idiom. As the decade progressed, black musicians and entertainers in search of work carried their music further and further afield, travelling the vaudeville and cabaret circuits that looped through the continent. One well-travelled circuit threaded from Chicago through Detroit, as far east as New York and Boston, and as far north as Montreal.

The island of Montreal was settled first by Indians, then by missionaries and fur-traders from France. Ideally situated at the junction of the St. Lawrence and Ottawa Rivers, accessible from the ocean and the Great Lakes, it became the transportation hub of the vast and powerful colony of New France that extended deep into the North American continent. The colony imported black slaves from the West Indies as early as 1628, almost a full decade prior to the arrival of the first slave ships on the shores of what later became the southern United States. Slavery, however, never became important to the fur-trading economy of New

France. The slaves worked mainly as domestics, whereas in the American colonies in the South, slave labour became essential to an agricultural economy based on large plantations.

The first great influx of blacks into the Canadian colonies did not take place until a century and a half after the beginning of the slave trade, when the American colonies rebelled against British rule. The United Empire Loyalists fleeing the American Revolution brought their slaves with them to Canada and settled mainly in Nova Scotia. The British authorities in turn enticed American slaves to desert the rebellious colonies by promising them freedom and land in Canada. At the same time, black freemen were arriving from the American colonies in search of land to farm. In all, some five thousand blacks entered Canada during the American Revolution. While slavery remained legal in the Canadian colonies until 1834, slavery had virtually ended by the 1820s. The last known private advertisement for slaves in Canada was in Quebec City in 1821.

A second wave of blacks entered Canada from the United States on the "underground railway," a legendary escape route for runaway slaves that has contributed to the erroneous myth that most blacks in Canada

The St. Antoine district in 1896, hemmed in (at the top) by the Canadian Pacific Railway tracks connecting to Windsor Station and (at the bottom) by the Grand Trunk Railway. Mountain Street runs perpendicular to the tracks (centre right). *Photo by W. Notman, Notman Photographic Archives.*

are the descendants of slaves. In fact, while several thousand slaves escaped to Canada, mainly to southern Ontario, a great many returned to the United States after the end of the Civil War and the abolition of slavery in 1865. By 1890 there were only fifteen thousand blacks living throughout the Canadian colonies, and it wasn't until West Indians began immigrating to Canada in large numbers in the 1940s that the country's black population increased significantly.[10]

At the peak of the great black migration in the United States, there were less than one thousand blacks living in Montreal, and perhaps as few as half that number; there are no official figures. It took the establishment of Montreal as a major railway centre to create a visible black community in the city. The Grand Trunk Railway and the Canadian Pacific Railway (CPR) were both operating out of the city by 1880, and black men began trickling into Montreal in search of work as porters. Most of them came from the United States, mainly from New York City. Hotels sprang up around the two railway companies' nearly adjacent stations, and the wealthier whites who had once regarded the neighbourhood as a suburb of the city's harbourfront core, three kilometres to the east, moved up the hill and further away from the river. The spacious homes they left behind were converted into rooming-houses or subdivided into small apartments. Here the black porters, some of them with families, took up residence. The strip of St. Antoine Street (still pronounced Saint-Ann-Too-Wine by older, English-speaking residents) running west from Windsor Station beside the CPR tracks became the main street of a small but thriving black community. Hemming the district in on its south flank were the tracks of the Grand Trunk Railway, running parallel to St. Antoine Street a few blocks away.

The black porters returned to the St. Antoine district from their runs looking for excitement and diversion, and they had money in their pockets to pay for it.[11] The seeds were thus sown for a "sporting," or vice and nightlife, district in the black neighbourhood. The first black club opened in 1897, on St. James Street, just south of St. Antoine. The Recreation Key Club, as it was known, was officially a private club; in fact, it offered liquor and illegal gambling to anyone known to the doorman.

Montreal's black community might have remained minuscule had the railways not decided to make Montreal their centre for hiring and training porters. As a result, the population of the district multiplied from an estimated three hundred blacks at the turn of the century to as many as three thousand by the end of the 1920s, providing fertile ground for the "sporting" entrepreneurs. Historian Robin Winks has written of the impact of this rapid social change on the district:

> There Negro prostitution, gambling, and other illicit activities developed, especially in the 1920s as other blacks moved in from Harlem to escape Prohibition. Each summer the St. Antoine dis-

trict grew, with temporary porters, redcaps, and the "flitting element" who came to the [horse] races. In 1897 the first Negro cabaret had opened its doors; by 1928 there were three.[12] In 1922 the Nemderoloc Club ("coloredmen" spelled backwards) became the center for the sporting crowd and was the object of persistent police raids, winning the intense dislike of the stable Negro population. But neither porters nor "sports" were inclined to take out citizenship or to enter into the mainstream of Negro Canadian life.

Thus the Montreal Negro gained a reputation—on the whole a false one—for loose morals, transiency, and a lack of interest in Canadian values. Unfortunately there was sufficient truth in the stereotype to add to the burden of white inconsistency carried by Canadian Negroes during the 1920s. Educational, social, and sanitation standards were low in "the district," the death rate exceeded the city average, and public transport was poor.... Trust companies became the absentee [property] owners of the district,... few structures were improved, and the vicious spiral downward to the slums was rapid.[13]

Music was an important ingredient in the social life of the black community, and there was certain to have been a contingent of local black musicians to play for dances, weddings, parades, and picnics. But we can only guess at what this largely amateur black music sounded like, or

 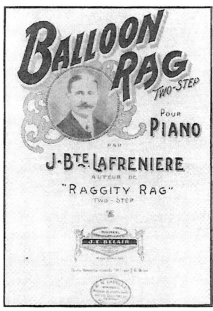

Sheet music of two compositions by Jean-Baptiste Lafrenière, Montreal's first known ragtime pianist. *Alex Robertson Collection, Concordia University Archives.*

A popular song composed and published by Willie Eckstein, whose photograph appears on the cover of the sheet music. *Alex Robertson Collection, Concordia University Archives.*

how much of it was heard by whites, even those living in the district. It is unlikely that whites began frequenting the black clubs in any significant numbers until the clubs began importing entertainers from the United States later in the 1920s.

The jazz craze that swept across the border from the United States into Canada in the wake of the ODJB recordings offers a convenient starting point for the story of jazz in Montreal. But the seed did not fall on unprepared soil: Montrealers had already embraced American popular music and culture through vaudeville and film. And they had already been exposed—unconsciously for the most part—to ragtime, which enjoyed public exposure in Montreal through the work of a handful of white professional theatre pianists.

The first person known to have performed ragtime in Montreal (others preceded him elsewhere in Canada[14]) was a francophone theatre pianist named Jean-Baptiste Lafrenière. He was a trained musician, born in the village of Maskinonge about 150 kilometres downstream from Montreal on the north shore of the St. Lawrence River. He earned his living in several Montreal theatres in the first decade of the twentieth century, then died in about 1911 while only in his late twenties. Lafrenière was a prolific composer, of marches, waltzes—and three rags. Though he died in obscurity and was never recorded, Lafrenière was the only resident musician known to have performed ragtime in Montreal at the peak of the music's worldwide popularity. Why there were not others is open to conjecture, but the history of jazz in Montreal is full of such time lags between the rise of new musical styles in the United States and their absorption by local musicians.

Montreal's three other known ragtime performers didn't begin working professionally until the ragtime craze had already passed. Eckstein, widely proclaimed as Canada's master popular pianist during the 1920s and 1930s, was born to European immigrants in Pointe St. Charles, a predominantly Irish, working-class district of Montreal. A child prodigy, he had absorbed six years of conservatory training at the piano by the time he was twelve. But his family was too poor to allow a potential wage-earner to accept a scholarship and continue studying music, so the young Eckstein embarked on a career in vaudeville. He performed on stages across North America and Europe dressed in a Little Lord Fauntleroy suit and billed as "The Boy Paderewski." Though Eckstein stopped growing at four feet nine inches, the musician in him outgrew his vaudeville role, and in 1906 he returned to Montreal, eighteen years old and stage-wise. Immediately he embarked on a second career as a theatre pianist, one which lasted until the "talkies" rendered him obsolete twenty-four years later. Not suprisingly, Eckstein's dazzling virtuosity and willingness to share his knowledge attracted younger pianists eager to follow in his footsteps. Among them were Montreal's two other known ragtime performers, Harry Thomas and Vera Guilaroff.

Thomas served his apprenticeship at Eckstein's side, and his playing was indelibly marked by the exposure. Returning from his first recording sessions in Chicago and New York, Thomas settled into a full-time job behind the piano at the Regent theatre. There Guilaroff, another self-taught immigrant from England, began substituting for him at the age of twelve. When Thomas left Montreal three years later to work as a theatre pianist in Halifax, Nova Scotia, Guilaroff took over his job at the Regent. Thomas eventually returned to Montreal, but seemed never to recover from the blow to his prestige wrought by the advent of the "talkies." He lived in destitution, performing in third-rate bars, until his death. Guilaroff's career was a happier one. When the "talkies" arrived, she set off to tour the United States with a band, then returned to Montreal and worked extensively with Eckstein on radio and in nightclubs. Later tours took her to England, Europe, and the Bahamas, and she eventually performed on television.

While Eckstein, Thomas, and Guilaroff recorded prolifically in Montreal and the United States, none ever became a jazz musician, though one record company made an overblown attempt to sell Guilaroff as "Canada's Premier Jazz Pianist" during the 1920s.[15] They were, nevertheless, celebrated as technically proficient pianists—in Eckstein's case an outstanding one—and as popular entertainers working in the mainstream of Montreal's entertainment industry. More importantly for jazz, they served double duty as advance heralds of improvised black music: each performed and recorded ragtime mainly for white audiences, and in so doing gave Montrealers their first exposure to a black American musical style.

Vaudeville provided further glimpses of authentic black music.[16] From the beginning of the century, American performers had been appearing on theatre stages in Montreal. Some theatres, like the Gayety, the Loew's, the St. Denis, the Princess, and the Palace, could seat two thousand people. The performers ranged from slapstick comedians, female impersonators, and acrobats, to singers, dancers, ventriloquists, and silent-movie stars such as Buster Keaton. Almost anything passed in the name of entertainment, from pie-throwing to punches: some vaudeville shows featured prizefighters on stage in sparring matches. To top off the shows there were chorus lines of high-kicking dancers, most of them recruited from towns and cities along the vaudeville circuit. In the province of Quebec, however, the prevailing Catholic morality discouraged all but the most disreputable young women from dancing on stage.

By the end of the 1920s, French-speaking performers in Montreal and Quebec City had organized their own vaudeville troupes and developed their own routines and theatrical "bits" for local consumption. But before they captured the local French market, all of the shows that appeared in Montreal played in English and originated in the United States. So, too, did the music that accompanied them. Pit orchestras com-

Vera Guilaroff. *Photo courtesy of Jim Kidd. John Gilmore Jazz History Collection, Concordia University Archives.*

prised of local musicians read the show music from scores written in the United States. Ragtime, blues, and fragments of other black musical styles crept into some of the shows, increasingly so after the jazz craze began in 1917. During the 1920s, all of the great touring black shows from the United States had blues and gospel singers and choirs in their casts.

Some vaudeville shows featured American instrumentalists on stage as well. Most of these musicians were white, but newspaper advertisements as early as 1918 publicized the occasional black performer appearing on Montreal stages. In that year, the Four Harmony Kings appeared on a stage at Sohmer amusement park in the east end of the city, the same year that singer/dancer Florence Mills appeared at the Gayety theatre. America's Greatest Coloured Jazz Band appeared at the Gayety in October 1920. Sometime about 1921 a black quartet toured Canada on the vaudeville circuit and may have performed in Montreal; led by pianist Bobby Brown, the group included saxophonist Binjie Madison, who later recorded jazz with Louis Armstrong and King Oliver. And for one week in September 1924, the touring company of the all-black musical revue *Shuffle Along*, written and produced by the great black composing team of pianist Eubie Blake and singer Noble Sissle, played at His Majesty's theatre in Montreal.

A heavy velvet curtain swooped across the stage, nipping at the heels of the departing chorus girls. The chatter of the audience rose to an intermission crescendo as the house lights flared. Then, from the upper reaches of the piano in the darkened orchestra pit, a tinkling of notes clamoured for attention. A few heads turned, the tinkling became more insistent, and then a full-handed explosion of rhythm set the shuffle of feet in the aisles ablaze. *"Aie! C'est Slap Rags!"* someone shouted. *"Y joue le blues!"*

James "Slap Rags" White was indeed playing the blues, and ragtime, in Montreal, at about the same time that the jazz craze was sweeping across the border into Canada. He was playing the blues the way he'd heard them played by other black musicians, on the South Side of Chicago, in Harlem, and in all the black roadhouses he'd visited on his travels around the United States. By 1918 or so, he'd made his home in Montreal, a smiling eddy of a city in the torrent of migratory America. How White stumbled upon Montreal is not known. It is not even certain that he was the first professional black musician from the United States to settle in Montreal after the birth of ragtime. But if there were others before him, their names are lost to history. Perhaps White heard about Montreal from the porters on the trains; perhaps he heard of the city from the five saxophone-playing brothers from southern Ontario whose ragtime and novelty band he is believed to have recorded with, on saxophone, in Camden, New Jersey, in the summer of 1916. He may even have joined the Six Brown Brothers[17] for a tour of the vaudeville circuit

28

and passed through Montreal previously. There can be little doubt, however, that what enticed White to stay in Montreal—as it did so many black musicians after him—was an abundance of work and the city's hospitality.

At a time when race relations in the United States were still scarred by the memory of slavery, and when discrimination in jobs, housing, justice, and social life remained glaring and endemic, Montreal must have appeared like an oasis in a desert of hostility to itinerant black musicians. The city was by no means a model of racial harmony: blacks were barred from many hotels and nightclubs, and they encountered unmistakable, if subtle, discrimination in many aspects of their daily lives. But at least black musicians of the 1920s could work on the same bandstand as whites, could share a meal with them at the same table, and could enjoy the company of white women without fearing the lynch mob. "It was like coming into your mother's arms," said saxophonist Randolph Whinfield of his arrival in Montreal in 1922. "The white musicians wouldn't let anyone call us those names. And the women loved us— they spoiled us!" Though racial harmony in Montreal soured noticeably in the 1930s as the Depression fueled white resentment of minorities, and gangsters tightened their control over the nightclubs, the first wave of black musicians arriving in Montreal in the 1920s found the city a welcome haven from the fear and tension which afflicted their lives south of the border.

Availability of work was Montreal's other great drawing card. Until the late 1950s, when television studios began to provide regular employment for musicians and performers, jazz musicians across North America depended for their survival on the nightclub industry. Where nightlife flourished, so did the musicians—and so did jazz. During the 1920s, Montreal's nightlife was booming, setting a pace that was to be the envy of most of the continent for almost three decades. Alcohol oils the gears of the nightclub industry and pays the salaries of its workers, and in Montreal alcohol flowed more liberally than anywhere else in North America. This fact alone made the city a popular destination for touring musicians and entertainers.

At the height of the jazz craze, Montreal was the only large city in North America to avoid total Prohibition on the sale and consumption of alcohol. Prohibition legislation was in force throughout the United States for fourteen years, from 1919 to 1933, and though illicit alcohol was widely available, nightclubs suffered as customers went off in search of speak-easies. In Quebec, many rural communities had opted to prohibit alcohol within their jurisdictions by 1918, but the large urban centres—Montreal included—resisted the continent-wide trend to temperance. In February 1918 the Quebec government passed legislation tightening laws on alcohol sales and promised to impose total Prohibition on 1 May 1919. Before it could do so, the federal government passed legislation permitting provincial referendums on the question. A month before total Prohibition was due to begin in Quebec, male voters went to the polls and overwhelmingly embraced a compromise: spirits would be available only under medical prescription, but beer, cider, and light wines would be freely available from licenced dealers. Many municipalities that had previously voted themselves dry quickly opted to go wet again.

Less than a year later, the Quebec government realized that its new alcohol law was being flagrantly abused in Montreal, where officials estimated that three-quarters of the city's 700,000 residents opposed Prohibition of any kind. Spirits were freely available in the city through a thriving black market in phony medical prescriptions and illicit stills. More ominously for Montreal's future, gangsters had moved in from the United States to organize major smuggling operations. Alcohol poured from Quebec into the United States and the rest of Canada, where total Prohibition was in force. Narcotics consumption was also on the rise in the city.

Under pressure from pro-temperance groups worried about Montreal's dissolute atmosphere, the Quebec government moved quickly to take control of the sale and distribution of alcohol throughout the province. In February 1921 a provincial liquor commission was established and government-run liquor stores were soon selling spirits to the public without prescription, one bottle at a time. At the same time, nightclubs and hotels were granted licences to sell beer and wine, something they had previously been denied, and the legal drinking age was set at eighteen years. This enlightened approach to alcohol regulation made Quebec—and Montreal—unique in North America. Other Canadian provinces began repealing their Prohibition laws between 1923 and 1926, but they maintained strict regulations about when and where alcohol could be consumed.[18]

Due in large measure to alcohol, Montreal developed an international reputation for good times in an era when Prohibition was inhibiting nightlife almost everywhere else on the continent. Nightclubs, cabarets, and bars thrived; vaudeville theatres, amusement parks, and dance halls, though not licenced to sell alcohol, benefited from the heady climate. Together the city's entertainment venues offered a wealth of employment to musicians fluent in the latest styles of popular music. As word about the city spread, musicians drifted to it in search of work. In this way black musicians from the United States began appearing in Montreal almost immediately after the onset of the jazz craze.

In January 1918, the Clef Club Jazz Band, an all-black orchestra drawing its members from New York City's black musicians' union, was booked into the Palais de Danse in Montreal[19]—the first professional black band known to have played in the city. That summer, American bandleader John Philip Sousa brought a sixty-member band to Dominion Park in the city's east end, where it performed for sixteen days; it may have included black performers. Sousa's was the most successful popular concert band of its day, and its music was heavily doused with

A popular American song of the Prohibition era touts Montreal's reputation for free-flowing liquor and good times. The lyric reads, "Speak easy, speak easy, and tell the bunch, / I won't go east, I won't go west, got a different hunch: / I'll be leaving in the summer, and I won't be back 'till fall, / Goodbye Broadway, Hello Montreal."

ragtime and black American folk music. Other black musicians from the United States soon appeared in Montreal; most stayed awhile and then journeyed on.[20] Slap Rags White was the first of them to make the city his home.

Few details of White's background, or of his fifteen-odd years in Montreal, have survived. He apparently came from New Orleans and had lived for a while in Chicago, where he earned a reputation for playing ragtime with his hands behind his back.[21] Once settled in Montreal, he worked in theatres—playing the organ, as well as the piano—and probably in nightclubs and other places, too. He seems to have also found work as a "music writer," the occupation he listed beside his name in the Montreal directory of 1925.[22] White's compositional talents were probably employed by vaudeville acts and local dance bands, with whom he may have played saxophone in addition to piano. He died in Montreal in 1933, deeply mourned by local musicians.

Reaching Montreal hard on the heels of Slap Rags White was another black pianist, Millard Thomas. Born in the coal-mining country of southwestern Illinois, not far from the banks of the Mississippi and the city of East St. Louis, Thomas had been living in Quebec City for two years before he decided to move to Montreal, arriving probably during the winter of 1918-19. Thomas was a trained musician who had studied organ and composition at the University of Nebraska. He led a ragtime orchestra in Shreveport, Louisiana, hometown of his bride, then travelled across the continent, stopping in Chicago in the summer of 1917 before moving on to Quebec City, possibly with a band in tow. In the predominantly francophone provincial capital he worked as "musical director" of the Princess theatre, where his duties probably centred around leading the pit orchestra for vaudeville shows. In January 1919 the Palais de Danse in Montreal announced the appearance of the Famous Chicago Jazz Band—a name so strikingly similar to the one Thomas used for his band during the following nine years in Montreal that there can be little doubt that this engagement marked his Montreal debut. By 1920 Thomas had formed a publishing company in Montreal and was on his way to establishing his band, now called the Famous Chicago Novelty Orchestra, as the leading exponent of black music in the city during the 1920s.

The band established its credentials in Montreal during an engagement that lasted at least two years at the Starland theatre, a vaudeville house on St. Lawrence Blvd., the north-south artery known locally as "The Main" which divides city streets into east and west. At the Starland, in the years around 1922, the Famous Chicago Novelty Orchestra played jazz before and between the local French acts it was hired to accompany. The band's description as a "novelty orchestra" suggests it was also featured as an act itself. Novelty numbers were a mainstay of vaudeville bands and typically involved zany costumes, outrageous antics, and sometimes homemade instruments—all combining to make a slap-happy but often highly musical routine. This comic performance reflected the way in which white audiences of the day viewed black music. Given the opportunity, Thomas's musicians were also capable of playing authentic jazz: in the 1920s that meant syncopated dance music with improvised passages and a flavouring of the blues.

Thomas was hired to play at dance halls, amusement parks, and probably nightclubs, and he varied the size of his orchestra—anywhere from five to nine musicians—to meet his employer's budget, a common practice. Local radio stations broadcast the band live from their engagements, demonstrating the versatility of the musicians in programs ranging from popular dance music to light classics and numbers featuring individual instrumentalists. It was most likely as a novelty act that Thomas's crew was engaged to play at the official opening of the Mount Royal hotel on 20 December 1922, a rare honour for black musicians. Thomas eventually left Montreal with his family in 1928. He settled in New York City, where he composed and performed music for the stage and the church, including an oratorio and an opera.

While musicians such as Slap Rags White and Millard Thomas were laying the foundation for jazz in Montreal, the white dance bands and their less discriminating fans were avidly embracing the ODJB's version of jazz. Montreal dance halls were flooded with white dance bands, many of them sporting the fashionable words "jazz" or "syncopation" or "novelty" in their names to capitalize on the craze. From the United States came such bands as Banjo Wallace's Jazz Band, which worked at the Jardin de Danse in March 1918 and then, in February 1919, began a long engagement at the Palais de Danse, using the name Yama Yama Jazz Jazz. Nineteen eighteen also saw the Dixie Jazz Band, the Original Tango Jazz Band, and the Original Kentucky Jazz Band appear in Montreal. Arthur C. Hand and his California Ramblers played frequently in Montreal, beginning in 1920, as did several bands from American impresario Harry Yerkes's stable.[23] Nineteen twenty-one brought the Manhattan Jazz Band, Dinty Moore's Rag Pickers, O'Hare's Novelty Orchestra, and Simone Martucci's orchestra to the city. Martucci, an American society orchestra leader prominent in Canada in the early 1920s, recorded some forty tunes in Montreal, using such names as the Jazzbo Band and the Champion Jazz Band. Isham Jones brought his dance band—one of the top white bands of the decade—directly to the Mount Royal hotel from Chicago, in 1922. Saxophonist Bennie Kreuger, a veteran of some of the ODJB's recordings, brought his own orchestra to the Venetian Gardens in 1924. During the same year, the popular and widely recorded Original Memphis Five appeared in town,[24] and Ben Bernie's orchestra played at the Princess theatre.

Perhaps the greatest pseudo-jazz event to steamroll across the Canadian border in the early 1920s was led by the self-proclaimed "King of Jazz," Paul Whiteman. A pudgy, balding violinist, he amassed a small

The **Melody Kings**, circa 1923. Left to right: John Tipaldi (violin), Billy Munro (piano), Andy Tipaldi (banjo, leader), Harry Luci or Rip Doucette (trumpet), Alex Lajoie (alto saxophone), Rip Doucette or Harry Luci (trumpet), Leo Dufault (tenor saxophone), Al Gagnon (trombone), Rob Roy (drums). *John Gilmore Jazz History Collection, Concordia University Archives.*

fortune at the head of a world-famous orchestra which at times swelled to more than thirty musicians. Whiteman later employed many of the best white jazz musicians of the era, including the brilliant cornetist Bix Beiderbecke, but these musicians had yet to join the orchestra in 1924 when it set off on a six-week tour of fifteen cities, including the Canadian capital, Ottawa. The tour ended at the St. Denis theatre in Montreal on 1 June. Billed "An Experiment in Modern Music," the program played on the tour is remembered chiefly because it premiered "Rhapsody in Blue," a work commissioned by Whiteman from composer George Gershwin. Whiteman intended the program to be educational, but its portayal of jazz was pretentious and misleading. The opening number, announced as a demonstration of "the true form of jazz," was the ODJB's by-then famous "Livery Stable Blues," complete with whinnying barnyard sounds from the horns.[25]

American musicians were not the only ones to take advantage of the thirst for jazz in Montreal. Local white musicians rushed to meet the demand for dance bands capable of playing in the new style, and local jazz bands began surfacing as early as 1919. Among the first on the scene were pianist Eddie Layton's Jazz Band, the Cyclone Jazz Band, Eckstein's Jazz Band (led by Willie Eckstein's brother Jack, a violinist), and Munro's Jazz Band (led by pianist Billy Munro, whose song "When My Baby Smiles At Me" became a hit for American bandleader Ted Lewis in the 1920s). The early 1920s saw countless other local musicians jump on the jazz bandwagon in such groupings as Percy's Novelty Jazz Band, Layton's Singing Jazz Orchestra, Alexander's Jazz Kings, the Westmount Syncopated Orchestra, and various "jazz bands" bearing the names of neighbouring municipalities such as Lachine, Outremont, and Westmount.

But the standard-bearer of the resident white bands was led by an Italian banjo-player from New York City who migrated to Montreal sometime between 1917 and 1919, apparently with the nucleus of a band in tow. Until 1928 Andy Tipaldi led a bouncing, tightly arranged dance band of from five to nine musicians which eventually became known as the Melody Kings. Advertised as "Canada's Premier Dance Orchestra," it played at Montreal's leading dance halls, appeared as a vaudeville act in city theatres, broadcast over local radio, and recorded extensively. Though its jazz content was minimal, the Melody Kings may have briefly included trumpeter Johnny Dixon, a former Canadian Army bugler who went on to become an acclaimed and widely recorded "hot" trumpeter in Europe. Other veterans of the band, including Billy Munro, trombonist Al Gagnon, and saxophonist Alex Lajoie, eventually became bandleaders themselves. Tipaldi, meanwhile, grew rich by investing his earnings from the Melody Kings on the stock market. When the market crashed in 1929 he was wiped out. After an ill-fated attempt at running a nightclub, he devoted the rest of his life to strengthening and presiding over the Musicians' Guild of Montreal.

Though the gulf between the white and black conceptions of jazz during the 1920s was considerable, this did not appear to sour relations between black and white musicians in Montreal. In any event, there were probably no more than twenty-five professional black musicians living in the city during the first half of the decade, and their white colleagues likely regarded them more as a curiosity than a threat. More significantly for the promulgation of jazz in the city, the white and black musicians had the opportunity to work together in the same bands—a practice unheard of in the United States at the time. This fact fostered a climate of exchange and cooperation: the whites, many of whom had benefited from formal musical training, helped the blacks, who were more often self-taught, to improve their reading skills and instrumental technique; the blacks, for the most part closer to the roots of jazz and its essentially aural tradition, offered the white musicians advice on phrasing, rhythm, and instrumental sonority.[26]

But if some of the white musicians developed a genuine respect for the new black music and a desire to fathom its subtleties, their admiration was by no means widely shared by the public at large, and especially by the older generation. North America's obsession with jazz and the frenzied social dancing that accompanied it provoked a shrill outcry from the white Establishment, who saw in the fad nothing less than the decline of Western civilization and Christian morality. Evidence of the reaction against jazz was a headline in the Montreal *Herald* in 1922: "Jazz's Day Is Done and White People Will Come to Their Senses." In the story which followed, an interviewer quoted Russian dancer Theodore Kosloff, star of a film then showing in Montreal, as saying, "Jazz is doomed. The white part of North America is rapidly approaching a 'morning after' disgust with her spree of sensual, negroid dancing."[27]

Some of this hysteria was imported *carte blanche* from the United States through such periodicals as *Maclean's* magazine, which in 1921 published a summary of an article from the *Ladies' Home Journal*, an American publication. Under the headline "Where Does Jazz Lead To?" *Maclean's* printed American author Anne Shaw Faulkner's answer: to girls abandoning their corsets, to a decline in worker productivity, and ultimately to "barbarism and bolshevism." Wrote Faulkner:

> That it has a demoralizing effect upon the human brain has been demonstrated by many scientists.... Jazz disorganizes all regular laws and order; it stimulates to extreme deeds, to a breaking away from all rules and conventions; it is harmful and dangerous, and its influence is wholly bad.[28]

This public obsession with the word "jazz"—both by its imitators and its detractors—seems to have reached its peak in Montreal in the early 1920s. By the middle of the decade the number of local dance bands calling themselves "jazz" bands had noticeably declined. That jazz continued to develop as a rich musical idiom despite this early onslaught of misrepresentation and commercialization is both a measure of the wealth of the black musical tradition and a credit to the tenacity of its most devoted exponents.

There was, however, another factor which helped jazz survive and spread, at least in the United States. This was the rapid growth of the recording industry. The size of the black population in the United States created a market for recordings of black performers, particularly blues singers and jazz bands. The white-owned record companies, recognizing the profits to be made in what they called the "race market," rushed to fill the void. "Race records" poured into stores in black neighbourhoods; inevitably, they also found their way into the hands of appreciative white listeners. In this way, jazz in the United States was documented and widely disseminated. Young musicians, black and white, learned to play jazz in part by imitating recordings of their favourite performers.

Canada, too, had its recording industry, but its influence upon early jazz in Montreal was slight. The few records that were made by black musicians living in Canada were sold almost exclusively in the United States. At the same time, American companies rarely bothered to send their recordings of black jazz and blues artists to Canada. In both cases the reason was the same: the Canadian market for black music was judged too small to be profitable. As a result, Canadian musicians were denied easy access to recordings of authentic black music at a time when a derivative white jazz was flooding the entertainment marketplace. Had it been otherwise, musicians living in Canada might have made significant stylistic contributions to the evolution of early jazz; instead, they were left groping for direction, and the innovations were all made south of the border. Nevertheless, the story of the birth and infancy of Canada's recording industry provides further insight into Montreal's entertainment industry in the early decades of the century.

Montreal was the birthplace of the Canadian recording industry and the only city in Canada where musicians could record until after the Second World War. The history of the early recording industry in Canada, told by Edward Moogk in *Roll Back The Years*,[29] is essentially a family history—that of Emile Berliner and his two sons. Berliner was a self-taught German scientist who immigrated to the United States in 1870, when he was nineteen years old. There he invented the gramophone, a wind-up machine which produced sounds from pre-recorded flat rubber discs—the precursor of what we now call "records." Berliner's discs were a major advancement on the wax cylinders then being used to record sound. At first he tried to manufacture and sell his invention from his own company in Washington, D.C., but eventually he sold the patent to a man who used it to found the Victor Talking Machine Company. Regretting, perhaps, that he had lost control over his invention, Berliner applied for a patent in Canada. When that was granted, in 1897, he moved to Montreal, planning to be the first to record French Canadian music—and so capture the Quebec market.

Two years later Berliner opened a factory on Aqueduct Street in the St. Antoine district. There he began assembling gramophones and manufacturing—though not recording—gramophone discs. The discs were copies pressed from original "master" recordings imported from the United States, England, France, and Germany. Berliner's brother Joseph, who had in the meantime established the Deutsche Grammophon company in Germany, supplied some of the masters for the infant Berliner Gramophone Company of Canada. Business began picking up, and in 1900 Berliner's American-born sons, Herbert and Edgar, moved to Montreal to work in the chain of music stores which their father had bought in the city to sell his products.[30]

Competition for the Canadian market was heating up. Columbia established a pressing plant in Toronto, and Edison began distributing its recordings from the same city. But Berliner remained ahead of his American rivals, partly by ignoring wax cylinders and concentrating exclusively on discs, the technology of the future. Meanwhile, the Victor Talking Machine Company made its bid for the Canadian market by offering Berliner an exclusive licence to manufacture and distribute Victor records in Canada. Berliner accepted the offer in 1901—but he was too ambitious to be content for long operating a branch plant for Victor.

By 1909 Berliner had built a recording studio on Peel Street and opened a custom-made, three-storey factory and five-storey office building further west on St. Antoine Street. Herbert Berliner was appointed vice-president and general manager of the operation, and the Berliner

Gramophone Company began to record its own master records in Montreal. The senior Berliner, who remained president, followed his original hunch and brought local French singers and musicians into his recording studio, aiming to outdistance his American parent company in the Quebec market. He also began recording popular white American musicians and bands in Montreal. Some were recruited from the ranks of the American musicians working in hotel ballrooms and dance halls in the city; others were brought to Montreal especially to record. Once Prohibition began in the United States, Berliner had little difficulty convincing musicians to make the trip to Montreal.

CABLE ADDRESS
"COMPOCO" MONTREAL

TELEPHONES { WALNUT 0685
{ LACHINE 562

THE COMPO COMPANY LIMITED

CANADA'S LARGEST RECORD MANUFACTURERS

131-141 EIGHTEENTH AVE.
LACHINE MONTREAL.
CANADA

Courtesy of Jim Kidd.

In 1918 the Berliner family history took a curious twist. Herbert Berliner established an independent record-pressing plant called Compo in the Montreal suburb of Lachine. No one knows what motivated him to do so while he was still managing the Berliner operation, but the two companies apparently remained on good terms for a couple of years, and even held joint staff picnics. Compo began by simply pressing records for several American labels, including Okeh and Gennett. Then, in the spring of 1921, Herbert and his younger brother quarrelled. Herbert resigned from the Berliner company, leaving Edgar to manage affairs, and took some of Berliner's top executives with him to Compo. From that point on, the two companies were bitter rivals.

Compo immediately began its own recording operations in a bid to outdistance Berliner. Competition in the industry, however, was becoming more intense. The Berliner company had captured the French Canadian market and was negotiating a new relationship with Victor. Columbia and Edison had Toronto tied up. And to complicate matters, the marketplace was becoming flooded with small companies manufacturing record players: Montreal alone had more than half a dozen manufacturers before the end of the First World War.

Herbert Berliner elected to push Compo into the rapidly expanding race market. Herbert was no lover of black music, but he saw in the American race market an opportunity to expand his business horizons. In the summer of 1923 he launched his own race label at Compo, calling it Ajax.[31] Herbert rented a studio on West 55th Street in New York City and began recording black musicians and singers there, including singer Mamie Smith, Fletcher Henderson's orchestra, and the Canadian-born pianist Lou Hooper. He transported the masters to Montreal, pressed them into records at his Compo plant, and shipped the records back to the United States for distribution to stores in black neighbourhoods. The records sold for seventy-five cents each. Some were even shipped to the West Indies. But so specialized did Herbert consider the market for his Ajax race records that he didn't even bother to distribute them in Canada. However, the Compo plant manager apparently took some of the early Ajax records to a restaurant or tailor shop on Mountain Street in the St. Antoine district.[32] This was the only known place where Compo's race records could be bought in Canada, though how long the store continued to stock them is not known. As for the American companies, some of their race records were shipped to Canada, but they were assigned low priority in marketing and distribution.[33]

Compo's race records sold poorly right from the beginning. Within a year, the company was issuing recordings of popular white musicians on the same label in a desperate attempt to keep it alive. Before the label disappeared in the summer of 1925, Herbert Berliner recorded some of the black musicians living in Montreal. Ultimately, only eight jazz records by Montreal blacks were issued on Ajax: four by Millard Thomas and his Famous Chicago Novelty Orchestra, one solo piano record of Thomas playing two original blues compositions, and three records featuring clarinetist Theodore West from the Famous Chicago Novelty Orchestra, accompanied by a piano and a kazoo. For reasons known only to Herbert Berliner, Thomas's solo piano record was also issued on Compo's most important label, Apex. As a result, of all the black musicians recorded in Montreal during the decade, this single record was the only one ever marketed in Canada.[34]

Meanwhile, the local white musicians were enjoying much more exposure on records, most of them recorded in Montreal for the Compo and Berliner companies. Willie Eckstein, a close friend of the Berliner family, issued more than sixty tunes, playing solo and in trios. The Melody Kings issued forty-two tunes; Harry Thomas issued thirty-eight; and Vera Guilaroff, a friend of Herbert Berliner, issued ten. None of this music was, strictly speaking, jazz, though it might have been difficult to convince fans and record buyers of this at the time.

Of the two Montreal recording companies, the one run by the wayward Herbert Berliner retained its independence from the United States the longest. His brother, Edgar, allowed the Berliner Gramophone Company to be taken over by its American parent in 1924. It was renamed the Victor Talking Machine Company of Canada. Five years later the senior Berliner died in Washington, and Victor operations in both Canada and the United States were taken over by the Radio Corporation of America (RCA), which created the RCA Victor label.

Edgar Berliner resigned as president of the Montreal operations in 1930 and died twenty-five years later in California. The Canadian division of RCA retained recording studios in Montreal until the late 1970s.

Compo's history was more illustrious. Besides concentrating on recording Canadian performers, it was the first Canadian company to issue recordings made electronically, with a microphone replacing the archaic bell of the old acoustic recorders. A year later, in 1925, it was the first Canadian company to issue records of radio broadcasts. Compo survived the Depression, in part through Herbert Berliner's willingness to diversify: the plant took on work manufacturing recording cylinders for dictation machines and transcription discs for radio, and even used its presses to turn out floor tiles for a while. In 1935 Compo became the Canadian presser and distributor for the Decca company of the United States, but in 1950 Decca bought out Compo. Fourteen years later Decca was in turn swallowed by MCA, which eventually shut down the old Compo plant in Lachine. Herbert Berliner continued to be involved with the operations in Lachine until his death in 1966.

A 1924 recording by Millard Thomas and his Famous Chicago Novelty Orchestra on Compo's race label, Ajax. Though the record was recorded and manufactured in Montreal, it was not issued in Canada; instead, it was marketed to black audiences in the United States through Compo's office in Chicago. *Alex Robertson Collection, Concordia University Archives.*

Montrealers who owned radio sets during the 1920s were no better off than those with gramophones when it came to hearing music performed by blacks. Radio was in its experimental phase during the first half of the decade; by the end of 1920s Montreal still had only two radio stations.[35] Initially, these stations were on the air for only a few hours a day. They prided themselves on live broadcasts, and used records only for interludes and test broadcasts. There was more than pride involved in this policy, however. The sound quality of acoustical recordings was primitive. Because electrical impulses were not used either to record or play back these records, broadcasting them required placing a radio station microphone in front of the speaker bell of a gramophone—with nearly indecipherable results. Nevertheless, Emile Berliner arranged a weekly promotional broadcast of some of his records over XWA in Montreal as early as 1920. The program, called "His Master's Voice Victrola Concerts," was probably more a curiosity for radio audiences than a satisfying listening experience.

In fact, relations between the recording industry and radio stations in North America were far from cooperative during most of the 1920s: both were competing for dominance in the rapidly growing home entertainment marketplace. It wasn't until the advent of electrical recordings in the middle of the decade, with their gratifying leap in fidelty, that radio stations began broadcasting records in any great numbers. By the end of the 1920s, records were a regular part of radio programming, a fact that could have helped to disseminate jazz in Canada—except that there weren't many race records in the country to broadcast.

What Montrealers did hear on local radio was live popular music, and on at least one occasion live jazz. CFCF brought Willie Eckstein and singer Gus Hall into its studio in 1919 for the first live radio broadcast of a music performance in Canada. Four years later the station made its first live broadcast from outside the studio when technicians took a microphone to the Regent theatre and stood it beside the piano of Vera Guilaroff. "Remotes," as these broadcasts were called, quickly became a staple of radio across North America, providing wide public exposure for musicians—most of them white. CKAC offered the first known remote broadcast of a black band in Montreal when it placed a microphone in front of Millard Thomas and his Famous Chicago Novelty Orchestra at the Island Amusement Park in 1923.[36]

By the end of the 1920s, radio had become a fixture of North American life. Government regulation of the airwaves and the formation of radio networks in the United States resulted in better reception from distant stations.[37] Montrealers could tune in to powerful stations in New York City, Chicago, and elsewhere, and listen to records and remote broadcasts of the top American musicians and performers. While race records and black performances were broadcast only rarely at first, and only on select stations, another door was nevertheless opening for the spread of American popular music, including jazz, to Montreal.

41

CHAPTER TWO

1925 to 1940

The ferry edged away from the wharf and nosed into the current. On the upper deck, four musicians took up their instruments. The beat and call of their banjoes and saxophones spilled across the river. For twenty minutes the hot summer air rang with the four men's music, and with the laughter and clapping of the passengers who had gathered around. Then the vessel slowed, turned, and wrestled free of the current, and the sounds of the approaching shore mingled with the strains of the last tune. Extending his derby hat, Smitty thanked the departing passengers for their tips, then joined his fellow musicians for a moment's rest while the ferry loaded for the return trip.

Smitty was Elmer Smith, a schooled saxophonist and piano player from Boston who had settled in Montreal in the mid-1920s. There he met other black musicians from the United States who were making their homes in Montreal. Some of them regularly rode the number ninety-one streetcar out to the town of Lachine, a suburb on the island of Montreal just west of the city. They worked the three car ferries that ran in a continuous circuit from the foot of 34th Avenue across the St. Lawrence River to the isolated Mohawk community of Caughnawaga.[1] The ferries, operated by Canada Steamship Lines, linked the island of Montreal with a highway running south to the American border, and to New York City beyond. They also provided the Mohawk with their only access to Montreal. The ferries remained in service until the Mercier Bridge opened in 1934.

How many musicians actually played on the ferries is not known. Three who are known to have worked with Smitty were another Bostonian, saxophonist Eddie Perkins, and two banjo players, Wiley Teasley and Eddie Simms. Smitty himself worked the ferries often enough to court a young Mohawk woman, who became his wife. Playing on the boats was a pleasant job when the weather was good, and it didn't interfere with the other work the musicians found in the vaudeville theatres, dance halls, and nightclubs that thrived in Montreal

The Sir Henri, one of three ferries linking Lachine on the island of Montreal with the Mohawk village of Caughnawaga and the highway running to Malone and other points in New York State. Black musicians from Montreal performed for tips on these ferries. *Courtesy of Archives du Musée de Lachine (V11 b-1).*

in the 1920s. Work for musicians was plentiful—so plentiful that hard on the heels of Slap Rags White and Millard Thomas came a second wave of black American musicians who had heard tales about the exciting city and ventured north. Smitty and his friends were part of this second wave. By the end of the decade, it had drenched Montreal with talent and with the sounds of the latest black music.

Some wandered to the city alone through the late 1920s and early 1930s, beckoned by friends or spurred by a spirit of adventure. There was Herbert Augustus Johnson, another saxophonist from Boston who had lingered in Harlem before journeying north. There was trumpeter Mack McKenzie from Pittsburg, who had toured most of the United States in bands but decided to put down roots in Montreal. And then there were the musicians who came from places south of the border that old friends and fans could no longer remember—pianist Nina Brown; violinist Arthur Provost; saxophonist and vaudeville performer Bob Everleigh; pianist Arthur Davis, whose girth saddled him with the affectionate nickname "Mister Five by Five"; and drummer Willie Wade, whose loud, driving, and infectious beat would make him the favourite drummer of visiting show girls for more than two decades to come.

Other musicians rolled into Montreal in convoys of automobiles stuffed with instruments and suitcases. One group to arrive in the city, probably in 1929 or 1930, was a touring band put together by a drummer named Johnson from Pennsylvania. He brought with him his three sons—Benny, Henry, and Frank—and three other brothers from the Pittsburg area—Andy, Bill, and Arnold Shorter. The eighth and final member of the band is believed to have been a trumpet player named Jimmy Jones, who vanished into obscurity at the end of the Second

Adrien Paradis. *Photo by O'Neil's Photos, courtesy of Adrien Paradis Jr. John Gilmore Jazz History Collection, Concordia University Archives.*

World War after fifteen years at the centre of Montreal jazz. The Shorter Brothers Band—Andy Shorter directed them on stage—broke up soon after it arrived in Montreal, probably for the simple reason that six of its members liked the city too much to carry on touring. Father Johnson and Arnold Shorter returned to the United States, but the rest of the group eased into the spirit of the city and found new jobs. Three of them—Frank Johnson, Andy Shorter, and Bill Shorter—spent the rest of their lives in Montreal.[2]

It wasn't until the early 1930s that the first generation of Canadian-born jazz musicians began to appear on the Montreal scene. Some, like six of the Canadian Ambassadors band, and saxophonist Bill Kersey, came from southern Ontario. Others grew up in Montreal's own black community: pianist Ilene Bourne, drummer Freddie Blackburn, alto saxophonist and pianist Harold "Steep" Wade, and a couple of young saxophone-playing brothers named Hugh and George Sealey. And from the white, francophone population of the city came three young musicians who went out of their way to learn to play the new black music first-hand at jam sessions: violinist Willy Girard, tenor saxophonist Adrien Paradis, and pianist Robert Langlois. These three men's routes to jazz were particularly arduous, since they had to surmount a linguistic as well as a cultural barrier to gain entry to the unilingually English and almost entirely black jazz community in Montreal. Adrien Paradis became known to the musicians as "Eddy"—sometimes "Eddy Paradise." Robert Langlois became "Bob." Girard, shy and soft-spoken, was always just "Willy." They mastered jazz far better than they did English, a factor that in Girard's case especially was to deter him from following a career to near-certain fame in the United States.

Little is known of Paradis's youth; and Girard's story will be told later, with that of the Louis Metcalf band in which his career reached its peak. But Langlois's coming to jazz reveals much about Montreal's early jazz scene. His older brothers and cousins all played the piano, and, as might be expected, he showed an interest in music at an early age. While still a child, Langlois was given a harmonica by his aunt, and he began to play it by ear. He spent all his spare time learning the latest popular tunes from the radio and records, and he was especially fond of the music of Willie Eckstein, whom he idolized. The young Langlois used to skip classes in the afternoons and go to the Strand theatre on St. Catherine Street, just to hear Eckstein play. Once, when he was twelve or thirteen, he played hookey and summoned up the courage to go to Eckstein's home.

> He [Eckstein] asked me what I wanted. I answered that I wanted to hear him play, just for me. He was dumbfounded, but he sat down at the piano and played for me. Then he asked me if I played the piano. I said no, but told him I played the harmonica. He made me play for him, and then he said, "I have a radio program, would you like to come on it?"[3]

Elated, the boy appeared on Eckstein's show the very next day and was invited back for several subsequent appearances. They played duets together on the air, harmonica and piano. It was this firsthand exposure to Eckstein's brilliant piano playing that inspired Langlois to take up the piano.

Langlois's father, however, had different ideas. Worrying that his son would succumb to the drugs and alcohol which he associated with the lifestyle of the popular musician, he sold the family piano, hoping to thwart the boy's ambitions. But the young Langlois would not be dissuaded; he began teaching himself to play on a neighbour's piano. At fifteen he quit school and went to work delivering bailiff's notices; from his six-dollar weekly salary he saved up twenty-five dollars, bought a piano at a bailiff's auction, and—enduring his father's fury—had it delivered to the family home.

When the storm blew over, Langlois began taking private lessons with a dance-band pianist named Pierre Drolet, who brought his eager student along to the halls where he worked. After the dances were over, Drolet would take Langlois around to the city's nightclubs, rounding out the teenager's musical education with firsthand exposure to the popular music of the day. Langlois soaked it all in. He was most impressed by the black musicians he heard and began seeking them out wherever he could. One day he rode the streetcar out to Belmont Park, an amusement park on the north side of Montreal island, to listen to the black band that was appearing at the dance pavilion there. Finding the band without a piano player, he asked if he could sit in. Soon the black musicians were inviting Langlois to attend late-night jam sessions at a private meeting room on St. Antoine Street they called the Clef Club. There, one night, Langlois met the American jazz pianist and entertainer Fats Waller, who was appearing uptown at the Loew's theatre. He also encountered Adrien Paradis and Willy Girard, who by their own circuitous routes had found their way to the Clef Club room, the hub of the city's black musical community. The three young whites jammed with the black musicians whenever they were invited; once Langlois performed Gershwin's "Rhapsody in Blue" from memory and drew a great round of applause.

By the early 1930s Langlois was playing occasional dance jobs with the black musicians. Once he worked three weeks with a black band at a hotel in Magog, a small town east of Montreal. In Montreal, however, nightclub owners who hired black musicians to accompany their black shows didn't want to see whites in the band, no matter how talented they were. Langlois, like other aspiring white jazz musicians, was thus confined to working in white bands in the city's nightclubs. The music played by the white bands was further removed from the black jazz he loved, but it offered its own rewards. Not the least of these was the fulfillment of a childhood dream to play piano duets with his idol, Eckstein. While still in his early twenties, Langlois teamed up with

Robert Langlois (at piano, right) with Willie Eckstein's (piano, left) band at the suburban Chateau St. Rose during the summer of 1941 or 1942. The band included leading members of the first generation of francophone Quebec musicians to embrace jazz. Back row, left to right: unidentified waiter holding bass; Roy Decair (drums); Marcel Scherer (trumpet); unidentified (trombone). Front row: Pete Gravel (bass, holding clarinet); Willy Girard (violin); Adrien Paradis (tenor saxophone, clarinet, flute); Stan Simons (alto saxophone); Tony Sabetta (alto saxophone). *Photo by Editorial Associates, courtesy of Robert Langlois. John Gilmore Jazz History Collection. Concordia University Archives.*

Eckstein to work at various nightclubs and theatres; the two men sat at their own pianos and were accompanied by the house orchestra. Spanning as he did both the white and black sectors of Montreal's jazz community, Langlois became widely respected by subsequent generations of francophone musicians, both for his musicianship and for his openness to later styles of jazz, including bebop and free jazz. When he retired in 1981, Langlois's name was still relatively unknown to the city's English community, yet to the francophone musicians and fans, he had attained something of the status of a father-figure.

What began as a trickle of black music into Montreal in the early 1920s had become a torrent by the time the Depression struck in 1929. Black music had found its way into the city's dance halls, nightclubs, and vaudeville theatres, and onto the cruise ships and ferries that plied the St. Lawrence River. By 1925 the Gayety theatre was regularly presenting black performers and "coloured jazz orchestras." During the winter of 1925-26, for example, its program included the Seven Syncopators, comedian and clarinetist George McClennon, and a musical revue with a cast of seventy—half of them black performers, including blues singer Lena Wilson and bandleader Joe Jordan with his Ten Sharps and Flats. In 1929 a touring company from the New York musical *Blackbirds* ended its North American tour at His Majesty's theatre in Montreal.[4] The large movie theatres, too, began importing top black acts directly from the Cotton Club in Harlem, including Fats Waller and the jazz bands of Cab Calloway and Duke Ellington. Other American bands appeared at dance halls: Fletcher Henderson brought his fifteen-piece band directly from the Roseland Ballroom in New York City to the Palais d'Or in Montreal for a one-week engagement in 1934, the first stop on a North American tour. Meanwhile, Lou Hooper, the Ontario-born pianist and composer who had already made some one hundred race records in New York City, had arrived in Montreal in about 1933. For the next six years he played in clubs, taught piano to such local youngsters as Oscar Peterson, and imported black shows from the United States to the Monte Carlo club in the St. Antoine district, in which he was a part owner.

Clubs featuring black entertainment were opening in abundance. Sometime in the 1920s one of the most legendary of these so-called

Herb Johnson's band at the Chinese Paradise Grill in Chinatown, late 1930s: Arthur Davis (piano, arranger); Freddie Blackburn (drums); Herb Johnson (tenor saxophone, clarinet); Herbert Augustus Johnson (alto saxophone, clarinet); unidentified (trumpet). *Courtesy of Herb Johnson. John Gilmore Jazz History Collection, Concordia University Archives.*

"black clubs," the Terminal club, opened on St. Antoine Street across from Windsor Station. The Terminal's shows were modest compared with others in the city, but the club became an informal after-hours meeting place for visiting black entertainers and musicians, and the scene of countless jam sessions. A few blocks west of the Terminal, past the Boston Café where the railway porters congregated, was Rockhead's Paradise, which opened in 1928 and was the only Montreal nightclub actually owned by a black. It was destined to become the most famous black club in Canada. Walking a zig-zag route north and east from Rockhead's, towards The Main, one passed several clubs which presented black shows and musicians intermittently during the 1930s: the Kit-Kat Cabaret, the Washington Club, the Cosy Grill, the Cotton Grill, and the Embassy. Then, within a radius of a few blocks around the corner of St. Catherine and The Main, were the "east-end" clubs that regularly featured black shows: the Boulevard, open by 1928, the Commodore, the Hollywood, the Blue Sky, Connie's Inn, and the Montmartre. The Rendez-Vous dance hall on The Main featured black bands, too. In nearby Chinatown, the Chinese Paradise Grill adopted a black show policy for a while.[5] Even some of the "sporting houses," as the brothels were discreetly called, had black music, usually provided by a solo pianist. The tips were said to be so good at some of these houses that the musicians paid the brothel-keepers for the privilege of sitting down at the piano. Finally, music may also have been played at some of the hideaways favoured by the black musicians, places remembered only by such names as Chauffeur Charlie's and Papa Greenspoon's.

Daybreak, 7 May 1935. Eight men slept fitfully on army cots, fully clothed against the cold of a late spring night. The only heat in the dusty storage room behind the dance pavilion came from a kitchen toaster, its cord trailing from an overhead light socket, its tiny coils glowing red in the grey dawn. Fortune was looking kindly upon the Harlem Dukes of Rhythm. Opening night of their summer tour of southern Ontario had been a success. It was the middle of the Depression, but they had work.

Jimmy Jones had packed his musicians,[6] their matching white suits, and their instruments—three saxophones, a trombone, a guitar, a drum kit, and Jones's trumpet—into a hired bus the day before in Montreal. For more than five hours they had lumbered southwest along the St. Lawrence River and on to Kingston, a college town on the shore of Lake Ontario. The posters were shouting from every street corner: "Canada's Finest Coloured Dance Orchestra," playing all week in the pavilion at the town's lakeside amusement park. The boys had been in high spirits. It looked as if it was going to be a good summer, at twenty-five dollars a week per man.

Some of the musicians in the band had been scuffling all winter, working two jobs back to back when they could find them, and subsisting on the generosity of other musicians when their luck ran out. Club

LOOKIE! LOOKIE! LOOKIE!

HERE COMES

JIMMIE JONES

AND HIS

HARLEM DUKES OF RHYTHM

CANADA'S
FINEST
COLORED
DANCE
ORCHESTRA

STAGE
RADIO
AND
DANCE
BAND

FLOOR SHOW
FUN AND ENTERTAINMENT
DON'T MISS THIS

NAPANEE ARMOURIES
THURSDAY, MAY 16TH

Hanson & Edgar Ltd., Printers, Kingston

owners had been reducing the size of their bands as the Depression cut into their profits; some clubs were even cancelling shows and cutting back on musicians' salaries. People just weren't going out as much as they used to, or spending as much on food, drinks, and tips. Many of the musicians, and especially the blacks who were harder hit by the economic crisis,[7] had been leaving the city in search of work. Some put together travelling dance bands or accompanied small shows to towns and smaller cities throughout Quebec and as far afield as the Atlantic Provinces and northern Ontario, where black performers were still regarded as something of a novelty. Meanwhile, the arrival of the "talkies" at the end of the 1920s had put theatre pianists out of work as well.

Montreal was not alone in exiling some of its talent during the Depression. Musicians wandered about the continent, stopping wherever they could find work. Countless numbers of unemployed musicians left New York City; some drifted north through New England, and a few ended up in Montreal. One who arrived in 1935, two years after leaving Harlem, was saxophonist Herb Johnson. His reputation had reached the ears of the enterprising Jimmy Jones, who enticed Johnson to Montreal with the prospect of a summer tour with his Harlem Dukes of Rhythm.

Working at an obscure hotel in a sleepy town somewhere was one thing, but a summer on the road playing dance pavilions with Jones was special. The musicians liked working with him: he swung hard, he played loud and exciting solos, and he pushed the music as far as possible into the realms of jazz without alienating the dancers. Jones liked to have fun, too, on and off the bandstand. He especially liked to gamble, and his bandmates sometimes had to drag him away from a good game when it came time to hit the stage.

Jones had come from the United States; no one remembered from where exactly. Some say he arrived in Montreal with the Shorter Brothers Band and refused, like most of the other members, to leave. He was a strong trumpet player with a good feeling for the blues. He must have been a skillful talker as well, for he succeeded in convincing a booking agent in Belleville, Ontario, to line up a summer's worth of engagements for his Harlem Dukes of Rhythm.

Fortune, however, changed her mind after that jubilant opening night in Kingston. A Toronto band was touring the same circuit just ahead of

(left): Poster used to promote Jimmy Jones's tour of southern Ontario during the summer of 1935. The photograph shows the Harlem Dukes of Rhythm prior to the tour; left to right: unidentified (saxophone); Herbert Augustus Johnson (alto saxophone, violin); Willy Wade (drums); Arthur Davis (piano, arranger); Sidney Flood (president of the Canadian Clef Club, not a band member); Frank Johnson (trombone); Henry Johnson (tenor saxophone); Jimmy Jones (trumpet); Benny Johnson (guitar). Two changes were made for the tour: Bill Kersey (tenor saxophone) replaced the unidentified saxophonist, and Herb Johnson (tenor saxophone) replaced Henry Johnson. *Courtesy of Herb Johnson. John Gilmore Jazz History Collection, Concordia University Archives.*

the Harlem Dukes of Rhythm, and the Montreal band arrived at their next stop to find a town full of footsore and penniless dancers. Poor organization by the booking agent contributed to the disappointing turnouts: sometimes the band's publicity posters arrived in a town just as the band was packing to move on. When one town cancelled its booking in June, the musicians had to borrow money to eat, then telegraph Belleville to ask for an advance on their next week's salaries.

The band's musical reputation, however, remained unsullied, and word of their prowess travelled suprisingly fast. The Silver Slipper nightclub in Toronto sent the band a telegram inviting it to audition for an engagement. Unfortunately, the telegram was intercepted by the man who drove, and owned, the band bus. Fred Hinds quickly calculated that if the Harlem Dukes of Rhythm landed a lengthy engagement at the prestigious Silver Slipper, they would abandon their tour, leaving his bus idle. Hinds concealed the telegram from the musicians and notified the Silver Slipper that the group had broken up. By the time the treachery was uncovered, the musicians had completed their wearying tour and returned to Montreal. The invitation was apparently never renewed.

Back in Montreal, the members of the Harlem Dukes of Rhythm returned to the life of underemployment and insecurity common to local musicians during the Depression. Faced with enduring hardship, the city's black musicians found solidarity and a creative outlet at a unique room on St. Antoine Street called the Clef Club. The jam sessions that began there at three o'clock every Thursday morning were the social and creative side of an organization formed by Montreal's black musicians to try to improve their lot. When they weren't talking business, the meeting room—in a converted residential flat above a store—reverberated with jazz and the laughter of members and their guests, including visiting black entertainers and musicians, and a few local white musicians like Bob Langlois and Willy Girard. On the third floor a gambling game was usually in progress.[8]

The seed of the idea to organize may have been planted by black musicians from New York City where, in 1910, bandleader James Reese Europe had created the Clef Club to further the cause of black music and musicians.[9] The first attempt at forming a similar organization in Montreal didn't come until 1928, when a violinist named Arthur Provost signed up at least twenty resident black musicians and formed the Canadian Coloured Clef Club. The group held meetings and performed concerts of European classical music at a room near St. Lawrence Blvd., then faded from view in the early years of the Depression. It was revived sometime after 1932 by a clarinetist who apparently worked as a Red Cap baggage porter at Windsor Station. Under Sydney Flood's guidance, the Clef Club rented a room on St. Antoine Street and in 1935 became an all-black union local, number 11, of the Canadian Federation of Musicians (CFM).

There were good reasons for the black musicians in Montreal to organize. The hospitality and abundance of work which had endeared Montreal to them in the 1920s faded away during the 1930s. As the Depression worsened and unemployment soared, blacks, Jews, and other minorities experienced a marked deterioration in the city's racial climate. Nazi rallies were held openly. It is difficult to assess to what degree the working conditions of black musicians actually worsened during the Depression, because so little is known about employment practices in the Montreal entertainment industry prior to 1935. But one thing is certain: black musicians were frequently out of work during the Depression. This fact alone brought into stark relief longstanding discriminatory practices, barriers which had been more easily tolerated by the musicians during previous years of prosperity.[10]

One barrier was the refusal by the most powerful musicians' union in the city to admit blacks as members. This was the Musicians' Guild of Montreal, Local 406 of the American Federation of Musicians (AFM). The guild was not unique: AFM locals in the United States also barred blacks. Nor was the guild alone in Montreal in using race as a criterion of membership in a musicians' association. The smaller, now defunct Canadian Federation of Musicians had established a local for white musicians in Montreal in 1934, comprised mainly of musicians disenchanted with the American union. A year later the CFM chartered the twenty-one members of the Clef Club as an all-black local. The blacks thus achieved membership in a union, but only on the fringes of power in Montreal. Greatly outnumbered by white musicians in the CFM, and overwhelmed by the powerful AFM guild, they had little means to challenge a more insidious racial barrier in the city.

This second barrier was an unwritten understanding, between the AFM guild and employers, that black musicians would not be hired to play in bands in hotels and most of the nightclubs on the west side of the city centre.[11] Blacks referred to this area of the city as "uptown" because it was a short, uphill walk from St. Antoine Street. Wages were higher in the uptown nightspots, which helps explain why the guild was eager to reserve the territory for its white members. But racism was also at work: most of the uptown establishments simply didn't want to see blacks on the premises, whether as paying customers or as employees. A few uptown clubs did experiment with black entertainment for brief periods during the 1920s and 1930s, giving black musicians an occasional chance to work on or near the west-central strip of St. Catherine Street. For the most part, however, black musicians were confined to the "east-end" clubs on or near St. Lawrence Blvd., and "downtown" on St. Antoine Street.

Racial considerations influenced nightclub policies in other ways, too. Club owners insisted that all-black bands play the music for all-black shows, and that white bands play for white shows. When a club changed the colour of its show, the band had to change as well, no mat-

Two Montreal bands of the 1930s. (top) At the Club St. Michel: Harold "Steep" Wade (piano); Eddie Perkins (drums); George Sealey (tenor saxophone); Benny Montgomery (trumpet); Randolph Whinfield (alto saxophone). (bottom) Herb Johnson's band at the Roseland Ballroom in Montreal: Herb Johnson (tenor saxophone, clarinet); Hugh Sealey (alto saxophone, clarinet); Elmer Smith (piano); Freddie Blackburn (drums); Clyde Duncan (bass). *Top photo by Jack Markow, courtesy of Evelyn Sealey. Bottom photo by La Photo Modèle, courtesy of Herb Johnson. John Gilmore Jazz History Collection, Concordia University Archives.*

ter how capable the outgoing band might be of playing the new show's music. This tradition prevented black and white musicians from working together on nightclub stages in Montreal through the Depression; it wasn't until the mid-1940s that mixed bands were seen with any regularity, and some clubs were still insisting on all-black or all-white bands as late as the 1960s. Outside of the nightclubs, racially mixed bands found work only in some dance halls, theatres, and community centres. Meanwhile, not only were black customers refused entry to the uptown night spots, but they were also barred from some of the east-end clubs featuring black shows. White patrons, of course, had access to all of Montreal's clubs; indeed the black clubs depended for their survival on white patrons, because the city's black community was too small to support them. Interracial dancing, a scandalous suggestion uptown, was permitted in the black clubs.

Against this backdrop of racial discrimination and economic hardship, the Clef Club tried to protect the livelihood of its members. It drew up a contract and a list of bylaws, intended, in the organization's words, to "relieve some of the grievous injustices, to end some of the mutually destructive difficulties, to ameliorate some of the suspicion and distrust that has long been a festering impediment to a happier and more profitable understanding between decent, capable musicians and decent, responsible employers."[12] For the most part, the bylaws were conventional union regulations about terms of employment and internal procedures. But in one respect they were daring: they declared the intention of the Clef Club to restrict the influx of more black musicians from the United States into Montreal.

To this end, the bylaws prohibited a Clef Club bandleader from hiring a foreign musician until the leader had satisfied the local that no Clef Club musician could do the job. So important was the issue considered to be that permission to hire a foreigner required the consent of a majority of Clef Club members voting in a secret ballot. A foreign musician who succeeded in obtaining work with a local bandleader was required to join the Clef Club and to pay membership dues before playing a note of music in the city; anyone who neglected to do so would be denounced to Canadian immigration authorities.[13] This was a curious set of bylaws, considering that some of the Clef Club members were themselves recent arrivals from the United States. Clearly, however, the black musicians who had settled in Montreal had come to identify themselves closely with the city and were hoping to protect the lean local job market from incursion.

None of this union activity appears to have benefited the black musicians in any tangible way. There is no evidence of deportations, or of punitive action against a club for unfair treatment of a musician, or even of the establishment of a minimum wage for the Clef Club's members. At the same time, the racial barriers remained intact and the musicians were frequently out of work. The tiny black local could not hope to influence either the economy or the AFM guild. The Clef Club's membership never exceeded twenty-five, and it frequently dropped below that figure when unemployed musicians failed to pay their dues, or left the city for months at a time to work elsewhere.

The city's racial barriers collapsed unexpectedly, as the world swung from Depression to war. Expediency, rather than a sudden flowering of conscience or outburst of anger, was the catalyst for change. Though the CFM never posed a serious threat to the AFM in Canada, the mere existence of a rival union hampered the AFM's efforts to establish firm control over the North American music industry. As long as musicians belonging to a rival union were available to work, an employer could flaunt AFM regulations and avoid punitive sanctions by severing its dealings with the American union and hiring CFM musicians instead. To consolidate its power, therefore, the AFM actively encouraged CFM musicians to defect. At the same time, the CFM musicians were realizing that they were missing out on job opportunities at workplaces firmly in the AFM camp. In Montreal, the CFM's white local held out for five years. Then, in October 1939, its president defected to the guild. Within two weeks, the remaining seventy-five CFM faithful followed him. The CFM white local simply ceased to exist.[14]

At some point the AFM guild realized that if it intended to drive the CFM completely out of Montreal, it would have to absorb the Clef Club musicians as well. Exactly how and when it did so is not known. No records have been found of any discussion of the issue at guild meetings. Nevertheless, other evidence suggests the guild began admitting blacks at about the same time that it absorbed the last of the white CFM musicians. A newsletter sent out by guild officials in November 1939 to inform members of the victory contains what appears to be a reference to the city's black musicians:

> The east-end boys are also realizing that they cannot improve their working conditions unless they join us. Confident in your present administration, they are joining us in great numbers and have shown, so far, a magnificent spirit; the cabaret situation in the east-end is disgusting; their plight is sad and in their distress they are extending their hands; in helping them organize we are also helping ourselves.[15]

Herb Johnson was vice-president of the Clef Club at the time. More than forty years later he was able to reconstruct from memory the sequence of events which led him to join the AFM guild. One day in late 1939 he received a call from an uptown club owner asking him to assemble a band to start work immediately. The white house band had apparently refused to continue working in a disagreement over money or hours. Johnson opened on a Saturday night, presumably with an all-black band. On Sunday morning he received another urgent telephone call, this time from Sydney Flood, president of the Clef Club. Flood asked Johnson to meet him at the guild immediately. When he arrived at the meeting, Johnson learned that the band he had replaced had filed a grievance against the club with the guild. In the guild's eyes, Johnson was working as a scab, an argument that carried little weight with either Johnson or the Clef Club since the guild had all along refused to allow black musicians into its ranks. But the allegations betrayed the guild's vulnerability to the black local.

Throughout the afternoon, the union leaders negotiated. The pressure was on the guild to admit Johnson as a member if it wanted him to boycott the club. If he didn't, the club would slip out of the AFM's control and the white bandleader's grievance might never be resolved. Eventually a deal was struck: Johnson agreed to quit his job at the club; in return, the guild agreed to allow Clef Club members to seek work uptown. Johnson did so, was offered work playing with a white bandleader in an AFM-controlled club, and immediately put the guild's intentions to the test by resigning from the Clef Club and applying for membership in the guild. He was accepted, becoming, by his own account, the first black musician to join the Montreal local of the American Federation of Musicians.

By the summer of 1940, the guild was issuing membership cards to black musicians. In theory, the blacks had won equal access to employment anywhere in the city. In practice, the uptown nightspots continued to be the almost exclusive domain of white musicians for years to come. For this reason, perhaps, the Clef Club musicians did not immediately flock to the guild. The black local survived for three more years. Its membership gradually dwindled, however, as musicians joined the army or grew weary of their isolation and went over to the guild. Finally, in the autumn of 1943, five remaining members of the Clef Club wrote to the headquarters of the All-Canadian Congress of Labour saying they could no longer survive as a union. They asked the congress to keep their charter in the drawer until the war was over, or until they could recruit new members. The Clef Club was never heard from again. Thereafter, Montreal musicians were represented by a single union whose power base lay in the United States.

INTERLUDE ONE

Echoes of 1928

Written documents of Montreal's jazz history are rare. The oldest written account of nightlife in the St. Antoine district is contained in "The Montreal Negro Community," a sociology thesis completed in 1928 by Wilfred Emmerson Israel. The words sit uncomfortably today, but they are all that we have, all that remain from the early years of jazz in Montreal.

Two Negro buffet parlors are being operated on St. Antoine street at No. 1256 over a tavern, and the other at No. 1323, over a Chinese laundry. Both premises have been former private residences. At No. 1256 the partitions between some rooms have been removed, giving greater floor space for dancing. For a period this location was known as the Owl Club. Membership and admission today is on a basis of being known to the management. These two houses are the Negro cabarets of Montreal.

The cabaret or night club is the night life of this group. During the day only the casual visitor is to be seen seeking admission. After 11 o'clock at night the patrons are to be observed drifting in the direction from their homes and from the auxiliary social centres in the sporting district. The jazz band, of piano, violin, and two saxophones, grind out the sensuous blue harmonies with a syncopation that sets the body in ready motion with sympathetic vibrations. With sounds of Broadway's favorites floating through the windows, lowered from the top, the patrons come in increasing numbers. By midnight these places are filled to their capacity. From then till daylight the dominance of the saxophone is challenged by the hilarity and laughter of both male and female voices. Nearby residents have, they claim, learned the words of "Follow the Swallow Back Home" and "Whispering," while struggling unsuccessfully to drop off in their blissful slumbers. Another claimed learning the piano version of "Girl of My Dreams."

The lady patrons of these cabarets are largely whites. These girls of the teen age and early twenties, some of whom are never seen in this district, except at night, come from all sections of the St. Antoine district.

Above the hill has its representatives also.... Coming from different sections of the city, they enjoy the freedom and abandonment of their new contacts. There is an emotional excitement to these girls from the fact of being in strange surroundings; the musical rhythm is most penetrating; the eating and drinking with the dark, soft-skinned male, supply that thrill and emotional release of unsatisfied wishes which she has sought for so long. Live, eat, drink and be merry, for tomorrow I may die has become her philosophy for this brief but fascinating period. The patriotic "God Save the King" at 5 o'clock in the morning brings the night's festivities to a happy conclusion. With the break up of these parties, the revellers are observed slowly wending their respective paths homeward. Often the young girls show facial signs of the glorious night that has been hers. Some walk after the pattern of the drunkard in their tired march home to rest for the frolic of tomorrow.

Excerpt from Wilfred Emmerson Israel, "The Montreal Negro Community," Master's thesis, McGill University, Montreal, 1928, 189-90. Street numbers may not correspond to present addresses.

You are cordially invited to attend the opening of

Connies Inn (Formerly The Frolics)

ON SATURDAY, MAY 20TH ... 9 P.M.

Featuring the highest calibre of colored divertissement direct from

the world **Famous Harlem.**

Incomparable dance rhythms by the Canadian Ambassadors,

Colored Kings of Jazz......

Blue Singers and Torrid Dancers to entertain yo

The pleasure-loving spirit of Harlem, carefree, happ

you'll find at CONNIES INN.

At **considerably reduced prices.**

NEVER A COUVERT OR

MINIMUM CHARG

Promotional brochure for the 1933 opening of Connie's Inn, the nightclub which provided the Canadian Ambassadors with its first Montreal engagement. Note use of French words in the text. Shown here are the front cover and inside, actual size. *Myron Sutton Collection, Concordia University Archives.*

CHAPTER THREE

Myron Sutton
and the Canadian Ambassadors

The polished metal door of the Voyageur bus swings open into the damp, December air. Niagara Falls, Ontario. Thundering nearby is the intractable, misting river. A man eases out of a parked sedan to greet his visitor. He wears a faded red ski jacket, an olive peaked cap, and freshly laundered workingman's trousers. A grey stubble peppers his face, but the bright eyes sparkling from beneath the cap and the taut muscles about his mouth belie his seventy-eight years. His handshake is firm: it's not difficult to imagine him gripping a welding torch, as he did every working day for almost thirty years. Stooping stiffly now, he settles again behind the wheel, his back hurting, but his voice crackling with high-pitched laughter. "I don't know much. I haven't got much to tell you. I hope you haven't wasted your time coming all the way down here."[1]

Myron Sutton was born in his parents' modest bungalow on Peer Street, Niagara Falls, in 1903. His father worked in a factory; his mother cooked and cleaned and ran the household. Mynie was their only child, and though none of the family was particularly musical, the boy's father sent him to the organist at a local church for piano lessons when he was nine. When he moved up from elementary school to Stamford Collegiate, he began playing the piano for the school dances.

Mynie was thirteen years old when the Original Dixieland Jazz Band's first record went on sale in the United States. New York State was visible, almost audible, across the Niagara River, and the jazz craze that swept the continent fueled the teenager's interest in the clarinet. By the time he was seventeen he had acquired an instrument of his own and started taking lessons; soon he picked up the alto saxophone as well.

Mynie persevered with high school, but devoted himself to music. He played clarinet in a local concert band, marching through the streets of Niagara Falls and playing for funeral processions. One summer he worked as a steward on a Lake Erie cruise ship sailing out of nearby Buffalo, New York. Eventually he started working across the border as a musician, too, playing clarinet and saxophone in a quartet in Niagara Falls, New York. The principal at Stamford thought enough of Mynie's abilities to give him fifty dollars to start a school band.

As Mynie's musicianship matured, his father began talking about sending him to a music conservatory somewhere in the United States, once he'd graduated from high school. It was not to be. One day when Mynie was playing with the quartet across the river, a pianist named Joe Stewart offered him a job in his dance band in Buffalo. Mynie abruptly quit school in the middle of grade twelve, shattering his father's hopes, and moved to the United States to join Stewart. It was 1924, Sutton was twenty years old, and his teenage dream of becoming a professional musician had come true.

The names, places, and dates trickle from his memory slowly, not with strain so much as with a certain reluctance to breathe again. It is all so long ago, so far in the distant past. He stands at the dining-room table in his house on Peer Street, three doors from where he was born, and thumbs the pages of a crumbling, overflowing scrapbook. Its old, glossy photographs, creased letters, and yellowed newspaper clippings document the travels, the triumphs, and the bitter frustrations of one of Canada's jazz pioneers.

"I didn't know anything about the blues before I got to Buffalo," Sutton ventures, searching for order in the unruly procession of memories wakened by the scrapbook and his visitor's curiosity. Looking back, he admits he didn't know much about jazz, either. Though he had been listening to records of black music back home in Niagara Falls, he hadn't spent much time trying to ad-lib his own melodies on the clarinet or saxophone. The older musicians in Joe Stewart's band took him along to jam sessions but he was too shy to play. He watched and listened, though, and after a while began ad-libbing a little when the occasion arose on the job. He was learning the kind of lessons they didn't teach at the conservatory.

After two years with Stewart, Sutton graduated to Eugene Primus's Birds of Paradise, one of the most popular bands in the Buffalo area.[2] One of the musicians in the nine-piece outfit was a young man from Georgia named J. C. Higginbotham, who had fled the drudgery of a General Motors factory in the North about the same time Sutton had dropped out of school. Higginbotham was set on making a name for himself as a big-time trombone player, and not long after Sutton joined

Twenty-three-year-old Myron Sutton with the Birds of Paradise, a New York State band which included trombonist J. C. Higginbotham. *Photo by Sattler, Buffalo, N.Y. Myron Sutton Collection, Concordia University Archives.*

The band bus that brought Myron Sutton back to Canada in 1927 with the Royal Ambassadors. *Myron Sutton Collection, Concordia University Archives.*

the Primus band Higginbotham defected to a travelling band. This was the Royal Ambassadors, a group of ten musicians from Cleveland, Ohio, who were working the territory around Buffalo in 1926. Higginbotham stayed with the Ambassadors for only seven months before latching on to a band headed for New York City, where he eventually found the fame he was looking for. But before he left the Ambassadors, Sutton caught up with him. The Canadian was looking for a way out of Buffalo, too—he'd been living there about three years, and the lustre had worn off the city. Higginbotham tried to persuade Sutton to join him on the road for New York City, but Sutton had his mind set on returning to Canada. He talked about home so often the Buffalo musicians had nicknamed him "Canada."

> Higginbotham wanted me to go to New York, and guys like that figured I was qualified to go to New York. But New York sounded *big* to me, and I just didn't want to be bothered. I really didn't. And maybe I'm sorry I didn't go. I could have possibly fitted in some place. But it just didn't appeal to me. The Royal Ambassadors had bookings in Canada, and so when I had a chance to go with them that's what I did.

Crowded into the back of a windowless wooden bus with nine other musicians and their instruments, Sutton's return to Canada was anything but triumphant. Still, it was springtime, and he was on the move. The Royal Ambassadors established a base in the village of Iroquois, Ontario, on the St. Lawrence River not far from the Quebec border: from there they rode out across southeastern Ontario, playing dance music and a few novelty numbers in one small town after another. A booking agent in Winchester, Ontario, lined up the jobs.

> The booker would take us to little towns like Perth, Ontario. They never saw coloured people before. The band was an oddity, and he played it for all it was worth. He made money, but that didn't make any difference to me. I was surviving. I had to survive, eh?

When summer ended, Sutton rode back to Buffalo with the band and worked there with it through the winter. The following summer the Royal Ambassadors were back in Ontario again. They kept this schedule up for at least two summers, possibly three. On one occasion, when the band was lazing around Iroquois with nothing to do for a day or two, Sutton and one of the trumpet players, Ted Brock, took a trip down to Montreal to investigate the stories they'd been hearing about the city. It was a hurried visit, but long enough for them to make the acquaintance of Elmer Smith and a few other musicians at the Terminal club on St. Antoine Street. The other two saxophonists in the Royal Ambassadors

The Cleveland-based Royal Ambassadors on stage in Iroquois, Ontario, during the summer of 1927. Left to right: Burroughs (trombone); unidentified (trombone); Lester Vactor (tuba, leader); Herbie Jenkins (trumpet); Rodrick Ray (drums, xylophone); Gudgell (piano); Bill Shorter (tenor saxophone); Andy Shorter (alto and baritone saxophones); unidentified (banjo); Myron Sutton (alto saxophone). *Myron Sutton Collection, Concordia University Archives.*

didn't make the trip, but Sutton and Brock's account of Montreal wasn't wasted on them: within a few years Andy and Bill Shorter would find their own way to the city, and stay the rest of their lives.

The Royal Ambassadors never made it to Montreal as a band, but they did work at the posh Gatineau Country Club in the hills of Quebec just across the river from Ottawa. They were a big hit with the white society patrons, and were apparently offered a long engagement at the club. But Canadian immigration authorities refused to extend the musicians' visas. Discouraged, they loaded back into their bus and returned to Buffalo, where they disbanded sometime around 1930. Out of work, Sutton went home to Niagara Falls alone.

He is seated now in an armchair in the living room. Though it is midafternoon, the curtains are drawn, and there is a timelessness to the diffused light and stillness of the room. His wife, Mae, is out shopping. Pictures of their grandchildren adorn the television set. Sutton is a modest man, and it is obvious he is uncomfortable talking about himself to strangers. He fidgets in the armchair, scraping a drink coaster back and forth across the fabric. There is a hint of impatience in his voice one moment, then a sigh of resignation the next; a crackling flame of laughter, then a whisper of pride: slowly he pieces together the story of the birth of his Canadian band.

Well, I got the idea that I'd rather stay in Canada than go back to the States. So, somehow I got in touch with this man at the Gatineau Country Club. I heard that he wanted a band—an all-coloured band. And so eventually I tried to find some boys that could play.

That proved to be a bigger problem than Sutton had ever imagined. Canadian immigration told him he couldn't bring American musicians into the country to work in his band until he had exhausted every effort in finding qualified Canadian musicians. The only black musicians Sutton could find in the region who were available to work were a piano player and a saxophonist. The Canadian immigration officers still weren't satisfied: they urged him to try to entice Canadian musicians back from the United States. Sutton first contacted Clyde Duncan, a banjo and guitar player he knew in Guelph. Clyde's older brother Lloyd, a tenor saxophonist who was working in Rochester, New York, agreed to come back. So did an Ontario-born drummer named Terry Hooper, who had settled in Cleveland. Getting Hooper back across the Canadian border, however, was another problem.

> Terry decided he's coming back to Canada. So we get down to the bridge [across the Niagara River]. None of us had any money and he wanted to bring his drums across. So they wanted us to pay duty on the drums, eh? We couldn't pay the duty, so the man says, "You have to take 'em back to the States." Well, I had some friends in the States—my mother's from there—so we decided we'd take 'em over there. We got over the river and they wouldn't let us go back into the States with the drums because he was a Canadian citizen. And we went through this for about an hour on the bridge, eh? Finally we said to the guys, "Let us take the drums over to the States, leave 'em there, we'll come over tomorrow and pay the duty and come home." So we did, and they let us go....
>
> Then Terry he had another hassle 'cause two of his kids were Canadian, two was born in the States. Anyway, he got that straightened out. So we got everybody except a trumpet player. We got three saxes—myself on alto and Lloyd Duncan on tenor and another chap from Windsor, I forget his name, and he played alto. We got John Walden on the piano and Terry Hooper was on the drums.[3] So now we needed a trumpet player, eh? So I went to the Immigration and told 'em what I had, and they said, "Well, if you can get a trumpet player from the States, preferably a West Indian boy, we'll fix it up so he can come over." So we did. We got this boy from Buffalo—Dave Burroughs was his name[4]—and they gave him a six-months permit to stay. That got renewed, and that's how we got the band started....

The musicians assembled in Guelph, hometown of Clyde and Lloyd Duncan. They brought with them whatever published "stock" arrangements of popular tunes they had collected from previous jobs, and they pitched in to buy a few more. But Sutton wanted the band to have a distinct sound and he began writing his own arrangements. Gradually these displaced the stock arrangements in the band's repertoire. Meanwhile, with Walden's help, Sutton was rehearsing the band, organizing the six members into a coherent, balanced unit. When it came time to pick a name for the group, Sutton remembered the band that had brought him back to Canada and thought, "What the hell—I'll call it the *Canadian* Ambassadors." Two days after Christmas 1931, the new band made its debut at the Gatineau Country Club. The management quickly expressed dissatisfaction with Walden's musicianship, and demanded he be replaced. Sutton assented and brought Brad Moxley, another Canadian from Windsor, Ontario, in to play piano.

The band was a hit at the Gatineau. On some nights fourteen hundred people crowded into the hall. A radio station broadcast the band live from the stage every night for thirty minutes. But after a year of working in the hills, the musicians became restless.

> At that time we were livin' in Ottawa, and Ottawa's a small place, eh? And they kept hearing about Montreal and they'd run down there on their days off and have a ball, and they got to the point where they just didn't want Ottawa no more. So we quit. We quit, and I said, "If you wanna go to Montreal, we'll go to Montreal." And we didn't have a damn thing to go to. So, I'd say, within two or three weeks we made contact, eh? But the band said, "You can't work, you gotta get us jobs." So they got in with a little group here, a little group there, and played, made ends meet, eh? But I couldn't play 'cause I was the leader of the band. They figured I would lose prestige if I worked with another group. I was starvin' with 'em, I ate toast, beans, and coffee, but I had prestige!

Sutton struggles for a moment to remember who else was playing jazz in Montreal during the winter of 1932-33 when the Canadian Ambassadors arrived.

> I don't think there was that much jazz in Montreal at all, actually, until we got in there and started to experiment and started playing the type of music that we were capable of playing, eh? You went to the Terminal club and they had maybe Smitty and a drummer and a saxophone player named Boston Herbie.[5] But it wasn't the type of jazz that we worked it up to be. And of course there was that violin player, Willy Girard—he was the only one who was playing any jazz. God, that guy could play! He used to come and sit in with us, and play. Beautiful music! There wasn't a

70

big band that come into town, Cab Calloway or any of them, that didn't ask Willy to join their band. He wouldn't go. He says, nah, he don't want no part of it. He was like that—like I was about going to New York.

For several months the Ambassadors freelanced individually in pick-up bands while Sutton circulated through the nightclubs, talking up his band and showing prospective employers his letters of reference from the Gatineau Country Club. Their determination to work as a unit paid off. A nightclub near the corner of St. Catherine Street and The Main was reopening with a black show policy. The location was already famous in the city: under its previous name, the Frolics, it had been home during Prohibition to a New York singer/hostess named Texas Guinan, who used to stand on a chair and shout "Hello, suckers!" as patrons walked in the door. Renovated and renamed Connie's Inn, the nightclub's new owners were vowing to bring the best of Harlem show biz to Montreal. Newspaper advertisements promised "the aristocrat of coloured floor shows" featuring "stunning Creole beauties," "famous sepian stars," and "incomparable dance rhythms by The Canadian Ambassadors— 'Colored Kings of Jazz.'" The band opened Connie's in May 1933, stayed on for the club's official opening in June, and was still there, working seven nights a week, when the New Year rolled around.

The nine-month engagement at Connie's Inn established the Canadian Ambassadors as the leading black band in Montreal. They were, in fact, the first organized Canadian black jazz band in the city's history—and quite possibly in all of Canada's.[6] Prior to the Ambassadors, only Millard Thomas and his Famous Chicago Novelty Orchestra had attained a comparable level of organization and stature in Montreal, but all of its members are believed to have been transplanted Americans. For six years during the 1930s, the name Canadian Ambassadors was associated with the best of Montreal jazz and black show biz, even during spells when the band was out of work, or out of town. No other black band in the city stayed together so long, became such an identifiable unit, and developed such a distinct repertoire of original arrangements.

Typically, the other black musicians in Montreal formed into groups when one of them landed a job, then disbanded once the engagement ended. There was little continuity even in the bands of such first-call leaders as Eddie Perkins, Jimmy Jones, and the Shorter brothers. As a result, leaders rarely wrote or commissioned written arrangements, and bands relied mainly on stock arrangements and impromptu, ad-libbed performances of popular tunes. The Canadian Ambassadors were different. Sutton added or subtracted musicians from the band according to the needs and budgets of his employers, but he maintained a loyal pool of musicians to draw upon. Some musicians left the pool over the six years and new musicians were brought in; but the presence of familiar faces and music on every job and the pride of belonging to a prestigious band engendered a sense of continuity in the Canadian Ambassadors that was unequalled by any other Montreal jazz band of the decade.

The Ambassadors' survival as an organized band during the Depression is explained first by the camaraderie of its members. All but one of the original Ambassadors were from southern Ontario, and all but a handful of the musicians who played with the band during its lifetime were Canadian citizens. This shared identity helped sustain individual members through periods of unemployment. "We were all Ontario boys," Sutton stressed, "so we stuck pretty close together. We had a kind of bond, eh?, and we looked after one another."

Sutton's leadership was a second factor. He tackled the business side of running a band with imagination and professionalism. He convinced a clothing store to outfit his musicians with custom-tailored uniforms at a major discount in exchange for a regular plug on stage. He collected letters of reference from club managers, radio stations, and booking agents. He printed up stationary with the name of the band in gothic lettering across the top, a list of prominent engagements down the side, and the band's "permanent address: 1742 Peer Street, Niagara Falls" across the bottom. He fed photographs and news about the band to local newspapers, to the American jazz magazines *Down Beat* and *Metronome*, and to the *Chicago Defender*, the leading black newspaper in the United States.[7] And when work became scarce in Montreal, he fired telegrams and letters off to prospective employers in Ontario.

But ultimately there was the music—spirited, swinging, and danceable. At the peak of the band's life, it had over three hundred tunes in its repertoire, many of them original arrangements. They were performed with the kind of relaxed, seemingly effortless, precision that comes after countless nights together on the bandstand.

> Our band was strictly a swing band, and we just swung, that's all. That's all we knew how to do. At that time, everybody liked swing, so they swung along with us! We never made ourselves *known* as a jazz band, but they just took it for granted we was a jazz band. Uptown in the big hotels they had a different type of music than we had. They had ballroom music. There might have been a barrier there that we never run against because we never tried to go for those jobs, eh? I guess there was restrictions around Montreal about who played where, but I never run into it. But I guess maybe I was lucky.... When I quit at Connie's Inn, they had already contacted me to play at the Hollywood. And

then when I quit another job, they had already contacted me to play at another place. Once I got established I wasn't running around looking for work. The band sold itself.

Sutton pauses to leaf through his scrapbook. It's all there: the letter from the Gatineau for that first job, the ads for the official opening of Connie's ("Yea Man! The Hottest Spot in Town!"), a photo of the band in one of its uniforms—black bow tie, short jacket with wide lapels, and a stripe running up each trouser leg. He stops to read a clipping, no name of the newspaper, no date: "Splendid Record Achieved by Sutton's Canadian Ambassadors: Played before Governor-General...." He doesn't remember when; the clipping doesn't say. Probably the second time at the Gatineau. "They have the distinction of being the only colored orchestra to appear before His Excellency the Governor-General."[8] And that's all. Not enough to jog a memory. "It was just one of those society nights, eh?" The Ambassadors couldn't have stayed long that second time at the Gatineau: a few weeks, maybe; early 1934. Buster Harding was with the band that time. Played piano....

Buster Harding was originally from Buxton, a small black community with a rich musical history, off the highway in farm country near Chatham, Ontario.[9] His father, Ben, played violin and sang with vocal groups. Ada, his mother, played organ at the Baptist and British Methodist Episcopal churches. She also taught music in the community; Buster started lessons with her at an early age. When he was ten, the family moved to Cleveland, Ohio, where Buster continued studying classical music at a school. He also began taking private lessons in jazz arranging. He led his own band in Cleveland and worked with another band in Buffalo. Then, in his early twenties, he returned to Canada.

Harding may have worked with the Canadian Ambassadors at the end of its debut engagement at the Gatineau Country Club and gone to Montreal with the band from there; in any case he was spotted in Montreal, playing in a band led by Eddie Perkins, during the Ambassadors' first winter in the city. How often Harding worked with the Ambassadors is not known, though a photograph confirms he was with the band during its return engagement to the Gatineau in early 1934. More importantly, he wrote an unknown number of arrangements for the band; tragically, they have all been lost. It is possible that Harding spent as many as four years in Montreal, but his stay was probably much shorter, for there is no firm evidence of his working in the city after 1933. An unconfirmed story says he married an American show girl in Montreal and moved to the United States with her. He joined the musicians' union in New York City in 1937 and went on to leave his mark on jazz, principally as an arranger for many leading

73

The Canadian Ambassadors during their brief 1934 engagement at the Gatineau Country Club in Aylmer, Quebec. Surrounding Myron Sutton at the piano are, left to right: Clyde Duncan (bass); Buster Harding (piano, arranger); Oscar Summers (unknown instrument, probably trumpet); unidentified musician from Windsor, Ontario (saxophone); Lloyd Duncan (tenor saxophone); Terry Hooper (drums). *Photo by Déry of Hull, Quebec, courtesy of Mae Sutton. Myron Sutton Collection, Concordia University Archives.*

The Canadian Ambassadors in one of their custom-tailored uniforms during an engagement at the Hollywood Club in 1934 or 1935. Left to right: Terry Hooper (drums); Clyde Duncan (bass); Lloyd Duncan (tenor saxophone); Myron Sutton (alto saxophone); Lou Hooper (piano); L. Fletcher (trumpet); Mayfield (bass or guitar); Andy Shorter (alto saxophone). *Myron Sutton Collection, Concordia University Archives.*

American big bands, including those of Teddy Wilson, Cab Calloway, Count Basie, Dizzy Gillespie, Benny Goodman, and Artie Shaw.

Another pianist to work with the Canadian Ambassadors was Lou Hooper, second cousin to the band's drummer Terry Hooper. Lou Hooper was also born in Buxton, but he was raised in Michigan, where he received a rigorous musical training. He served with a U.S. Army band in Europe during the First World War and then earned a bachelor of music degree in Detroit. In 1921 he moved to Harlem, where he taught music, recorded extensively, and worked with some of the leading black performers of the day. He was a member of the *Blackbirds* touring company that travelled to Montreal in 1929, but it was almost four more years before he returned to the city to stay. Hooper worked with the Canadian Ambassadors during part of its engagement at Connie's Inn, where he accompanied a teenage Billie Holiday during her appearance at the club. Unlike Harding, Hooper seems to have had no driving ambition to return to the United States: he was, after all, approaching forty. Until the Second World War took him back to Europe to entertain troops, Hooper remained in Montreal, working extensively with Sutton, teaching and composing, and leading a men's choir.

Back from the Gatineau, the Canadian Ambassadors settled into a fifteen-month residency at the Hollywood club, just around the corner from Connie's Inn. The band had grown to seven members at the Gatineau with the addition of a bass; now Sutton enlarged it to eight: first with a banjo or guitar, then preferring a second trumpet instead. A local radio station broadcast the band live from the club, where it accompanied black shows and provided music for dancing.

In the summer of 1934, while the Canadian Ambassadors were at the Hollywood, they received a job offer from Toronto, at $235 a week. Sutton turned it down. It wasn't the first time he enjoyed the luxury of refusing lucrative work in the middle of the Depression: in each of the two previous years, the band had received offers of work in Ontario, but on each occasion the musicians had preferred to stay in Montreal. More tempting, however, was an offer of work at a summer resort in the Adirondack Mountains of New York State, half-way down the highway from Montreal to New York City. Sutton expressed polite interest in the job, but when the booking agent applied to U.S. Immigration for permission to import the band, he was refused. The agent appealed to his congressman for help in getting the Ambassadors in, but without success. Immigration refused to bend on its interpretation of recently enacted legislation barring foreign musicians from working in the United States.

The treatment the Canadian Ambassadors received under the so-called "contract labour laws" of the United States would be meted out countless times again to Canadian musicians attempting to break into

WAR

WILL BE DECLARED
ON
Sunday, April 8th at 8.30 p.m.
AT THE
STADIUM Ball Room
(COR ONTARIO & DELORIMIER STS)

GRAND ATTRACTION

Complete Club Hollywood Creole Revue

30 PERFORMERS 30

One hour of fast, Red Hot Dancing, Singing and Entertainment.

12 Beautifull Creole Dancing girls.

10 Star Feature Singing and dancers. Babe Wallace, M. C.

PLUS

Myron Sutton and his Can. Ambassadors

Canada's Hottest Colored Orchestra

A floor show you will never forget,

A night you will always remember.

Entire floor show by kind permission of the

CLUB HOLLYWOOD, where they are feature

3 times nightly.

Under the Personnal Direction of TED MARKS.

Promotional flyer announcing a 1934 battle of the bands which pitted the Canadian Ambassadors against several other dance bands. *Myron Sutton Collection, Concordia University Archives.*

the more lucrative and prestigious American marketplace. The laws had their origin in legislation passed by Congress in the 1880s which was intended to safeguard jobs for American workers by limiting the entry of foreign labourers. During the first two decades of the twentieth century, these laws were used to limit the influx of unskilled labourers. Professionals and artists were exempt, leaving the door to the United States open to foreign musicians. The newly formed American Federation of Musicians (AFM), however, moved quickly to close the door. Fearing that European musicians would take jobs away from its members, the union imposed sanctions on musicians and booking agents who attempted to import foreign musicians and appealed to European unions to keep their musicians at home. Those foreign musicians who did make it to the United States were barred from joining the American union. Meanwhile, the AFM was lobbying Washington for more restrictive laws. In 1932—just two years before the Canadian Ambassadors were offered work in New York State—Congress passed new legislation. Foreign musicians were barred from the country unless an employer could show that there were no American musicians capable of doing the job. Thus, a nearly insurmountable wall was erected around the United States against musicians from other countries, Canada included. Ironically, the AFM counted many members in Canada and hadn't especially wanted to block their entry to the United States. But the union could not induce U.S. Immigration authorities to let Canadian musicians into the country.

Canada already had similar barriers in place. An order in council passed in 1929 prohibited foreign labour under contract from entering Canada. Immigration authorities interpreted this to mean that foreign musicians—with the exception of concert groups and outstanding soloists—could work in Canada only if an equal number of Canadian musicians were employed for the same engagement, at the same salary, and for the same number of hours. This interpretation forced dance hall and nightclub owners to hire two bands of identical size—one, the American group they wanted to feature, the other a "standby" band of Canadian musicians. When, after the Second World War, Canada found itself suddenly short of skilled workers, the federal government passed a new order in council suspending the original restriction on foreign labour. In 1947 the door swung open again, with a resulting influx of American musicians into Canada. The United States did not accord similar privileges to Canadian musicians trying to go south.[10]

The fate of the Canadian Ambassadors was sealed: they would remain in Canada, enjoying local popularity, but never testing the limits of their ability and ambition in the more advanced and competitive American jazz market. Montreal was the leading city for jazz in Canada, and the Ambassadors had already played some of the most prestigious engagements open to black musicians in the country. South of the border, where jazz was born and where its master musicians were continuing to advance the art, the Canadian Ambassadors might have realized their collective potential; in Canada they could only mask their frustration with a happy-go-lucky indulgence in Montreal's pleasures. Few challenges awaited them now, except survival.

> We just put the States out of our mind. We knew we were missing out on more fame and money, but we were having fun. I guess some of the guys, you couldn't have pried them out of Montreal, because they were having a ball.... I never wanted to go back to the States, really. I knew I couldn't stand that pace. I would have been dead by now if I'd gone to New York. Look at all the guys I knew at that time, guys like Higginbotham—he's dead. Montreal was a slower pace of life. No, I didn't want the big city.

The Canadian Ambassadors remained at the Hollywood for more than a year, with occasional sorties to dance halls in Montreal and nearby towns. In June 1935 the engagement ended. This time there was no one waiting in the wings with another contract. The Depression was biting deeper, and steady work had evaporated. The band found a few week's work at an east-end dance hall, but Sutton began looking outside the city for something to sustain them. He fired a letter off to the man who managed one of Ottawa's leading nightclubs as well as a dance pavilion in neighbouring Hull. The reply was ominous: the Hollywood Gardens in Ottawa was in such dire straits that it was open only on Tuesday and Friday nights, and attendance at Luna Park in Hull was falling. However, the manager would be pleased to feature the Canadian Ambassadors; in fact he was willing to risk opening the Gardens on both Friday and Saturday nights for the band, and give them a Sunday night in Hull as well—providing the musicians would agree to work for nothing more than a percentage of receipts at the door. Sutton refused the offer. Instead, he accepted a night's work playing a moonlight cruise out of Montreal, and hastily patched together a summer tour of Ontario.

The Canadian Ambassadors' 1935 tour of Ontario was the first of three they would undertake to survive the dry summers of the later Depression years. But Sutton couldn't work miracles. He was forced to prune his band back to six musicians to make the tours feasible, and on at least one tour brought along a singer—Bernice Jordan—to enhance the band's drawing power. The group lashed their instruments onto the roof of a Cadillac, squeezed inside with their hired driver, and set off zig-zagging across the province from the shores of Lake Ontario in the south to the mining towns of Sudbury and Timmins, almost five hundred kilo-

The Canadian Ambassadors pose beside their car in North Bay, Ontario, during a summer tour of Ontario. Note bass tied to the roof. Clockwise from top: Willy Wade (drums); Lou Hooper (piano); Clyde Duncan (bass); Bernice Jordan (vocals); Mack McKenzie (trumpet); Myron Sutton (alto saxophone). Centre: Lloyd Duncan (tenor saxophone). *Myron Sutton Collection, Concordia University Archives.*

metres to the north. They never strayed into Quebec. They played strictly for dances, in pavilions, community halls, and schools. On one occasion they drove 150 kilometres from North Bay to Barrie, played one night, then drove all the way back to North Bay the following day in time to play for another dance. The further they pushed into the northern frontier, the rougher the working conditions became. On opening night in Sudbury, Sutton was shown a rope that he could unhook if the miners started brawling: the rope lowered a chain-link screen down in front of the stage to protect the musicians from flying chairs and bottles.

> Oh, we did a lot of pioneering. They had nothin' but dirt roads up there. We'd go to places where they never saw coloured people before. Everywhere we went we'd meet somebody. They'd take us here, take us there. It was rough, but we had a ball.

One tour was unexpectedly extended. An employer in Kirkland Lake refused to pay the band after it finished its engagement, stranding the musicians in the northern mining town without enough money for the journey back to Montreal. Winter was already settling in as Sutton took the matter to a lawyer. The local court said it didn't have the authority to rule on the dispute and told Sutton he'd have to wait until the travelling assize court arrived in Kirkland Lake to hear the case. It wasn't due until spring. After three months of wrangling and shivering, the musicians settled out of court for just enough money to get back to Montreal.

The Canadian Ambassadors were only rarely able to find work in Montreal's ailing nightclubs during the latter half of the Depression. They were forced to freelance individually, taking work with pick-up bands; Sutton himself sometimes worked for other leaders. More frequently, however, he led the house band at the Terminal club, which had become an after-hours meeting place for local and visiting musicians and entertainers. The owner of the St. Antoine Street nightclub liked Sutton and provided long stretches of employment for him on several occasions when the Canadian Ambassadors were idle. One engagement lasted twenty-two months, giving Sutton a respite from summer touring for one year. Unfortunately, the Terminal could afford to hire only four or five musicians, not the full Canadian Ambassadors. Sutton used members of the Ambassadors for his bands at the Terminal, and they played some of the Ambassadors' repertoire; the arrangements, however, were not easily adaptable to the smaller group, and the Terminal bands simply ad-libbed most of the music. Sutton was reluctant to dignify such groupings with the name of the Canadian Ambassadors; he preferred instead to advertise the band as Mynie Sutton's Swingsters, or simply as the Mynie Sutton Orchestra.

The Terminal club became home base for Sutton and his musicians between tours and more prestigious work as the Canadian Ambassadors. The musicians developed an affection for the club. It was a modest establishment, with music and small shows on the second floor and gambling on the third.

> The Terminal club was the kind of place where anything could happen. I saw Johnny Hodges come in there and blow my horn. I saw that guy puff jaws—Dizzy Gillespie—come in there. Duke Ellington came in and sat behind the bar. Anybody's liable to come in there. It was just a joint, but it was a well-known joint. They had three or four girls they'd put up, show girls from out of town, and they'd go around to the tables and sing. Sometimes they'd get up and dance, do a little fifteen-minute show, but it was on a small scale. It was just another joint. And I'll tell you, they had a sloppy cook in there. He had grease from one end of his apron to the other. But that was the best fried chicken in Montreal!

He's laughing now with the memories of those nights almost half a century ago. The Terminal club! Pot-bellied stove and bare floors. Jam sessions. Fights. Bino and the other waiters, big as football players, they would break a port bottle over the stove and challenge anybody who got out of line. The Terminal club—not as fancy as Rockhead's Paradise, not as well known either. "But things happened down there that didn't happen at Rockhead's, 'cause people

The TERMINAL

"Bringing Harlem to Montreal"

Presents

● **Ruble Blakey**
Singer, Dancer, M.C.

● **Creme "Exotic" Danseuse**

● **Cliff Bookman**
"Tapsody in Blue"

● **Birtie Warfield**
Lovely to Look At

● Bernice Moxley——*"Copper-Colored Gal"*

Dance to MYNIE SUTTON'S SWINGSTERS

Delicious Fried Chicken—St. Antoine & Windsor—MArquette 0500

There's a Heat-Wave
at the TERMINAL!

Montreal's Show-place of Sepia Attractions

Presenting

● **Ruble Blakey** —Emcee, Singer, Dancer

● **Birtie Warfield** —"Gardenia Girl from Tahiti"

● **"Chickie" Collins**   —   ● **Bernice Moxley**

● **Mynie Sutton's Band**

Championship Fried Chicken — St. Antoine and Windsor

SWING IS KING

AT THE TOWN'S SEPIA HIGH SPOT!!

A New and Fast Moving Floor Show
Direct from World-Famous Harlem

● Ruble Blakey—Emcee and Sweet Singer of Songs

● La Lolita—"Heat-Wave"

● Myrtle Wilson—Exotic Dancer

● Bea Morton—Torrid Singer

● Gladys Ridley—

● King of Swing—
Mynie Sutton and His Orchestra

"Sepian Sophisticate"

You've never tasted such Fried Chicken!

The
TERMINAL

St. Antoine, off Windsor St.

Clippings from Myron Sutton's scrapbook. *Myron Sutton Collection, Concordia University Archives.*

came in to the Terminal to relax—and Rockhead was out for that big buck."[11]
A lot of things happened down there....

We'd have a lot of rich people come into the Terminal club, and they'd wanna be secluded, eh? So they'd come in and keep the band. Maybe the bartender would come up and say, "When everybody goes, you guys stay here and play, because Mr. So-and-So is gonna stay." And the guy would spend about three or four hundred dollars, and he'd pay the band another fifty dollars or so just to play an extra hour.

Very few coloured people came in there, because it was an after-hours joint. When the big places closed uptown, people would come down and have a few more drinks. The gamblers would come down, the hustlers, the prominent people—it was a mixture. And we stayed late, till four o'clock sometimes. The doorman wouldn't let everyone in. He knew the clientele.

It went through a period there at the Terminal club where the English people tried to have a theme song, like "There'll Always Be an England." So we'd play that but the French wouldn't stand up. English would stand up at attention, French people wouldn't stand up. So when we got through playing the song, the English people wanted to fight the French people 'cause they wouldn't stand up. So then we'd have to play "God Save The King," or queen, or who the hell was in power then, and they'd all stand up again! I used to carry a piece of iron under my seat. I never had to hit anybody, but I would have. Some of them guys were crazy if you get 'em half drunk.

There wasn't too much vice. The only thing was, if you ordered champagne, the first bottle was champagne, and maybe the next few bottles was watered. And the odd time maybe a girl would take a trick out, but that was her business, eh? And if some of those chicks could latch onto a guy with a few bucks, well, they'd get 'em drunk enough and roll 'em. One time, I remember we had a pretty girl working there. She rolled this guy for his money, eh? I'll never forget this. She took the money up in the ladies' dressing room and hid it. So the next intermission, Willie Wade [the drummer] went up there and found the money —and he hid it! And you know, this girl called the detectives in to find where the damn money was, and they searched the whole joint—and it wasn't even hers! But Willie got the money. Things like that happened, you know?

But there was a lot of rackets. I've seen the bartender make up the order and they deliver the booze to the Terminal club in the morning. Then the vice squad'd come by in the afternoon and impound it, eh? Then in order to get the club working that night, or the next day, you had to go and buy back your booze for thirty percent more than what you paid for it. I've seen that happen!

Entertainers and staff line up in front of the Canadian Ambassadors at the Montmartre, 6 October 1937. Musicians left to right: Willy Wade (drums); Harold "Steep" Wade (alto saxophone); Myron Sutton (alto saxophone); Benny Montgomery (trumpet); Bill Kersey (tenor saxophone); Brad Moxley (piano). Bassist Clyde Duncan was added later. Standing beside Willy Wade is club owner Adolphe Alard; club manager Willie Legare is standing below and between Sutton and Montgomery. *Photo by Roger Janelle. Myron Sutton Collection, Concordia University Archives.*

I've seen the rackets going on, and they were big stuff, but it didn't bother the musician because he wasn't involved. He was little guy on the totem pole....

I'll tell ya, I was in another joint once down on St. Lawrence Boulevard. I forget the name of the club now, but it was after-hours and we were up there having clams and beer. Jesus! Here comes the guys in there with machine-guns, stood at the door, and I'm telling you, everybody scooted under tables, under chairs, anything you could get under. They never fired a shot but they took hammers and broke all the bar and everything else. Gang, eh? So when I got out of there it was a long time before I went back! At that time, things were going on. But nobody ever bothered the musicians too much. What the hell, we were paid to do a job, that's all.

The last blaze of glory for the Canadian Ambassadors began in September 1937. The band was engaged to launch a new black show policy at an east-end nightclub called the Montmartre, on St. Catherine Street a few doors west of The Main. Sutton, who had just finished his twenty-two-month stretch at the Terminal club, opened with a six-man band, including a young Montreal-born alto saxophonist named Harold "Steep" Wade. The club was so successful that within three months a seventh musician was added; Sutton brought bassist Clyde Duncan back into the fold. The band worked at the Montmartre through the winter and on into the summer of 1938. It was on top of the world again, and Sutton composed a simple, jumping riff tune to serve as the Ambassadors' theme song. He called the tune "Moanin' at the Montmartre," an incongruous title at the time, but one which proved to be prophetic.

After nearly a year at the Montmartre, the Canadian Ambassadors fell victim to the kind of racial stereotyping and discrimination that has shaped the course of jazz history so often since its beginnings. The Montmartre decided to switch to white shows. Bowing to convention, the management laid off the black musicians and replaced them with a white band. Fortunately, an offer of work arrived from a club in Toronto at about the same time. The Silver Slipper booked the Ambassadors to open in September 1938. This time, union problems beset the band.

Bitterness clouds Sutton's memory. He's not anti-union, he just didn't want to be bothered with all that. There's not a word about unions in his scrapbook: no cards or union contracts, no mention that he was a member of the Clef Club. His voice becomes laboured; he doesn't really remember the details, but he thinks some of the Toronto musicians were worried because the Canadian Ambassadors had a reputation: they wanted to keep the Ambassadors out, so they put pressure on their union.

Sutton had signed a two-hundred-dollar-a-week contract with the Silver Slipper, on the Ambassadors' own stationary. When the eight musicians arrived in Toronto for the engagement, Sutton was called before the union local and challenged for not arranging the contract through the proper union channels. It is not clear which union challenged his right to the job, the American Federation of Musicians or the Canadian Federation of Musicians—the latter may already have collapsed in Toronto by the fall of 1938. In some fashion or another, however, Sutton reached a compromise with the union: the Ambassadors could work out their one-month contract at the Silver Slipper, on condition that they didn't remain in Toronto afterwards seeking other work.

True to his promise, Sutton didn't solicit other work in Toronto. He did, however, accept brief engagements for the Canadian Ambassadors in Hamilton and Windsor. The band returned to Montreal at an opportune moment: a job had suddenly become available at Connie's Inn. But

There's Plenty of Action at

THE MONTMARTRE

59 St. Catherine St. W.

The only REAL coloured show in Montreal,
with Mynie Sutton's Swing Oknystra
ZIPPY - SPICY - SPARKLING - RED HOT

DINE   *No Couver Charge*   BEER

DANCE   **PL. 7368**   WINE

A. ALLARD, prop.
W. LEGARE, mgr.   HARRY MILLER, H.W.

Clipping from Myron Sutton's scrapbook. *Myron Sutton Collection, Concordia University Archives.*

something was in the air: club managers, trying to divine public taste, were uneasy about the Montmartre's recent switch from black to white shows. The Canadian Ambassadors had been at Connie's only a few months when the club followed the trend to white entertainment.

> When the Montmartre changed policies, that's one of the reasons that the band went into trouble. Because when *they* changed policies it looked like the whole town changed policies. The last engagement we had with the big band was at Connie's. We tried to hold our band there with the white show. And we *played* for the white show—we played their music. But then the white show started to get bitchy. They said we weren't playing the type of music that they wanted, and so they changed the band.... And so that put you out in the field again, and you started struggling.

Struggling got too hard, you kept cuttin' your band down, and everybody started working with somebody else. That's about how it was. From there on it was just struggle with small groups.

The trend to white shows in the city was only a phase; black cabaret would return to fashion. But Sutton, discouraged and out of work, was not inclined to take a long-term view of things. It seemed to him as if no one had any more use for a large, tightly knit black band. For the next two years he used his Ambassadors in small groupings, whenever he could find work as a leader. For much of the time, however, Sutton himself freelanced as a sideman.

> The music scene in Montreal was at a low ebb. I was knocking around playing with George Sealey and others, just playing a gig here, a gig there. I wasn't doing anything definite. And then my cousin come down and he said, "Well, you might as well go back with me. Your mother's not that young any more, and there's nobody around Niagara [to look after her]." I didn't have any brothers or sisters or anything, so I figured it was time to come home.

Sutton had probably already decided to move back home when he was booked to lead three jazz concerts in the spring of 1941, at Victoria Hall in the prosperous, anglophone suburb of Westmount. Four Ambassadors and two other local musicians were hired for the band. Sutton brought in as a special guest the musician he had admired the most when he arrived in Montreal eight years earlier: violinist Willy Girard. The program notes for the concerts were unsigned, but if Sutton didn't have a hand in writing them, he would have had no qualms about endorsing their sentiment:

> Jazz as produced by Montreal musicians has been ignored far too long by jazz lovers in this city. This is not the fault of the public for they have never been able to go to a "club" and listen to a group of musicians play truly good jazz as a unit, but rather they have to keep their ears open all night long so as to hear a certain saxophone or trumpet who may be allowed to make a few short solos during the evening.
>   That we have good musicians in Montreal goes without saying, but they are split up into so many different orchestras that we seldom get a chance to hear a group of them play together. We have tried to gather together some of the finest jazz artists in Montreal to play for you this afternoon, and we sincerely hope that you will enjoy the music that you are about to hear.[12]

Sutton's hopes about the Montreal jazz scene were rekindled by the

Myron Sutton with the Casuals, during a 1971 engagement at a motor inn in Niagara Falls, Ontario: Rod North (drums); Joe Hvilivitzky (electric bass); Marsh Goegan (piano). *Photo by Robert Wybrow. Myron Sutton Collection, Concordia University Archives.*

success of the concerts, which drew large crowds and favourable press coverage.[13] He began to have misgivings about his decision to return to Niagara Falls, but the family commitment was too strong to break. As the date of his departure drew closer, he was overcome by pessimism about his future. Convinced that he would never again lead a band, he gave all of the Canadian Ambassadors' music to George Sealey, who had been part of the Victoria Hall concerts. He also gave Sealey his clarinet. Then, on some forgotten day in 1941, Sutton boarded a train and headed home to Niagara Falls; at thirty-seven going on thirty-eight, he had retired from music.

Sutton steps now to a wooden cabinet in a corner of the dining room and threads a spool of tape onto his reel-to-reel machine. The house fills with the warmth of an alto saxophone, vibrato broad and rich, paraphrasing "Embraceable You." The recording is of a quartet called the Casuals that has been playing weekends around Niagara Falls for the past few years. The swell and pulse of the organ, the clinking of glasses, and the laughter and chatter of voices could have been recorded at any Legion hall or hotel wedding reception across the country. But there's something about the saxophone, tired as it sounds, that induces you to listen. "I've always tried to base my style on a little bit of Johnny Hodges," he offers above the music. "But before Hodges, there was nobody to copy from. So you had to work up a little style of your own, eh?" The tape winds on through one standard after another. Then he switches off the machine and returns the reel to its box. He has other home recordings on the shelf, all of them made since he returned to Niagara Falls in 1941. "Ya, some company or other recorded the Canadian Ambassadors," he says, the smile fading from his face with the memory. But the recording was never issued, and no one knows what happened to the master. "I don't have it. I never heard it." He turns from the cabinet and settles slowly back into the armchair, picking up the thread of the story again. "I had no intention of continuing in music once I got back to Niagara Falls...."

Sutton went looking for a day job. With eleven years of high school, he found a position as a time-keeper in a factory. The white workers, however, resented having a black man checking on them, and when it became clear their hostility would not abate, Sutton resigned. Nearing forty, he decided to become a welder. He went to work at a factory that manufactured railroad track—and remained there for twenty-nine years.

Niagara Falls wouldn't let Sutton forget his music. Not long after he returned, someone talked him into putting together a band for a dance. The ten-piece outfit—all white except for Sutton—was an instant hit, and he decided to keep it together for occasional weekend jobs. The band played for dances around the Niagara peninsula until the end of the Second World War, when smaller groups became more fashionable, and affordable. From that point on, Sutton did most of his playing in small combos like the Casuals.

He even let himself be talked into getting involved with the Niagara Falls local of the American Federation of Musicians: for thirty years he sat on its executive board. He married, raised a family, and became a community man. He founded a chapter of the Canadian Brotherhood Club and served as its president for the rest of his life. He joined the Legion and the British Methodist Episcopal Church. He taught music to local youngsters at his home. In his later years the honours rolled in. The musicians' union made him a life member. The Niagara Promotions Association honoured him for community service as a musician. The local newspaper published a lengthy story about him when he retired. And, occasionally, he would receive a long-distance telephone call from some stranger asking about his band.

The stories exhausted, he leads the way through the kitchen and down the stairs to his basement hideaway. It's a low-ceilinged room at the end of a dark passageway. A tiny, curtained window. An old sofa and chairs. An old record player. On the walls, framed black-and-white photographs: souvenirs from another life: a teenager holding his first saxophone; the Royal Ambassadors posing with their instruments; and there (pointing proudly now)—his Canadian band: at the Gatineau, the Hollywood, the Montmartre, the Silver Slipper. There's another big frame with a portrait and the story they wrote about him for his retirement. And a plaque from the union honouring his long service. But he's stooping at the closet now, pulling out a leather case. It's his saxophone. He holds it up, affectionately: an old French Selmer.

His wife calls down the stairs. The roast and sweet potatoes are ready. He slips the saxophone back into its hiding place and opens the door to the darkness. "So. I don't know if I've been much help to you, but, ah...."

Six months later. In newsrooms across Canada, editors scroll through stories pouring nonstop from wire service printers, looking for news to print. Canadian dollar hits record low. Israeli invasion of Lebanon continues. Charles and Diane take newborn son home from hospital. Amidst the day's headlines, a brief item comes over the Canadian Press wire:

> MONTREAL (CP)—Funeral services were held in Niagara Falls, Ont., this week for Mynie Sutton, a forgotten Canadian jazz great who was a fixture of Montreal's racy nightclub scene during the 1930s.
> Sutton, who died of cancer June 17, was 78....[14]

CHAPTER FOUR

The Big Band Era

Montreal during the Second World War was an anomaly among Canadian cities: it was both a focal point for the country's war effort and a theatre for dissent. Factories turned out armaments, the armed forces trained soldiers in nearby camps, and ships loaded supplies and personnel in the city's harbour. Yet most francophone Montrealers were opposed to involvement in the war, and the sheer frivolity and extravagance of Montreal nightlife mocked the exhortations of Canadian leaders to sacrifice and sobriety.

Much of this popular opposition to the war effort was the festering of an old wound. The province's majority francophone population had long resented the political, commercial, and cultural domination of their lives by English Canada. The nation's call to arms was perceived in Quebec largely as a call to defend England, the country which had militarily conquered the French colony two centuries previously. Quebec nationalism, long endemic among the province's francophones, would erupt with revolutionary political and cultural fervour during the 1960s; during the Second World War it found calmer, though no less threatening, expression through opposition to Canada's war efforts.

The country moved quickly to contain the challenge. Quebec Premier Maurice Duplessis was running for reelection in 1939, the year the war began. An outspoken opponent of conscription, Duplessis pledged that if his Union nationale party was returned to power, the province would dissociate itself from Canada's war efforts. The Union nationale was defeated, not because of its platform, but through federal intimidation of the province's voters: all of the Quebec members of the federal cabinet threatened to resign en masse, leaving Quebec without any representation in the Canadian government, if the province returned Duplessis to power.

Montreal's mayor met with harsher treatment. In 1940 Camillien Houde proclaimed that Quebecers would support the Italian dictator

Benito Mussolini, Hitler's partner in fascism, rather than Canada's wartime allies, which included England. Federal authorities promptly arrested Houde for counselling the populace to oppose conscription and he spent the next four years interned in a camp reserved for enemies of the country. Neither Houde nor Duplessis lost the support of their constituents: they were returned to power at the earliest available opportunity. Moreover, midway through the war, three out of every four Quebecers voted against conscription in a national referendum.

Such overt expressions of Quebec's feelings about the war enraged patriotic English Canadians. Yet the unabashed frivolity of life in Montreal that was as much an expression of contempt for the war effort fascinated the country. Armed forces personnel stationed in the area indulged in every pleasure, licit and illicit, which the city had to offer. Official efforts to enforce rationing and inspire a spirit of sacrifice in Montreal were continually frustrated. The wartime Liberal government of Joseph-Adélard Godbout which replaced the Union nationale cancelled many liquor permits in Montreal in an effort to dampen the city's nightlife; many nightclubs were closed as a result, and musicians were thrown out of work. But illegal bars known as "blind pigs" continued to thrive, serving alcohol around the clock while escaping prosecution by bribing municipal authorities and the police.

By 1944, when Duplessis and Houde were both reelected, all pretence at moderation in Montreal had been abandoned. Even the armed forces, whose officers patronized the blind pigs, began to worry about the city's corrupting influence. Alarmed by the high incidence of venereal disease among servicemen stationed in or near Montreal, or who were passing through the city, the Canadian military threatened to place the city out of bounds for all soldiers unless municipal authorities clamped down on prostitution.[1] City hall obliged by closing the brothels—temporarily; they were allowed to reopen soon after the war ended.

Whatever moral outrage Canadians felt about Montreal's wartime lifestyle, curiosity about its delights ran high. *Maclean's* magazine sent a writer to Montreal in 1944 to investigate the tales emanating from the city. Jim Coleman returned to his editor in Toronto intoxicated with what he had witnessed:

> Demon rum may be rationed in other sections of the country, but there is enough medicinal spirits in Montreal to float the entire Atlantic Fleet up St. Catherine Street. Cigar smokers in other cities may be haunting streetcar stops, waiting for some fortunate [citizen] to discard a butt, but in Montreal you can buy cigars by the handfuls. When a surprised visitor inquires about this apparent anomaly in the national distribution system, the Montrealer merely shrugs his shoulders and looks significantly toward the heavens....

Everywhere the *Maclean's* writer turned he encountered people with money to spend—and no shortage of places to spend it. Taverns, bars, blind pigs, gambling dens, and dance halls were filled to overflowing. Tickets to theatres, wrestling matches, and hockey games were frequently sold out.

> From dusk until the milkman starts his morning rounds, the town [glows] like a Roman candle. Tired businessmen, expatriates who have fled briefly from the more arid sections of the country, money-heavy warworkers, and young men and women of the armed services keep the merry wheels spinning.... Regardless of how one feels about such things in wartime, there is the inescapable fact that the entertainment business in Montreal is booming as never before.[2]

This mixture of wartime prosperity, abundant alcohol, and legions of young armed forces personnel looking for amusement provided a fertile environment for big dance bands in Montreal. They sprang up in abundance soon after the war began, and they thrived beyond its conclusion into the late 1940s. Every weekend as many as ten bands could be found playing in and around the city, each one drawing from several hundred to more than a thousand local youths and off-duty service men and women. Audiences flocked to them: to dance, to court, to fall in love, and to say good-bye. The music they did it to was swing, the jazz style of the day. The big bands made jazz more popular than it had ever been before.[3]

Jazz had always been closely linked to dancing. Ragtime had unleashed a craze for social dancing among North American youth that continued unabated through the early years of jazz. The music of the Original Dixieland Jazz Band and its imitators, and the swing style of jazz that followed during the 1930s, was essentially dance music. That was its role in society. Playing music for people to dance to—whether for performers on a nightclub stage or for patrons on a dance floor—was how most jazz musicians earned their living. The artistry of early jazz existed within the confines of the music's commercial function.

In Montreal, dance halls sprang up quickly as jazz's popularity spread across the continent. The Venetian Gardens and the Roseland Ballroom were both operating in central Montreal by the early 1920s. In the suburbs, accessible by streetcar, huge dance pavilions were built, some of them with walls that folded open to let in the summer breeze. Amusement parks and beaches on and around the island of Montreal opened their own dance halls.

The peak of this craze for social dancing coincided with the most tumultuous event that can overtake any generation of youth: a war.

MONTREAL'S BIGGEST NEW YEAR'S EVE FROLIC AND DANCE ......

Sat. Dec. 31st at 10 p.m.

THE LIONS CLUB PRESENTS

DUKE
ELLINGTON
"HARLEM'S ARISTOCRAT OF JAZZ"

Come and
Enjoy An
Outstanding
Vaudeville
Show and
Dance To
Your Heart's
Content

Form a Party
NOW —
Get Your Seats
In Advance
And Avoid
Disappointment

AND HIS WORLD FAMOUS

ORCHESTRA
Through Arrangement with MILLS ARTISTS INC., N.Y.

Plus VAUDEVILLE SHOW

SEATS ON SALE THURS. DEC. 15th AT FORUM
Tickets can now be obtained from members of the LIONS CLUB
SARRAZIN and CHOQUETTE PHARMACY — STATION CHLP —
All seats are reserved — Net proceeds to Lions Welfare Work.

GENERAL
ADMISSION **$1**50
PLUS TAX

FORUM

BOX
SEATS **$2**00
PLUS TAX

Promotional flyer, 1938. *Courtesy of Walter de Mohrenschildt.*

From the mid-1930s to the decline after the Second World War of what came to be called the Swing Era, North American youth were infatuated with swing music. They saw in it an escape from the hardships of a world they were inheriting and, for some, a symbol of revolt against the middle-class values of their parents. The big bands and their jazz soloists were the pop culture heroes of the day. The jitterbug and other dances they inspired expressed a reckless affirmation of life and love in a world marching towards death.

An entire book could be written about the big bands that enlivened Montreal during the 1940s. In addition to the numerous bands from the United States that played in Montreal on tour, there were at least a dozen big bands resident in the city, and possibly a good many more. The local big bands ranged in size from ten to fifteen musicians. Several were full-time bands employing professional musicians; the rest were semiprofessional, weekend bands comprised mostly of part-time musicians moonlighting from day jobs in offices and factories. Countless numbers of musicians and singers passed through these bands: most of their names will be lost with the disappearance of the generation that danced to their music.

In Montreal the big-band craze was a white phenomenon. There was not one big band in the city led by a black musician, and throughout the 1940s only four black musicians are known to have played in any of the resident big bands.[4] In this respect, the city was a microcosm of North American culture: though the big-band style of jazz was created by black musicians in the United States, had its roots in black American music, and reached its highest artistic expression in the American black bands of Fletcher Henderson, Duke Ellington, and Count Basie, white musicians playing a derivative, more commercial version of black music achieved wider exposure and greater financial success.

The popular media, and especially radio, played a powerful role in fueling the big-band craze and shaping public taste for swing. The white youths who flocked to dances in Montreal, as elsewhere, expected to encounter white bands playing easily accessible, often sentimental, renditions of the hit tunes they were hearing over the radio—hits which were in turn the product mainly of white bands from the United States. Overt racism also discouraged black participation in the big-band phenomenon. Colour bars, both on stage and on the dance floor, continued to be enforced at some ballrooms and dance halls in Canada well into the 1940s. White bandleaders who might have been ready to use black musicians were wary of the obstacles a mixed band might encounter in finding work. Those who hoped to play out-of-town engagements knew as well that hotels could not be counted on to accommodate black travellers.

Cab Calloway's orchestra packs them in at the Chez Maurice Danceland on St. Catherine Street near Mountain. Leading bands from the United States performed regularly in Montreal during the Swing Era. *Courtesy of Armand Samson. John Gilmore Jazz History Collection, Concordia University Archives.*

Montreal's full-time big bands provided a valuable source of income and experience for the city's white jazz musicians. About a half-dozen of these professional big bands existed during the 1940s, though not all of them were active at the same time and personnel frequently overlapped.[5] The professional bands were generally engaged for an entire summer season to play at a suburban dance pavilion or at a beach resort or amusement park. During the rest of the year, they worked in the city, usually at the Chez Maurice Danceland, a spacious former nightclub on St. Catherine Street West near Mountain, or at the Auditorium, a nightclub on Ontario Street near Bleury where dancing was the principal attraction for several years. The Auditorium was the only dance hall in the city that sold alcohol; all of the others were unlicenced, to attract teenagers under the drinking age and people who could not afford nightclub prices. Flasks of alcohol were often smuggled into dances, however.

The Chez Maurice Danceland regularly featured big bands from the United States, complementing the larger, intermittent spectacles of touring bands at the Forum hockey arena. Montreal's professional big bands served as standby bands for these foreign attractions: the local musicians usually opened the show then sat back and let the visitors take over, sometimes returning to the stage later during the visiting band's break. This working arrangement gave Montreal musicians a chance to hear their idols at close range, and occasionally even sit in with an American band. Opportunities to work with American bands were rare and highly coveted. Frank Costi was tenor saxophone soloist with Roland David's big band at the Chez Maurice Danceland when the popular Jimmie Lunceford big band was brought in from the United States. One of Lunceford's tenor players had been barred entry to Canada for the tour. Impressed by Costi's playing, the American bandleader invited him to sit in. The white Montreal saxophonist worked with the all-black American band for the rest of its engagement at the Chez Maurice, then went on to finish the Canadian leg of Lunceford's tour, playing through Ontario. Lunceford wanted Costi to stay with the tour as it crossed back into the United States, but U.S. Immigration vetoed the idea.

In contrast, the musicians who played in Montreal's part-time big bands were a curious species.[6] Many of them were genuinely interested in jazz, and a few could play authentic jazz solos. But most of them, despite a youthful enthusiasm for swing, could do little more than read the music put in front of them. Collectively they contributed to the popularization of jazz through the saturation of popular culture with big-band swing. As individuals, however, they were marginal to the city's jazz community: they had little contact with the professional musicians, and disappeared quickly from the jazz scene with the passing of the big bands. Ironically, it was a part-time big band which left the greatest mark on Montreal jazz history. Long after the music of the Johnny Holmes Orchestra has been forgotten, the band will be remembered for the role it played in the development of Montreal's first international jazz star, Oscar Peterson.

Johnny Holmes was born into a white, working-class family in central Montreal. He quit school at twelve to start bringing in some money as an office boy. He also taught himself to play the cornet and read music. With a few tips from his father and older brother, labourers who played cornet and trombone respectively, the young Holmes advanced quickly; he took only a handful of private lessons. By fourteen he had switched to trumpet, and his musicianship had matured to the point of attracting an offer of employment from one of the fledgling symphony orchestras that were struggling to fill the void left by the dissolution of the Montreal Symphony Orchestra at the onslaught of the Depression. The orchestra, however, could only offer Holmes six dollars a week, a dollar

Roland David's orchestra at the Chez Maurice Danceland, 26 February 1944. Trumpets left to right: Norman Calvert, Maynard Ferguson, Joe Christie Sr., Al Kane; trombones left to right: Frank Taplitizki, Joe Bell; saxophones left to right: Frank Destello (baritone), Tony Mazza (alto), Adrien Gaboury (alto), Frank Costi (tenor), Roland David (tenor, standing); others: Rita Gail (vocals), Armand Samson (guitar), Jimmy Malone (drums), Bert Brown (bass), Joe Stroble (piano). *Joe Bell scrapbook, courtesy of Jack Litchfield. Concordia University Archives.*

less than his office job paid. The family could not afford the loss of income, and he declined the offer.

It was a cruel blow to a youthful dream, but a propitious moment for Montreal jazz. Seeking another outlet for his talent, Holmes began playing beside his father and brother in a large orchestra at a Pentecostal church on Drummond Street just below St. Catherine. Encouraged by the teenager's enthusiasm for music, the orchestra leader formed a second musical group at the church, a twenty-two-piece brass band. The leader also showed Holmes the basics of arranging. The young trumpeter quickly began experimenting with voicings for the brass instruments, and over the next few years he wrote a large repertoire of arrangements for the band. He also tutored many of the younger brass players in the church, collecting twenty-five cents for a half-hour lesson from those who could afford to pay.

Like others of his generation, Holmes was captivated by the sound of swing. In 1940 he helped form a part-time swing band called the Esquires. The ten-piece band thought of itself as a cooperative outfit, but the members soon assigned Holmes—at twenty-four the oldest mem-

A Montreal band led by trumpeter Bix Belair (standing) at the Roseland Ballroom in 1948, with Freddie Nichols (baritone saxophone) and Frank Costi (tenor saxophone, seated). *Photo by Marcel Deschamps, courtesy of Frank Costi. John Gilmore Jazz History Collection, Concordia University Archives.*

ber—the task of managing their business affairs. He also bore the key musical roles of lead trumpet and soloist. As the war siphoned off the band's original members one by one, Holmes shouldered more and more of the responsibilities. Eventually the band began appearing under the name the Johnny Holmes Orchestra.

The change in name signalled a change in the quality of the band's music as well. Most of the local big bands were content to play published stock arrangements of hit tunes. Not Holmes: he gradually replaced the Esquires' collection of stocks with original arrangements, three-quarters of them his own, the rest contributed by other band members. When Holmes heard a tune on the radio he liked, he called to his wife to take down the lyrics while he transcribed the music by ear; the resulting scribbles he quickly transformed into an arrangement for the band. Holmes's writing took into account the strengths and weaknesses of individual musicians in the band. Slowly, the Johnny Holmes Orchestra developed a repertoire and sound which distinguished it from the other bands in Montreal; Holmes likened its sound to that of the Les Brown orchestra, a respected white American band of the Swing Era.

Holmes established a base for the band at Victoria Hall in Westmount, where he produced the dances himself. He rented the hall, guaranteed the musicians' salaries out of his own pocket, hired people to sell tickets and soft drinks, and paid for all of the publicity. The gamble paid off quickly. By 1942 the Johnny Holmes Orchestra, enlarged to fifteen musicians plus two vocalists, was packing Victoria Hall every weekend with eight hundred dancers.[7] Line-ups formed outside two hours before the dances began. One night, a thousand people crushed into the hall before Holmes realized he had erred with the ticket numbering; he was reduced to begging two hundred fans to leave with a promise of a guaranteed entry the following weekend.

Holmes was a glutton for work, on the bandstand as well as off. He ran between his place in the trumpet section and his spot at the front of the band, where he both conducted and played solos. "We'd start at nine," he remembered. "By ten-thirty I'd have to make a complete change of clothing. I was soaking. I'd change again at midnight, and then once more after the dance." He claimed to have lost an average of seven pounds a night at dances, simply through perspiration.

When he first started organizing the dances at Victoria Hall, Holmes had been working as a salesman for a pharmaceutical supplies company. As the band's popularity grew, however, so did his earnings. In 1944 he quit his day job to devote himself fully to the band. For the next six years, it provided him with a comfortable living, though it remained a part-time orchestra working only two or three nights a week. Holmes invested heavily in the band. He consistently paid his musicians above the union scale; he bought his own stage props and sound and lighting systems; he hired work crews to truck the equipment to engagements and prepare the stage; and for some dances he even hired nightclub acts to perform a mini-show for the teenage audiences.

The band was rarely without work. CBC radio broadcast the band live from Victoria Hall for several months, fueling its local popularity. Calls came in for company and school dances. There was a steady stream of one-nighters at hotels, military depots, high schools, and colleges in the Montreal region, and occasionally as far afield as Queen's University in Kingston, Ontario. In 1946 the musicians all took their summer holidays at the same time and set off on a two-week tour of Ontario in a chartered bus; Holmes had lined up bookings from Windsor to North Bay, though bypassing Toronto. They were a tight band: in addition to weekly rehearsals, the musicians gathered regularly at Holmes's apartment to listen to the latest records of American big bands.

Despite its semiprofessional status, the Holmes band was one of the most successful big bands in Montreal. It even managed to secure work at the Chez Maurice Danceland from time to time, and on one occasion outdrew the American big band of Stan Kenton. Montreal's professional

Johnny Holmes and Oscar Peterson during one of their regular meetings at Holmes's apartment, 1944. *Johnny Holmes Collection, Concordia University Archives.*

musicians were fans of the Holmes band: on a night off they would sit in the balcony at Victoria Hall, listening to its arrangements and swing. They were also listening, with steadily growing admiration, to the band's gifted young pianist.

Oscar Peterson was seventeen years old when he joined the Johnny Holmes Orchestra in 1942. The war was swallowing up young men, and Holmes had lost two pianists in quick succession to the army, just as his band was beginning to take off at Victoria Hall. Holmes was still casting around for a new pianist when saxophonist Art Morrow showed up at rehearsal one evening with a nervous black teenager in tow. Young Peterson didn't have any experience working in a big band, though he'd been playing in a student dance band at his high school. Eager to impress Holmes, he unloaded every musical idea and cliché he knew into the first tune the band asked him to play. Holmes wasn't impressed; but as the rehearsal ground on, the bandleader began to see a glimmer of hope in the teenager's hyper-exuberant playing. "He was a diamond in the rough," Holmes recalled some thirty years later from retirement. "He already had amazing technique, but he shot everything in the first chorus."

Oscar Peterson poses with his family in one of a series of photographs commissioned by the Canadian Pacific Railway, for whom his father worked as a porter. Left to right: brother Chuck, father Daniel, mother Olivia, sisters May and Daisy. *Courtesy of Canadian Pacific Archives.*

With Morrow's encouragement, Holmes took Peterson aside during a break in the rehearsal and tried to explain to him what was required of a big-band pianist. He asked Peterson if he had ever listened to Tommy Dorsey's band. When the teenager said he had, Holmes advised him to try playing like Dorsey's pianist, Joe Bushkin—filling in behind the saxophones, but not trying to dominate the band. "He got it right the first time," said Holmes. "He played just like Bushkin."

At the end of the rehearsal, Holmes hired Peterson, then went one step further. He fixed a date with the pianist for a private get-together, to go over the band's music. The meetings became more regular as a friendship developed. Over the next two years Holmes and Peterson met several times a week, for up to two hours at a time. Holmes played only rudimentary piano, and there was nothing he could show Peterson about keyboard technique. He did, however, coach the young pianist on jazz conception and delivery, playing records to illustrate fine points of phrasing and performance. The influence on Peterson's playing was profound. "I was overdoing boogie-woogie and was completely lost for slow tunes," Peterson told a magazine in 1946, after making his first recordings. "Holmes was responsible for changing this; he built up my technique and was responsible for the style I put on records."[8]

Peterson brought to the Holmes orchestra a burning passion for music, fueled by years of practice and sustained family encouragement. The fourth of five children born to West Indian immigrants in the St. Henri district of the city, he had begun playing music even before he had learned to read. His father, Daniel Peterson, had been a sailor in his youth, and while working on the ships had taught himself to play an instrument resembling a small organ. Daniel married and settled in Montreal, and became a railway porter. He showed his wife, Olivia, how to play the instrument he had learned on the ships, and both also learned to play the piano. Each child that came along was taught to play the piano and a brass instrument and was encouraged to pass their learning on to their younger brothers and sisters. One of Oscar's older brothers, Fred, was a gifted pianist who dabbled in jazz but died of tuberculosis at sixteen. Another older brother, Chuck, lost a hand in a factory accident but became a professional trumpeter.

Oscar began playing trumpet when he was five years old. Two years later he contracted tuberculosis and was confined to hospital for thirteen months. When he emerged, his lungs were cured, but weakened. Heeding the doctor's advice, Daniel Peterson decided his son should take up the piano. The boy began playing hymns and classics under the tutelage of his older sister, Daisy, who worked, like their mother, as a domestic. Daisy eventually earned a diploma in music from McGill Conservatory and became a highly respected teacher in the city. Several Montreal jazz musicians besides Oscar have credited her with their formative musical training.

Daisy tutored Oscar, but it was Daniel Peterson who set the pace and content of study. Before leaving on a portering run, Daniel would assign each of the Peterson children something to learn during his absence. Returning home, he called the children one at a time to the piano and insisted they perform their lessons. Poor effort was punished with a strap.[9] There was a lighter side to music in the Peterson home, though. The children played in a community band which practised at the Peterson home and performed at church and community halls. Oscar's appetite for music was seemingly inexhaustible. "I used to practice from nine a.m. to noon," he later told an interviewer. "Then, after lunch I'd go from one to six. After dinner I'd practise again from seven-thirty until my mother would drag me away so the family could get some sleep."[10]

When Oscar was eleven, he began studying with Lou Hooper, the veteran Harlem pianist and former member of Myron Sutton's Canadian

Ambassadors. At fourteen he began lessons with Paul de Marky, Daisy's classical teacher at McGill. The Hungarian-born de Marky assigned Chopin études to Oscar and showed him how European composers such as Debussy had built rich, soft chords. Peterson's biographer, Gene Lees, has written: "Hooper is Peterson's link to the Harlem of the 1920s, his deep early root into the earth of Willie the Lion Smith and James P. Johnson. And de Marky is the link to Liszt and the great Nineteenth Century tradition of bravura piano playing...."[11] De Marky also encouraged his pupil's growing interest in jazz.

By the time he was in high school, Oscar was already exhibiting an awesome keyboard technique. He loved to impress his schoolmates by playing boogie-woogie at near-impossible tempos, a feat that earned him the nickname "The Brown Bomber of Boogie-Woogie." Montreal High School was teeming with aspiring musicians, including a young trumpeter named Maynard Ferguson and his brother Percy, who played saxophone. Percy led the school's Victory Serenaders, which provided Oscar with his first dance-band experience. Daniel Peterson disapproved of his son playing jazz, but Oscar's mother encouraged him, believing there might be a future in it.

At fifteen Oscar won an amateur contest organized by a local radio personality. He began broadcasting fifteen minutes a week on CKAC. It was the first of a series of radio appearances that, by the end of the Second World War, had exposed Oscar's talents to listeners across the country. Bolstered by his popularity on radio and encouraged by older musicians, Peterson resolved to quit school and commit himself to a career in music. His father supported the decision but added a corollary. "The strongest memory of my dad is the day that I came home and told him I wanted to leave high school," Peterson recalled some forty years later. "He told me I could leave, not to be another piano player, but to be the *best*."[12]

Despite a determination to conquer which had been instilled in Peterson by family, teachers, and friends, the young pianist who joined the Johnny Holmes Orchestra in the autumn of 1942 was far from self-assured. For one thing, he could not go unnoticed on the bandstand. According to Holmes, Peterson was the first black musician to work regularly with any of the local big bands. Breaking ground was sometimes painful. Once, the Holmes band was engaged to play for a private dance organized by the International Order of the Daughters of the Empire (IODE) at the posh, uptown Ritz-Carlton hotel. A few days before the engagement, Holmes received a telephone call from the hotel. The manager had just learned about Peterson's presence in the otherwise all-white band, and he told Holmes bluntly that he didn't want a black musician in the ballroom. Holmes politely informed the manager that

Oscar Peterson on stage at Victoria Hall with the Johnny Holmes Orchestra. In the background are drummer Russ Dufort and guitarist Armand Samson. *Johnny Holmes Collection, Concordia University Archives.*

Peterson was the band's star pianist: the orchestra didn't work without him. If the Ritz forced cancellation of the engagement, Holmes vowed to place an advertisement in the *Gazette* stating that the Johnny Holmes Orchestra could not play at the Ritz because blacks weren't allowed in the hotel. The conversation ended abruptly. Later that day, Holmes received a second call from the hotel manager. Members of the IODE had intervened, bringing the hotel to its senses. Peterson could appear at the Ritz. Not content with the moral victory, Holmes kept Peterson in the spotlight throughout the dance, calling one piano feature after another all night long.

Peterson was not the only black musician to play with Holmes's band. Steep Wade substituted for Peterson for a couple of weeks once when Peterson was ill, and George Sealey played briefly in the band's saxophone section. Though both Wade and Sealey were strong jazz soloists with considerable nightclub experience, neither succeeded in blending comfortably, and unobtrusively, into the band's ensemble sound. "That was typical of the Negro musicians," Holmes said, "because they never had a chance to play with these big bands."

Peterson blossomed with the band. As time passed, Holmes recognized that his pianist was a major contributor to the band's success and popularity. He acknowledged Peterson's drawing power by paying him more than any other band member; eventually Peterson was earning a living from the band, the only member besides Holmes to do so. Holmes also began including Peterson's name on the band's publicity flyers and newspaper ads, billing the band as "the Johnny Holmes Orchestra with Oscar Peterson." He gave Peterson liberal solo space in his arrangements; a popular ballad called "Dark Eyes" became Peterson's feature number. Finally, Holmes began turning the last fifteen minutes of every dance over to Peterson and the band's bassist and drummer, giving the pianist the first taste of the trio format that was to become the staple of his career. Recalled Holmes:

> The last fifteen minutes we played all the slow and dreamy music so the kids could dance very close together. We just let Oscar play. He'd call the tunes.... But he'd be playing, say, "Body and Soul," and someone in the band would call out another tune, say "I Surrender Dear." And he'd have to incorporate that right away into "Body and Soul," whether it was on the third beat of the bar or whatever. He never got hung up once. And they were calling out ridiculous things, classicals, everything. He would never get hung up at all.... The band idolized him. The greatest audience he had was the band.

One day during the winter of 1944-45, Peterson told his mother he'd

Johnny Holmes fronting his orchestra at Victoria Hall in April 1946. Left to right, trumpets: Wilf Gillmeister, Joe Caruso, Sy Cooper; saxophones: Arnold Gibb (baritone), Bob Redmond (alto), Art Barsky (tenor), Art Morrow (tenor); trombones: Jean Vadeboncoeur, Toller Thompson, Bob Swetland. *Photo by Hugh Franki Advertising Photographs, Reg'd. Johnny Holmes Collection, Concordia University Archives.*

like to make a record. She suggested he telephone one of the record companies and tell them what he'd just told her. He called Hugh Joseph, the man in charge of RCA Victor in Canada. By coincidence, Joseph himself had been considering calling Peterson, whose reputation had reached him.[13] With a firm offer of a recording contract from Victor, Peterson turned to Holmes for advice. The bandleader effectively became Peterson's manager for his first recording contract and session. Though Peterson insisted on writing a twenty percent commission for Holmes into the contract with Victor, the bandleader never collected on it.

Peterson's first recording session took place on 30 April 1945 in a Montreal studio. RCA Victor matched Peterson with two older local white musicians, bassist Bert Brown and drummer Frank Gariépy. The two 78 r.p.m. records that resulted from the day's work sold thousands of copies. Over the next four years, RCA Victor issued twenty-nine more titles recorded by Peterson in Montreal, with a variety of rhythm sections. "They weren't too representative of my playing at the time," Oscar later claimed;[14] nevertheless, they caused a minor stir in Canada for the raw virtuosity of the piano playing, which encompassed boogie-woogie, swing, and, in the last records, a tentative foray into the latest jazz style, bebop.

Holmes had long recognized that Peterson's talents demanded a wider audience and greater musical challenges than the big band could provide. He began encouraging the pianist to think about his career. Peterson, however, was reluctant to go. He trusted Holmes's musical and business judgement, and he felt bound by loyalty and friendship to the man who had given him so much help and encouragement. "He was also afraid," said Holmes. "I was security to him. He was paid well, and he was from a poor family." Peterson had also married and started a family of his own while working with Holmes's band.

The world, however, was drawing Peterson out. In February 1946 he performed a concert of jazz and classics at His Majesty's theatre. "It isn't every 20-year-old Negro pianist who can fill a house the size of His Majesty's Theatre and send his audience into ecstasies of appreciation on the occasion of his concert debut," began a review in the *Herald*. "When the fact is considered that he is a jazz pianist, whose speciality is swing and boogie-woogie, the occasion becomes the more impressive." The review is worth quoting at length, for its observations are revealing:

> Young Peterson, who made his local concert debut with an established reputation as the result of his radio programs and recordings, gained in musical stature and public acceptance last night to a degree seldom encountered in the field of popular music.
>
> It may be well to point out that the young Negro pianist has established a following locally that regards him as the finest jazz pianist in the Dominion. In their eyes and ears he can do no wrong; and for the sake of the record it must be recorded that he very seldom falls into error on the technical side of the popular idiom.
>
> Peterson, while making an impressive debut, is not yet a great jazz pianist. He is very, very good, but there still remains considerable study, practice and the gaining of experience before he can take what appears to be his destined place among the ranks of the truly great jazz pianists of this continent.
>
> Last night he showed he had the makings. His sense of rhythm is highly accurate; his knowledge of tone patterns truly remarkable in one so young. The famed left hand, kept under wraps for part of the concert, was allowed to break loose at appropriate intervals, and the effect was to send his competent bass and drums accompanists into a pronounced, if brief, jam session.

> The weakest part of his presentation, and it is one that can be eliminated when he becomes more familiar with the program he will present in his cross-Canada tour, proved to be in the lack of confidence he displayed in improvising on such numbers as Chopin's Prelude in A Major and Addinsel's Warsaw Concerto....[15]

The reviewer was mistaken about the extent of Peterson's upcoming bookings. That year, Holmes organized a few two- or three-day excursions into Ontario for Peterson, booking him for trio concerts using rhythm sections picked up along the way. Holmes drove Peterson to the engagements. On one trip they had a car accident: Holmes was hospitalized, but Peterson was unhurt and travelled on alone to the engagement.

Peterson finally made the break with Holmes in the spring of 1948, after five-and-a-half years in the fold and twenty-five issued titles. He let go of one secure job to accept another—at the head of his own trio at the Alberta Lounge, a nightclub facing Windsor Station just around the corner from St. Antoine Street. Radio station CFCF broadcast the trio live from the club. During his two-year residency at the Alberta Lounge, Peterson spent most nights after work sitting in and socializing with the Louis Metcalf band at the nearby Café St. Michel, where he immersed himself in bebop. Visiting American musicians were invariably stunned on first hearing Peterson, whether at the Café St. Michel or elsewhere. Lou Hooper's son, Lou Hooper, Jr., was at the Chez Maurice Danceland one night in late 1948 when the pioneer bebop trumpeter Dizzy Gillespie brought his big band in from New York City for a two-night stand:

> On the first night, Oscar was there, and pretty soon people were shouting out, "Get Oscar to play! Let Oscar play!" So finally Diz says, "OK, Oscar, come on, where are you?" They pulled out the most difficult piano chart they had. It was one of those things where the band wails, then stops dead, and the piano's supposed to play. So they built up to this break, and we're all saying to ourselves, "Watch this!" And when the break comes, Oscar leans back and...

Momentarily lost for words, Hooper Jr. resorted to sweeping hand gestures and boiling vocalizations to convey an image of the tidal wave of notes that poured from the piano as Peterson laid into it with all fingers flailing.

> The whole brass section stood up and looked at him and said, "Who in the hell is *that*!" Diz just stared at him for a minute, then started shouting, "Blow! Blow! Go ahead and blow, man!" Then Oscar *really* got going. Well, from that point on the band just kept putting numbers in front of him so they could listen to him play.

We didn't go with them afterwards, but Oscar told us that Diz kept him up till about six o'clock in the morning at some after-hours club, keeping him playing, and he kept asking him, "Do you really *hear* them chords?"[16]

American musicians had been carrying stories of Peterson home with them for years. Count Basie had raved about him to *Down Beat* in 1944. Coleman Hawkins had been impressed by him in 1945. A year later, both Jimmie Lunceford and Basie apparently made special trips to Montreal to hear him play. Both big-band leaders tried to hire Peterson, but he refused to leave Holmes: he claimed the Montreal band was play-ing the same style of music as the American big bands, and paying him handsomely. Numerous other American musicians jammed with Peterson during stopovers in Montreal. All of which casts serious doubts on the accuracy of the legend that has grown up about how Norman Granz, the American promoter of the famous travelling Jazz at the Philharmonic concerts, first heard Peterson by accident one night in Montreal. Granz has recalled:

> Musicians like Coleman Hawkins had told me about this cat as far back as 1945, but I had never bothered to listen to him. Then one night in 1949 I had been visiting Montreal to prepare a con-cert and I was on my way back to the airport when I heard some music on the taxi radio. I asked the cab driver what record that was and he said, "It isn't. It's live—a trio playing at the Alberta Lounge." I said, "Turn around and go back into town."[17]

Granz's fateful meeting with Peterson at the Alberta Lounge that night may have been the first face-to-face encounter between two men whose lives would be closely entwined for years after. Yet, as Gene Lees has deduced, it seems highly unlikely that Granz had never before heard Peterson's piano playing. Basie, Hawkins, and other American musi-cians who were raving about Peterson in the United States were regular members of Granz's travelling Jazz at the Philharmonic shows, and they must have encouraged Granz to listen to Peterson, if not in person then on record. Furthermore, Peterson himself remembered that Granz criti-cized his boogie-woogie records during their first meeting at the Alberta Lounge. Lees has even suggested that Granz may have previously asked Peterson several times to appear with Jazz at the Philharmonic, but that Peterson kept insisting he wasn't ready.[18]

Regardless, on that night in 1949 Granz convinced Peterson to take a chance at stardom by performing in a Jazz at the Philharmonic concert at Carnegie Hall in New York City. Many years later Peterson told an inter-viewer that he had realized early in life that, as a black man, the only way to succeed as a musician was "to frighten the hell out of everybody pianistically."[19] That philosophy served him well at his American debut. Whether to avoid union and immigration problems, or simply to heighten the drama of Peterson's appearance, Granz did not include the pianist on the program. Instead, on the night of 18 September 1949, he simply called the unknown twenty-four-year-old up out of the audience and invited him to play. Within minutes, according to *Down Beat* reporter Mike Levin, Peterson "stopped the Norman Granz Jazz at the Philharmonic concert dead in its tracks...."

> Balancing a large and bulky body at the piano much in the fashion of Earl Hines, Peterson displayed a flashy right hand, a load of bop and [George] Shearing-styled ideas, as well as a good sense of harmonic development.
>
> And, in addition, he scared some of the local modern minions by playing bop figures single finger in his *left* hand, which is distinctly not the common practice.
>
> Further than this, Peterson impressed musicians here by not only having good ideas and making them, but by giving them a rhythmic punch and drive which has been all too lacking in too many of the younger pianists. Whereas some of the bop stars conceive good ideas but sweat to make them, Peterson rips them off with an excess of power which leaves no doubt about his technical excess in reserve.[20]

Peterson returned to Montreal a conquering hero, but he was soon to be swept out of the grasp of his local fans. Granz quickly signed him for Jazz at the Philharmonic. In 1950 Peterson surrendered the piano at the Alberta Lounge and began spending long periods away from home, performing and recording. Within four years of his Carnegie Hall debut, he had toured North America, Europe, and Japan, recorded close to two hundred titles in the United States, and been voted best jazz pianist in *Down Beat*'s polls of readers and critics. In 1958 he moved his home to Toronto.

Among the other young musicians who worked in the Johnny Holmes Orchestra was a young white trumpet player with a facility for high-note playing that served as his visa to the United States a year before Peterson's Carnegie Hall debut. Like Peterson, Maynard Ferguson was raised in a musical family, started playing music before he could read, and absorbed his ambition from demanding parents. Unlike Peterson's parents, however, the Fergusons were not content to cheer from the sidelines as Maynard, who switched from violin to trumpet at nine, and his older brother Percy, a budding saxophonist, felt their way in the world. Rather, they approached older musicians on their sons' behalf, seeking opportunities for the boys to play. They ushered them to dances and jam sessions, made sure the boys were paid, and even packed sandwiches for them to take on the job.

By the time Maynard entered high school, he already held a union card. He played with Peterson, two-and-a-half years his senior, in Percy's Victory Serenadors. Maynard, too, decided to quit school. His father, an elementary school principal, endorsed the move. At fifteen he began studying privately at the Conservatoire de musique du Québec in Montreal. His parents secured regular radio appearances for him in both Montreal and Toronto. The teenager was so shy that on one occasion a radio station called in a young actor to announce the tunes and chat with the host in Maynard's place, leaving the young musician with nothing to do but play his trumpet.

Maynard joined Holmes's band after Peterson. As Holmes remembered it, he was looking for a baritone saxophonist for his orchestra, and the call went out to Percy Ferguson. When Percy showed up at the rehearsal, he was accompanied by his father—and Maynard. The father laid down the terms: if Holmes wanted Percy, he'd have to find a spot for Maynard, too. Holmes, a trumpet player himself, wasn't impressed with Maynard's playing, despite the teenager's uncanny ability to play easily in the extreme high register of his horn.

> I didn't want Maynard. He had no chops at the time. His sound was horrible—scratchy and squeaky. He could already play those freak high notes, but he had no technique when it came to playing a jazz ensemble passage. He'd take a solo on "Stardust" and play five beats in the bar, three beats in the bar, anything. He just didn't have it.

Percy, Holmes felt, was the better musician of the two brothers, and the only one that met the standard of musicianship Holmes was trying to set for the band. But good baritone saxophonists were in short supply, and Mr. Ferguson stood firm to his condition. Holmes accepted Maynard into the band to gain Percy. He assigned Maynard the role of fourth trumpet, where he remained during his less than one year with the band.

The Johnny Holmes Orchestra was Ferguson's stepping-stone to the professional big bands. In the spring of 1943 Ferguson left Holmes to join Stan Wood's big band for its summer residency at Belmont Park; he continued with Wood at the Auditorium that fall and winter. Wood billed Ferguson as "The 15-Year-Old Trumpet Wizard." In the absence of any recordings of Ferguson made before he left Montreal, it is impossible to evaluate his musicianship as a teenager; nevertheless, his local popularity was spreading rapidly. After a stint with another local band at the Chez Maurice Danceland, Ferguson was called upon to organize his own big band for a summer job at the dance pavilion in his hometown of Verdun.

Business at the Verdun pavilion had fallen off drastically following an ugly battle there between angry servicemen and civilian zoot-suiters. To the men and women in uniform, the billowing zoot suits that were fashionable in Montreal during the war were an affront to the country's war effort. The government was encouraging citizens to conserve cotton and other textiles for use in military uniforms. Zoot suits, which squandered yards of material, were seen as symbols of opposition to conscription and national sacrifice. Off-duty servicemen frequently went hunting for zoot-suiters, their rage fueled by liquor and the frivolity of Montreal nightlife. One night a mob of servicemen stormed the dance pavilion in Verdun, using park benches to batter their way through doors and walls in their frenzy to get at the zoot-suiters among the crowd inside. Vicious fighting erupted. The band, terrified that the servicemen would turn on the zoot-suited musicians among them, played loudly and without stop as the riot raged around them for more than an hour. The military police eventually arrived to restore order, and ambulances ferried the injured to hospital. Miraculously, the musicians emerged unscathed. By the end of the evening, however, the Verdun pavilion and its reputation were heavily damaged.

Ferguson's job was to draw the dancers back to Verdun. Straining credulity to that end, he was billed as "King of the Trumpet." He had just turned seventeen. "I was just fronting the band, and the owners looked after the business end of it," he wrote some years later in *Coda* magazine:

> This was the first band I ever had, and actually we started out to zero business. It was just after the zoot-suit riots and the pavilion had a bad reputation. We used to start the job without one single customer in the place, but the band had a ball. Gradually the word got around and the crowds started flocking in.[21]

As the summer season of 1945 was drawing to a close at the Verdun pavilion, Ferguson contacted the owner of the Palais Royal dance hall in Toronto. The owner had heard Ferguson play with Stan Wood's orchestra and told him to stay in touch. Ferguson was immediately offered a month's engagement at the Palais Royal, leading his own sixteen-piece orchestra. For the next two years, Ferguson travelled back and forth between Montreal and Toronto with his big band. It wintered in Montreal, with lengthy engagements at the Auditorium and the Chez Maurice Danceland. Summers were spent at the Palais Royal and at Crystal Beach, an amusement park on the Lake Erie shore of the Niagara Peninsula.

Maynard Ferguson and his orchestra at the Auditorium. Left to right, trumpets: Tom Covey, Al Kane, Ferguson (standing), Joe Christie Sr.; trombones: Gordie Marsh, Gordie Martin; saxophones: Freddie Nichols (baritone), Tony Mazza (alto), Percy Ferguson (alto), Frank Costi (tenor), Roger Brousseau (tenor); others: unidentified vocalist, Dale Davies (bass), Jimmy Malorni (drums), Harold "Steep" Wade (piano), Richard Boudreau (guitar).
Courtesy of Pierre Brousseau. John Gilmore Jazz History Collection, Concordia University Archives.

> We were lucky, because all the time this band was together, we only had about three weeks without work. We worked steadily for three years with only a few weeks off. The band was undergoing constant changes all through this time, and with the average age of the boys around 30 you could say that I really had to learn a lot. My father and mother were handling the personnel changes and business arrangements, but it was up to me to get the music out. We used a number of trumpet features in that book [i.e., the band's repertoire], such as Bunny Berigan's "I Can't Get Started" and Harry James's "Concerto for Trumpet."[22]

Ferguson, still in his teens, had become a hot item on the professional dance band circuit. But the war was over, and the big bands were dying. The end of the Swing Era was noticeable first in the United States, where eight leading big bands—including Benny Goodman's—broke up at the end of 1946. Changing tastes in entertainment coupled with rising transportation and salary costs were making it increasingly difficult for big bands to survive, and especially to tour. Perhaps for these reasons,

Ferguson began rehearsing a sextet in Montreal during the winter of 1947-48, with an eye on a cross-Canada tour the following summer. Then, suddenly, Ferguson's ticket to the United States materialized in the form of an invitation to join a big band led by Boyd Raeburn. Ferguson abruptly disbanded his sextet and left for the United States to catch the tail end of the Swing Era. His brother Percy abandoned music at this time and turned to an academic career.

For the next few years, Ferguson worked as sideman and soloist in several of the leading big bands that survived the end of the Swing Era; after Raeburn he played with Jimmy Dorsey, Charlie Barnett, and Stan Kenton. He became widely known for his recorded solos, first with Barnett but more so with the the the Kenton band, where he served three years in the band and rose to the top of the *Down Beat* readers' poll. In the early 1950s, Ferguson settled in California and worked in Hollywood film-studio orchestras. Finally, in the late 1950s, he began touring at the head of his own scaled-down big bands, developing an enduring international following for his distinctive, bravura style of big-band jazz.

Canadian trends in music follow closely those in the United States, though generally at a cautious distance. Jazz has been no exception. The big-band craze started later in Montreal than in the States, and accordingly took longer to die out. Yet by the end of the 1940s, Johnny Holmes could see that an era was ending. Attendance at his Victoria Hall dances dropped off as the teenagers he had played for during the war married and began to raise families. Peterson and Ferguson, the heroes of the Montreal big band scene, had left the city. The dance pavilions were closing; the Auditorium was transformed into a nightclub called the Bellevue Casino. Holmes, with a wife and child of his own to support, hung up his horn in 1950 and found a job as a salesman again. His orchestra survived a year without him, then broke up.

Holmes remained out of music until 1959. In that year Ken Withers of CBC radio in Montreal sensed the country was ripe for big-band nostalgia. He invited Holmes to put together a new orchestra for a weekly radio show. For the next ten years, Holmes led, part-time, a series of studio big bands, featuring new arrangements and professional, studio jazzmen. CBC issued several recordings of these studio bands; ironically, no one had offered to record the original Johnny Holmes Orchestra with Oscar Peterson during its peak at Victoria Hall. In fact, no Montreal big bands were recorded during the Swing Era. Peterson was the last Montreal jazz musician to be recorded by either of the city's pioneering record companies, Berliner or Compo. By 1950, Toronto had usurped Montreal as the centre of the Canadian recording industry, and jazz was being recorded mainly by small, independent record companies—only a handful of which were based in Montreal.

CHAPTER FIVE

Louis Metcalf and the Arrival of Bebop

At the end of the Second World War, stage shows continued to be the staple of Montreal nightlife. Every night of the week, Sundays included, Montrealers could be entertained by singers, dancers, comedians, and acrobats at any of scores of nightclubs throughout the city. Accompanying each of these shows was a local band, and in many of these bands sat jazz musicians. To most of the audience, the musicians were anonymous. Their job was to play the music which the entertainers required for their acts and which the audiences required for their dancing between shows. Most of the musicians accepted their lot in life; few aspired to fame; only a handful succeeded in making their names known to the average nightclub patron. Yet of all the nightclubs that thrived in Montreal during the late 1940s, one stood out from the rest, not because of its shows, but precisely because of its musicians. "In all the other clubs I worked in," Herb Johnson reflected after forty-five years in Montreal, "people would ask, 'What time does the show go on?' But at the Café St. Michel, people would say, 'Is Louis Metcalf here?'"

Louis Metcalf, veteran trumpet player of the Duke Ellington orchestra and a string of other top American bands, achieved something quite remarkable in Montreal for his time: he transformed an inelegant show club into the city's first jazz shrine. With a mixture of business acumen and practised professional charm, Metcalf made the Café St. Michel a hallowed name in jazz communities across Canada and a required stop for musicians passing through town. In doing so, he pushed six Montreal musicians into the spotlight previously reserved for entertainers and ushered a fledgling new jazz style called bebop onto Montreal stages.

Metcalf was no stranger to Montreal when he began assembling the city's first bebop band at the beginning of 1946. As a young musician, dancer, and singer, he had brought his own nightclub revue up from

New York City in the early 1930s. A talented teenage singer named Billie Holiday had been part of that revue. Yet the season Metcalf had spent in Montreal with his revue was only a minor episode in his musical career: he had already recorded dozens of titles with Duke Ellington and other black musicians and singers, and he had worked alongside Jelly Roll Morton and Willie "The Lion" Smith, two master pianists of early jazz. Like other musicians who visited Montreal in the early years of jazz, however, Metcalf was impressed by the city's vitality, hospitality, and free-flowing liquor.

A spell of unemployment probably turned Metcalf's thoughts back to Montreal after the end of the Second World War. Since his first visit to the city, he had turned forty and added more credits to his name: he had worked with Fletcher Henderson's orchestra, led his own bands, and even run his own nightclub in New York City. Now unexpectedly out of work, he decided to go on the road with a band he had been leading at the Downbeat club on New York's 52nd Street in late 1945. With a tour of Canada apparently in the planning stages, Metcalf went on ahead of his band to Montreal, arriving probably in January 1946. There he discovered that Canadian immigration regulations prevented him from bringing his band into Canada.[1] With no engagement in New York to return to, Metcalf lingered in Montreal. Impressed by the wealth of local jazz talent, he decided to form a band comprised of local musicians to play the new style of jazz that was becoming popular among younger black musicians in New York.

Bebop was a radical departure in the evolution of jazz, and it was to Metcalf's credit that, schooled and practised as he was in the music of the 1920s and 1930s, he was ready to embrace the newly emerging style. All over the world, musicians, critics, and audiences of Metcalf's generation were rejecting the new music out of hand. Unable to grasp its innovations and penetrate its complexities, they heard little of beauty in bebop's richer harmonies, unconventional phrasing and rhythms, and headlong tempos. The older generation was especially offended by the arrogance displayed by the young bebop musicians towards nightclub audiences, and they predicted bebop would be the death of jazz. They were, of course, terribly mistaken, for as bebop matured, jazz attained another plateau of artistry, virtuosity, and emotional profundity. In the process, however, bebop shook jazz to its roots, challenging musicians to develop new musical skills and faster reflexes. Many of the older swing musicians were unable, or unwilling, to adapt and felt threatened by the radical changes in the language of jazz. It had, after all, happened very fast, as historian James Lincoln Collier has written:

> At the beginning of 1941 bop was only a handful of ideas tentatively being tried out by fewer than a half-dozen players. By 1942 it was being played by at least a few men. By 1943 it was circulat-

ing through the younger men in jazz; by 1944 it was a recognized, if controversial movement; and by 1945 [when the first pure bebop recordings were made in the United States] it had a public large enough to support it. And it was clear by then that bop was more than just a musical force; it was the core of a set of social ideas as well. Associated with it was an attitude that expressed itself in a habit of language, dress, and behaviour. This was what came to be called "cool"... and it had two meanings. On the one hand, it was a deliberate attempt to avoid playing the role of flamboyant black entertainer, which whites had come to expect. On the other hand, it was a send-up of what the blacks saw as the square, restricted world of the whites.[2]

There was, however, nothing radical about the instrumentation of the bebop combos, and the group Metcalf assembled in Montreal in early 1946 was no exception. Its front line of trumpet, tenor saxophone, and trombone was identical to the band he had left behind in New York City. Backing up the horns was a four-piece rhythm section of piano, guitar, bass, and drums.

Only one of the Montreal musicians recruited by Metcalf was close to him in age. Benny Winestone, thirty-nine, was a widely admired Glasgow-born tenor saxophonist and clarinetist who had been prominent on the British jazz scene during the 1930s. He had immigrated to Canada at the beginning of the Second World War, hoping to step from there into the United States. But though he worked briefly, and probably illegally, with pianist Jess Stacey's band in New York City in late 1945, and even subbed a few times in the Benny Goodman band, American barriers against foreign musicians prevented him from settling south of the border. For the rest of his life Winestone drifted back and forth between Montreal and Toronto in search of work, new musical challenges, and the ticket to the United States which eluded him to his impoverished end. He cloaked his frustrations in a veil of perennial good humour and inebriation; the jokes poured from his tongue in a nearly indecipherable concoction of Scottish brogue, Jewish humour, and black street argot. The box of Cow Brand baking soda which he carried with him everywhere to soothe his liquor-enflamed stomach was a source of constant amusement to his fellow musicians, who invariably joked about him being full of soul—and soda. Winestone, swallowing his medicine, would counter: "There ain't gonna be no Cow Brand next year, 'cause they gonna put *my* picture on the box!"

Standing cockily next to Winestone and Metcalf in the front line of the new band was Jiro "Butch" Watanabe, at twenty-one the youngest member. Born to Japanese parents near Vancouver, he had already crossed Canada three times. Driven eastward when his parents were interned by the Canadian government during the Second World War, he had made his way to Montreal, worked as a houseboy while finishing high school, then found a job in a war plant. The armed forces recruited him for intelligence work against the Japanese and sent him back to the West Coast for training. When the war ended, he returned to Montreal with an armed forces scholarship to study music at McGill University's conservatory. By his own account, Watanabe was a "brash, young brat" when he joined Metcalf's band. It was his first professional job as a musician; he was unable to sight-read and was still finding his legs as a soloist. Yet the band's drummer, Mark "Wilkie" Wilkinson, who had brought Watanabe into the band, saw promise in his playing and insisted Metcalf hold on to the young musician while he studied music at McGill by day and learned his lessons with the band at night.

Wilkinson, himself only twenty-four, was an obvious choice for Metcalf's band. Born to Swedish parents in Ontario, he was conservatory trained on piano but self-taught on drums. He had spent the early years of the Second World War playing drums in Lou Hooper's army band in England. Discharged from the army for medical reasons, Wilkinson had gone to New York City, befriended the pioneering bebop drummer Kenny Clarke, and witnessed the emergence of the new style of jazz in Harlem. Returning to Montreal to start his own career as a professional drummer, Wilkinson had quickly gravitated to the black clubs in the St. Antoine district.

Harold "Steep" Wade was the pianist in Metcalf's band. What the Montreal-born musician lacked in first-hand exposure to bebop, he more than made up for in harmonic imagination, irrepressible swing, and professional experience. Wade was twenty-eight when Metcalf recruited him, but he had already accumulated ten years of professional jazz experience in Montreal, first as a saxophonist and then as a pianist. Bassist Al King was about twenty-nine and a recent arrival from the United States; little else is known about him. Guitarist Gilbert "Buck" Lacombe, twenty-four, rounded out the rhythm section. A veteran of Don Messer's Maritime fiddle band and Stan Wood's Montreal big band, Lacombe couldn't have been back from the army show in Europe more than a few months when Metcalf snatched him up.

These were the musicians who first tried to play bebop in Montreal. Faced with the necessity of earning a livelihood as nightclub musicians, they could not take as much time as they needed to master the new style and repertoire of jazz before going public with it. Instead, they worked out arrangements of the popular tunes of the Swing Era and then attempted a bebop interpretation of the material. Montrealers greeted their first efforts coolly. Metcalf organized a series of concerts to introduce his band to the city, but, as he told *Record Research* magazine sixteen years later, "the crowds were not too good, so what we had to do was be versatile by adding dixieland and swing music to our repertoire."[3]

Within a few months of the band's formation, several events coincided which assured it serious attention in the city. First, Metcalf secured a steady engagement at the Café St. Michel, a nightclub on Mountain Street almost directly facing Rockhead's Paradise. The Café St. Michel specialized in black stage shows, but the club's manager seemed prepared to give Metcalf more latitude than most Montreal bandleaders enjoyed in determining the kind of music played in the short dance sets between shows. Metcalf's status as an American jazz star and his experience as a New York club owner provided strong incentives for the Café St. Michel to trust Metcalf's judgement on musical matters. Given this leeway, Metcalf quickly began shaping his band into a nightclub attraction. That he succeeded in doing so was due in no small part to the contributions of two highly talented and experienced musicians who joined the band shortly after it opened at the Café St. Michel.

Willy Girard was a short, painfully shy, French-speaking Montrealer who had begun playing Québécois reels on the violin at the age of four.[4] Private classical studies led to an offer of a position with the Montreal Symphony Orchestra while Girard was still a teenager, but he cast aside the opportunity and set off in pursuit of jazz. Through the 1930s he played professionally with white bands in cabarets and dance halls, but his reputation as an inventive and highly swinging jazz soloist was established mainly at jam sessions in the black clubs. The antithesis of a hustling musician, Girard was frequently without work and by the 1940s had begun taking day jobs to support his family. The thirty-eight-year-old musician had been without work for seven months when he decided to telephone his friend Buck Lacombe and ask the guitarist if he knew of any openings. By coincidence, Lacombe was overwhelmed with offers of radio work, at wages Metcalf could never hope to match. Three-and-a-half decades later, Girard sat in retirement in his Montreal home and laconically resurrected from memory that fateful conversation with Lacombe, and its outcome:

> I called Buck Lacombe. I knew he was working at the Café St. Michel, and I wasn't working. He said, "Do you want to take my place?"
>
> "Are you crazy? A guitar and a violin, they're not the same thing!"
>
> "Yes, yes, I'm serious."
>
> "Well, call your leader."
>
> He didn't call him. He called Steep Wade. *Maudit* Steep Wade said, "OK." They were all new musicians to me. I didn't know any of them, only Steep Wade.

Girard arrived unannounced at the St. Michel for afternoon band rehearsal. Only the head waiter greeted him.

> I didn't even take off my coat. I put my violin on the bar and I said [to the musicians], "I'm replacing Buck Lacombe."
>
> The bandleader asked me, "Isn't he here?!"
>
> I met the musicians—Wilkie, Butch, Benny Winestone. They didn't know me at all. They asked me, "What do you play?"
>
> "The violin. I'm replacing Buck Lacombe. I don't know if it's going to work."
>
> Steep was pleased. He introduced me to Louis Metcalf, and I told him, "Buck can't make it. He's too tired. He's doing too much work, too much radio work."
>
> "What's that thing, there?" Metcalf pointed at my case.
>
> "I play the violin. It's not the same as the guitar."
>
> He just looked at me. Then he continued talking to Steep Wade and I heard him ask Steep in a whisper, "How well does he play?"
>
> Steep said, "Oh, not bad."
>
> I said nothing.
>
> So Steep said to me, "Take your coat off." I did, and we got ready to play.
>
> I tuned my violin and all that. But I only had the microphone, the one they used for announcing. I didn't have an amplifier. Then Metcalf asks me, "What do you want to play?"
>
> "Oh, anything. Just play, play whatever you want."
>
> So he picks up his trumpet and starts playing a bebop tune. I'd never heard it before! So he plays. Then, all of a sudden—he didn't even look back at me—I just started playing. I swung it. Not a lot. I just teased him a little. He turned around to look at me. He was still holding his trumpet to his lips. And he listened.
>
> "Take another chorus!" he shouted.
>
> "Take another one!"
>
> "Take another one!"
>
> And I put more into it.
>
> He was overjoyed. "You're in!"
>
> We started practising the show right away.[5]

Shortly after Girard joined the band, Winestone departed, due either to illness or a conflict with the union. Musicians moving from one city to another were required to sit out a six-month waiting period while their union membership was transferred from their previous hometown to their new local. During this six-month probation, transferring musicians were only allowed to accept part-time work, so as not to take steady work away from regular members of the local. If Winestone had recently wandered into Montreal, the union probably objected to his taking a full-time job with Metcalf at the Café St. Michel. Metcalf himself seems not to have been hindered by this regulation. As a famous trumpeter who was creating work for six local musicians, the union may have considered him an asset to the local and decided to bend the regulations in his favour. During the first few months of the band's engagement at the Café St. Michel, Metcalf performed on a tiny circular platform next to the bandstand; in so doing he probably claimed, with the union's acquiesence, that he was a show attraction and was not actually working on the same bandstand as Montreal union members.[6] Winestone, however, could not command the same cooperation from the union. Whether for that reason, or because of illness, he was suddenly unable to continue in the band. Metcalf needed a tenor player—fast.

"One day I received a call from Louis Metcalf, and he asked me if I wanted to join the band," recalled Herb Johnson, who had been working mainly in uptown bands since the breakdown of the city's colour barrier and hadn't been paying much attention to the downtown scene. "I just happened to be looking for a gig. I didn't know any of the musicians in the band. Nor did I know what I was getting into—it was the hardest working band in Montreal!"

Metcalf knew of Johnson through *The Music Dial*, a black-owned and operated monthly magazine published in New York City which covered music, theatre, and the arts. Metcalf had served as treasurer of the publication in 1944; at the same time, Johnson had been contributing a regular column on the Montreal music scene and selling copies of the magazine by hand in the clubs. Johnson was a musician of Metcalf's generation: he was two-and-a-half years older than the trumpeter and had never played bebop prior to stepping into Winestone's shoes. His credentials, however, were impeccable. Johnson had been a professional musician for twenty-five years, beginning in dance bands in his hometown of Hartford, Connecticut, during the 1920s, and highlighted by five-and-a-half years in New York City working in bands led by Jelly Roll Morton, Benny Carter, Noble Sissle, and Kaiser Marshall. Forced out of Harlem by the Depression, Johnson had been working in Montreal since 1935, where he had earned a reputation locally as a reliable, hard-working bandleader and sideman, an excellent tenor player in the Coleman Hawkins tradition, and a champion of racial integration on the bandstand. In addition, he brought to the Metcalf band arranging skills which would prove invaluable.

By May 1946 the personnel of the Metcalf band had solidified; it would remain unchanged for the next three years. Whether by choice or by chance, Metcalf had gathered around him six musicians of different racial and ethnic backgrounds—a Canadian trombonist of Japanese

121

Louis Metcalf's International Band at the Café St. Michel, with guitarist Curly Reid sitting in. Band members: Steep Wade (piano); Louis Metcalf (trumpet, vocals); Willy Girard (violin); Al King (bass); Herb Johnson (tenor saxophone); Butch Watanabe (trombone); Wilkie Wilkinson (drums). Note small, separate bandstand for Metcalf. *Photo by Canada Wide Feature Service, courtesy of Herb Johnson. John Gilmore Jazz History Collection, Concordia University Archives.*

parentage, a French Canadian violinist, an American-born tenor saxophonist of mixed black American and French Canadian descent, a black Canadian pianist of West Indian parentage, a white Canadian drummer of Swedish parentage, and an American bass player of mixed black and Mexican blood. Though the calibre of the musicianship and the controversial nature of the music the group was attempting to play should have been sufficient to generate local interest, the media was fascinated as much by the band's cosmopolitan mix.

Metcalf's was not the first mixed band to play at the Café St. Michel—a white saxophonist named Irving Pall had led mixed show bands there and at Rockhead's Paradise as early as 1944—but it was still not yet commonplace to see black and white musicians working together on Montreal stages, and rarer still to see a band of such diversity led by a famed New York trumpet player who was himself part Cherokee Indian. The *Standard*, a Montreal tabloid, ran a two-page photo feature of the band in May 1946 with the headline "Mixed Band: Famed Jazz Musician Builds Unique Band." Reporter Ken Johnstone's article called the band "a challenge to racial prejudice," adding "the band sets a new high for jazz musicianship as well."[7] A year later, *Down Beat* magazine heralded the band in a story headlined "New Canadian Mixed Ork Wows Hot Jazz Fans." The article began:

> There's no novelty in Negro and white musicians making good music together, but when a group of seven men representing that many different nationalities are playing terrific jazz in a small Montreal night club—brother, that's news!

Calling the group "the most talked-about band in Canada," writer William Brown-Forbes added, without elaboration:

> They've had a few bad breaks because they were a mixed aggregation but this exhibition of prejudice has only made them more determined to stay together.[8]

Whatever the band members may have felt individually about their role as champions of integration, ultimately it was the challenge of the music and the prestige which Metcalf generated for the band which held them together for so long. For the first time in their Montreal careers, the musicians weren't taking second billing to the show acts. The Metcalf band continued to play the music required for the shows, and with all the professionalism Montreal show bands had become noted for on the entertainment circuit. But Metcalf gradually transformed the traditional intermission dance sets into mini-concerts showcasing the band itself.

"Montreal was a dancing city in those days," recalled May Oliver, who, with her husband Ed, helped manage Metcalf's business and personal affairs during his stay at the Café St. Michel. "People expected that if they went out to a club, sometime during the evening they would dance. For them to listen to something other than dance music was quite a thing. It was amazing that Metcalf was able to do it."[9]

Metcalf didn't do it overnight. His musicians needed time to learn to play bebop, and his audiences needed time to feel comfortable with the new music—and with their new role as seated spectators at a jazz performance. Before bebop, jazz was essentially dance music elevated, at its best, to an art. But bebop, at its purest and fastest, was simply impossible for nightclub patrons to dance to, a fact which seriously impeded its acceptance by the paying public. Bebop musicians across North America were encountering bewildered audiences and impatient nightclub owners: even as Metcalf's band was finding its legs at the Café St. Michel, Charlie Parker, bebop's messiah, was fired by a nightclub in California because his mixed bebop band simply wasn't drawing large enough audiences.[10]

"Louis knew where he wanted the band to go," Oliver continued, "but he'd been in the business long enough to know that you couldn't force it down people's throats. You led them there. It was like an education in jazz."

Metcalf was a charming and experienced host; he knew how to win the hearts of his audience. At the Café St. Michel he let the patrons get their fill of dancing during the first intermission set of the night. As the night wore on, he gradually replaced the danceable swing tunes with the new bebop music his band really wanted to play, while simultaneously drawing the audience's attention to the band. He sent Johnson and Girard down onto the stage in turn to perform featured solos: Johnson's version of "Body and Soul," a challenging test piece for tenor saxophonists ever since Coleman Hawkins had made it a jazz hit with a 1939 recording, was always popular with the audiences. By the last set of the night, the band was playing all bebop—and the St. Michel was packed with people listening.

The new music Metcalf's band was playing was only just spilling out of New York City at the time, and there were no Montreal musicians to turn to for help in learning to play the new repertoire. "We were the first band in Montreal to play bop," said Wilkinson. "Most musicians in town didn't really know what was happening." Added Johnson: "There may have been some musicians trying to understand the chord progressions [to the bebop tunes] which were based on standard tunes—because "Groovin' High" was simply "Whispering"—but we were the only band in town that was playing certain of those Charlie Parker-Dizzy Gillespie things note for note."

Learning the new tunes—which Parker and Gillespie had begun

Herb Johnson soloing with the Metcalf band. *Photo by Canada Wide Feature Service, courtesy of Herb Johnson. John Gilmore Jazz History Collection, Concordia University Archives.*

recording together in early 1945, at intimidating tempos—was no easy task. Left to their own resources, the band gradually built up a repertoire of jazz material through a rigorous schedule of unpaid, afternoon rehearsals—as many as three a week initially—and Johnson's tireless writing. Easiest to learn were the published arrangements of jazz standards, though these had to be modified to accommodate the unusual presence of a violin in the front line. The only source for the new bebop tunes, however, were the 78 r.p.m. records coming out of the United States. The band listened to these records repeatedly at rehearsals. Metcalf, who possessed a keen musical ear, would pick out fragments of the melody on his horn, then sing or hum them slowly to Johnson, who would scribble the notes down on manuscript paper. Collective efforts were required to decipher the more difficult bebop harmonies, with their unusual dissonances and frequent chord substitutions. "We were trying to learn something new," said Johnson, "something very, very new, and not one of us had instruction in the new chord progressions. We learned by ear."

With a sketch of the tune's melody and chord progression finally on paper, the band was ready to add the tune to its repertoire. If the front line decided to play the melody in unison, a common practice in bebop performances of the day, the musicians could begin learning the tune right away, by ear. If the band desired a written arrangement featuring more complex interplay of the instruments, the task was left to Johnson. It was a solitary and anonymous job but he tackled it with perseverance, often retiring to a corner of the band room during intermissions at the Café St. Michel to work out some detail. With parts for all of the instruments finally written out, Johnson brought the arrangement to rehearsal. Though the band played the show music from written parts, when it came time to performing their own repertoire on stage they prided themselves on playing without benefit of written music. A good part of their rehearsal time was therefore devoted to memorizing their material. In this fashion they eventually built up a repertoire of about one hundred jazz tunes. A handful of these were original compositions, mostly unwritten pieces developed collectively and based on a few simple riffs played over the blues or a standard chord progression.

In return for writing most of the band's arrangements, Johnson received an occasional bonus from Metcalf. Watanabe contributed about a half-dozen arrangements, but he preferred to write for the show acts, from whom payment was more certain. From time to time an outside musician would bring an arrangement for the band to try out, and the best of these also found their way into the book. In the band's later years a local alto saxophonist and self-taught arranger named Gerry Macdonald wrote several arrangements for the band.[11]

The music of Stan Kenton inspired the Metcalf musicians almost as much as that of Charlie Parker and the other pioneering black beboppers. Kenton, a white American bandleader and a crusading spokesman for modern jazz, led a series of large touring orchestras which played music far removed from the light commercial dance music of the day; some of it borrowed heavily from European music. Johnson admired Kenton and reorchestrated many of his published arrangements for the Metcalf band. Whenever Kenton appeared in Montreal, at the Forum or the Chez Maurice Danceland, Metcalf would arrange an hour off for his band on a weekday night so the musicians could run uptown and hear their idol. Returning to the St. Michel bandstand later, "we tore up the club because we were so inspired by Kenton's music," Johnson said. Members of Kenton's band would return the compliment, making the pilgrimage down to the St. Michel after work and sitting in with the Metcalf band. Eddie Safranski, Kenton's bassist, was especially encouraging to the Montreal modernists: during one week-long engagement with Kenton in Montreal, he spent every night after work sitting in at the St. Michel and attended an afternoon rehearsal of the band to coach the musicians through a new Johnson arrangement of a Kenton number.

"Louie Metcalf and his International Band—Canada's Greatest Jazz Band" proclaimed the souvenir cards sitting on the tables at the Café St. Michel.[12] The seven musicians had been playing together nightly for three years by 1949, and their fame had spread across Canada and into the United States. The Café St. Michel had become as famous with jazz fans as Rockhead's Paradise across the street had become with connoisseurs of black entertainment. The two clubs, between them, were drawing flocks of tourists to Montreal every summer, including many black Americans. They say you could spot licence plates from just about every state and province on the continent if you hung around the corner of Mountain and St. Antoine long enough on a hot summer night. Carloads of musicians from Toronto drove the 540 kilometres to Montreal just to hear the Metcalf band. And American musicians in town for engagements uptown routinely headed for the Café St. Michel after work to relax and enjoy the band. Some, like Conte Candoli, Ray Brown, and Art Pepper, sat in; others, like Sonny Rollins and Fats Navarro, waited for Wilkinson and Wade to lead them to an all-night jam session after the band had finished work.

Trumpeter Jack Long, an aspiring bebopper who was just completing high school in Toronto while the Metcalf band was in full flower at the St. Michel, was typical of the band's long-distance admirers:

I knew all about it in Toronto, even though I'd never heard a recording of it. In fact, I never *heard* the band! But I could tell you the names of all the players. Everybody in the jazz scene in Toronto knew about it.[13]

Notwithstanding the band's fame, the show still went on at the Café St. Michel. There simply wasn't a large enough paying audience in Montreal to support a nightclub featuring only jazz. So, twice nightly, three times on Saturday nights, Metcalf and his musicians donned their custom-made, no-lapel jackets, buried their noses in a thick folder of music, and earned their fifty-odd dollars a week each. The show music presented few musical challenges, and there was little in it to trip up the experienced sight-readers in the band. Watanabe was a liability at first, but like most musicians of the day he perfected his sight-reading on the job.

Girard faced the biggest obstacle: there was rarely anything for him to read. The music which the entertainers brought with them was written to accommodate a wide range of possible band instrumentations—but not the violin. On particularly complicated show numbers, Girard might sketch a violin part out for himself based on a leftover horn part. But most of the time he simply played by ear, filling in a harmony line on the spot while looking over Johnson's shoulder at the tenor saxophone part to anticipate any breaks or rhythmic highlights in the number.

"Challenge" dances were a staple of show biz, but Metcalf introduced a twist which helped to bring the band out from the shadow of the show. Instead of two tap-dancers challenging one another on stage, Metcalf set a single dancer up against his drummer. The act was never rehearsed. As the dancer neared the end of his act, Wilkinson would play a brief solo—perhaps four bars long—in which he'd improvise a catchy rhythm. The dancer would listen, repeat it beat for beat with his taps, pause, add a few more beats on the end, then turn and gesture at Wilkinson as if to say, "Beat that!" Wilkinson would accept the challenge and go one better, introducing a subtle twist to the rhythmic phrase and perhaps adding more on the end. Back and forth the challenge went, until one or the other conceded "defeat"—or the phrases became so convoluted that the pair, and the audience, doubled up in laughter, unable to go on.

Playing the shows was never too painful for the musicians; some of the music they actually enjoyed. They lived for the band sets, however, especially the late-night ones when the club let them stretch out on their favourite jazz material. Visiting American jazz musicians would be invited to sit in, providing on-the-spot schooling for the musicians in Metcalf's band who were always hungry for new ideas fresh from the States. On one occasion, Wilkinson subbed for an ailing Sonny Greer in

Duke Ellington's orchestra uptown, then ushered Ellington downtown after the concert to sit in with his former sideman's band.

Local musicians, too, sat in with the band, though only the best were invited to do so a second time, especially during regular club hours. Bassist Bob Rudd, who had worked with Noble Sissle and Lucky Thompson in the United States before settling in Montreal, was always welcome. In fact, Wade and Wilkinson would have gladly substituted Rudd on a permanent basis for King, whom they felt lacked commitment to the music. Metcalf, however, refused to turn King out of the fold. Lennie Copple, an amateur guitarist only in the sense that he earned his living by day in an office, was another favourite guest of the band. And then there was Oscar Peterson.

"Oscar practically lived at the St. Michel," Johnson and Wilkinson agreed. Already a local hero for his work with the Johnny Holmes big band and his trio recordings, Peterson spent countless nights at the St. Michel listening to the older Wade, whose playing he deeply respected. The St. Michel provided Peterson with firsthand exposure to bebop. It wasn't until 1948, when he began leading a trio at the nearby Alberta Lounge, that Peterson had the opportunity to try out the new music in a working situation. Before that, sitting in with Metcalf's rhythm section was his only opportunity to work at the new style. Near the end of a band set he would slide onto the piano bench and take over in mid-tune from Wade. With seemingly bottomless reserves of energy, he would launch tune after tune in quick succession as the front line slipped away for a rest, leaving Wilkinson and King on the stand, unable—and most of the time unwilling—to stop, until it was time for the band to reclaim the stand for the late show. "Every time a piano player came in with a piss pot full of technique—which Steep was lacking—[Wade would] get on the blower to Oscar and say, 'Come over and get 'im!'," Wilkinson said. "Oscar and Steep were very tight." In quieter moments, Johnson would seek Peterson's help with an arrangement he was working on. Peterson in turn used Wilkinson and King on some of his 1947 trio recordings.

It was during the band's jazz sets that Girard cemented his reputation as a soloist. For more than a decade prior to joining Metcalf, the violinist had been the toast of the inner circle of Montreal's jazz community. Now his talents were reaching a wider audience. Girard was, by all accounts, something of an oddity on the jazz scene—a white musician with barely a word of English in his vocabulary who swung hard and played dazzling solos on an instrument rarely heard in jazz. Welcome at any jam session, he nevertheless rarely socialized with the musicians, refusing drink or drugs. "It always seemed he was out of place," Wilkinson said, "just chewing on that pipe of his. He just didn't fit in." According to local legend, Girard's reputation had already reached New York City in the

1930s: Fletcher Henderson, having neither met Girard nor heard him play, sent him an invitation to come to New York and join his band—only to withdraw the offer when he learned Girard was white. The door to near-certain international fame was opened to Girard twice more during his first year in Metcalf's band when both Cab Calloway and Duke Ellington offered him a place in their bands. Metcalf told *Down Beat* in 1947:

> I've played with them all—Eddie South, Stuff Smith, Ray Nance —and I'll put Girard up against any or all of them. He's absolutely sensational! I'm not alone in that opinion either. Willy Girard is perhaps the only white musician prior to Django Reinhardt offered a spot by Duke Ellington. When Cab Calloway heard him he came back every night and raved.[14]

Local legend also recounts that Dizzy Gillespie once tried to take Girard to New York City. The violinist refused all offers to leave Montreal, pleading family responsibilities. Equally likely, Girard's shyness and lack of English held him back from testing the waters in the United States. During his tenure with Metcalf he travelled to New York City only once on a brief holiday; there he apparently left Thelonious Monk and Roy Eldridge reeling at a jam session—they could not believe a musician of Girard's calibre was still holed up in Montreal. But New York City was too overwhelming for Girard, despite its musical challenges, and he never went back. Metcalf considered himself fortunate to have such a devoted sideman: Girard apparently refused an offer of more pay to work in another club, preferring to stay with Metcalf where he could play more jazz.[15]

Metcalf's musicians played their fill of jazz on the weekends, when the music at the Café St. Michel continued almost nonstop. Saturday night the band came in early to play an extra show at 9:00 p.m., followed by their regular nightly schedule of shows at 11:00 p.m. and 1:15 a.m. Between shows they played their own music. By 2:00 a.m. the club was filling up with the late-night crowd. At 3:00 a.m. the St. Michel's breakfast dance started, though breakfast was little more than champagne and snacks, and the dancing quickly gave way to a heavy dose of jazz. By 9:00 a.m. the sun was pouring in the St. Michel's windows, the church bells were beckoning more pious Montrealers to mass, and the musicians were finally packing up their instruments after twelve hours on the job.

"Nobody cared about sleeping in those days," said Wilkinson. It was just as well, for less than seven hours later the musicians were back on the stand. Sunday afternoons were advertised as jam session time at the Café St. Michel, as they were at several other Montreal clubs. Metcalf organized the St. Michel sessions himself, and in true business fashion divided the time equally between pure jazz jamming, with other musicians sitting in, and a mini-show and dance, to advertise the St. Michel's nightly fare. The band collected whatever admission was charged at the door, to supplement their salary, and the club profited on the drinks. The afternoon session ended at 7:00 p.m., giving the musicians four hours to nap and eat before winding up the week with another two shows Sunday night, beginning at 11:00 p.m. "You practically left all your blood on that bandstand," said Johnson.

If the weekends were grueling, weekdays offered little respite. The shows changed on Mondays, usually every second week, and the band was expected to meet the entertainers at the club on Monday afternoons to run through the music for the new acts. The show rehearsals challenged little more than the musicians' ability to sight-read and stay awake after a near-sleepless weekend, but it meant an extra ten or fifteen dollars in each of their pockets. Ironically, most of the band members considered Metcalf to be below Montreal standards for show reading because he would take more than the once through which most of the other members required to feel comfortable with the new music. Other weekday afternoons were devoted to band rehearsals. These were unpaid, and Metcalf sometimes resorted to fines to ensure attendance.

Weekday nights offered more time for "hanging out," the perennial social activity of jazz musicians the world over. Girard and Johnson rarely indulged, preferring to head home to their families immediately after work. Watanabe, with classes to attend at McGill the next day, was also quick out the door, at least on weekdays. But the rest of the band, in various parties augmented by friends, show people, and other musicians, inevitably wandered off to eat after the last set.

The inseparable Wilkinson and Wade usually headed across the street to a Chinese restaurant, a favourite eating and meeting place with the musicians, entertainers, waiters, and prostitutes who earned their living on the corner. Once fed, the duo would wander off in search of a jam session, lugging Wilkinson's drum kit by hand. First stop was usually the Snake Pit, an aptly named bar on the ground floor beneath the Café St. Michel which occasionally hired small jazz groups but is better remembered for its jam sessions—and shadowy clientele. "You never knew who you were rubbing elbows with in there," said Wilkinson. "If it walked, if it crawled, if it talked—it was in there. It was rough!" It was also frequently too noisy to make jamming the pleasure it is meant to be, so the musicians would trudge up Mountain Street, under the railway tracks, to Aldo's, a small club owned by a retired professional hockey player named Jimmy Orlando and his brother Frank. The club was notorious, though by no means unique, for its popularity with the local gangsters, but it was hospitable to the jazz musicians and their friends, and there the jamming, drinking, and partying frequently lasted until morning.

Six weeks in a row, seven nights a week, the band kept up this working schedule, a typical one for nightclub musicians in Montreal. Union regulations entitled them to one night off a week, but rather than leave a club owner scrambling to find a replacement band to back his show for that one night, most bands worked six weeks straight and took the seventh week off in lieu. Most of the time, the "week off" was a misnomer. Since the musicians weren't paid when they weren't working, a week off was a week without pay, and most tried to hustle work elsewhere. Metcalf made a point of it. He booked his band into other clubs, or, more often, took it and a few show acts to play one-nighters in Quebec City, Granby, the Eastern Townships region of Quebec, and across the provincial border to Cornwall, Ontario. Few people outside of Montreal had heard of Metcalf the famous jazz musician: he arrived at one club in Quebec City to find himself billed as Louise Madcap—a liberal phonetic interpretation of what the francophone club manager had thought he'd heard over a long-distance telephone line.

Located at 770 Mountain Street just below St. Antoine. Cafe St. Michel is in the heart of Montreal's Harlem section and is known from coast to coast as The Cafe famous for the finest colored shows in Montreal. There is an early show and a late show every night with continuous dancing to Louis Metcalfe, his trumpet and his orchestra.

Souvenir postcard from the Café St. Michel. *Courtesy of Herb Johnson. John Gilmore Jazz History Collection, Concordia University Archives.*

On a typical trip to Quebec City, 250 kilometres north over poor, winding roads, Metcalf would arrange the musicians, their instruments and clothing, the entertainers, and their costumes and props, into three rented cars. He never let the musicians drive, insisting on hiring drivers for the night. They'd unpack and do a show at a dance hall or nightclub in Quebec City, then pile back into the cars and drive to a second booking at a bar or hotel somewhere out in the countryside. There they'd unpack again, and perform another show for the late crowd. That over, and whatever jamming and partying that followed, the entourage would collapse into the cars for the long drive back to Montreal along the river. Metcalf, a veteran of band buses and one-nighters, took the travelling in stride. May Oliver recalled the trips home:

> Louis, knowing that later on down the highway you're gonna hit the sunrise, he'd put his sunglasses on and button his coat up over his head. Then he'd fall asleep, sitting dead upright in the back seat. Later, I'd feel him grip my arm: "May! I'm blind! I can't see anything!" I was so tired I didn't even wanna laugh at him, so I'd just say, "Unbutton your coat, take off the glasses, and you'll see the sun, Louis."

On another week off, in May 1949, Metcalf rented His Majesty's theatre in Montreal for a concert, putting up the money for the production himself. The first half of the concert featured the Metcalf band in a jam session reunion with Benny Winestone and backing a guest singer from New York City named Tina Revere. The second half featured a tap dance act and Oscar Peterson's trio from the Alberta Lounge playing a survey of different jazz styles. A local newspaper reported a large and enthusiastic turnout for the concert.[16]

Yet even at the height of its popularity in Montreal, the Metcalf band was unable to reach audiences outside of Quebec and eastern Ontario. It never travelled far afield in Canada, at least partly due to the reluctance of Wade and Wilkinson to leave familiar territory: they were addicted to heroin, the narcotic that swept like a plague through the bebop generation of musicians; both worried about the difficulties and risks involved in finding suppliers in small towns and strange cities. There were rumblings of a recording contract, a booking at Massey Hall in Toronto, and an engagement at a big resort hotel in southwestern Ontario—but nothing materialized, for reasons that may never be fully known.

Clearly, the greatest opportunity for the band lay south of the border, and especially in New York City where bebop was the rage and Metcalf was well known. Because the band never recorded, one can only speculate about how it might have fared in the American jazz market. However, given the band's foreign origin, "International" make-up, and considerable stage experience, it is reasonable to assume that it would have achieved some popular success. In fact, Metcalf secured a booking for the band in New York City, probably in 1949; Johnson believed it was a double booking at the Savoy and Apollo theatres. U.S. Immigration, however, refused to grant the Canadian musicians permission to work in the country. Wade and Wilkinson's addiction may have been a factor, for the Royal Canadian Mounted Police (RCMP) regularly shadowed the two and would probably have shared their knowledge of the musicians' habits with American authorities, if consulted. In denying the band entry, however, U.S. Immigration authorities were only applying the nation's laws, which barred all foreign musicians except those judged to be of distinguished merit. What made the refusal so hard for the Metcalf band to endure was the fact that Canada had reopened its doors to U.S. musicians in 1947. Johnson suggested the band reapply to enter the United States not as musicians but as a show act, but the other musicians vetoed the idea. Metcalf relived the episode for *Record Research*:

> My Canadian International Band was a band of the future who were praised by such prominent leaders as Duke Ellington, Stan Kenton, Nat King Cole, and Dizzy Gillespie.... With their advice we tried to come to the United States. This was about the same

time that Oscar Peterson was being discovered. He made it to the U.S. but my band was refused permission by the U.S. immigration authorities.

We were going to be booked by Consolidated and everything was set. The Canadian union came to our aid to find out why the U.S. immigration authorities refused to grant us clearance. The Canadian union was of the opinion that if American musicians could work in Canada why could there not be a mutual exchange of Canadian musicians into the United States (and the peculiar matter of this was that the Canadian union was a subsidiary of the AFM and they were being treated like a discarded child)....

The Montreal union lawyer was given a cross-country runaround. I was called into the U.S. immigration office in Montreal and advised to forget it. They informed me that I should get myself a band of American musicians. And to add salt to the wounds my men were penalized for three years for even asking permission to visit the U.S. And just that penalizing day, Harry James blazed into the Montreal Forum with 28 men all from the U.S....

Here's a case where six Canadian musicians couldn't get into the U.S. but 28 musicians could come from the U.S. into Canada. This incident put the whole band in the dumps. I may sound bitter, but after years of dreaming and preparing to come to the U.S. with our solid reputation, we got kicked. This so disheartened me that we disorganized and I returned to the U.S.[17]

Metcalf's account of the breakup of his International Band glosses over, with understandable intent, a disintegration that in fact took more than a year. The exact sequence of events during the band's last year remains uncertain, but piecing together all available evidence, the following account seems most probable.

Metcalf's popularity in Montreal prompted him to consider buying a nightclub in the city: perhaps he relished complete freedom in deciding what kind of music and shows his band would play. The Café St. Michel was an obvious choice, and it was apparently for sale in 1949. If Metcalf tried to buy it, he failed, and the club came under new management. Metcalf's long-established authority at the club may have been challenged. In any event, he left the St. Michel in August 1949 and took his band to either the El Patio or the Casino Français, two larger nightclubs on The Main; he ultimately worked at both clubs, and continued hosting jam sessions, at least at the El Patio.

A wave of desertions followed. The musicians, discouraged by their inability to get into the United States, had little to look forward to. They had fallen from their perch at the Café St. Michel, whose very name had become synonymous with jazz in Montreal—thanks to their efforts.

There was no shortage of show work for the band in other clubs, but things would never be the same again. They were exhausted, and embittered, by a three-year struggle that had taken them nowhere.

Immediately after the move from the Café St. Michel to The Main, Johnson handed Metcalf his two-week notice of resignation and returned to the Café St. Michel to work in Russ Meredith's mixed show band.[18] Benny Winestone came back into the fold to take Johnson's place, though Leroy Mason also played tenor sax in the band at some time during its last year. Wade, Wilkinson, and Girard all eventually left the band as well, though Wade hung on until the summer of 1950. Metcalf used Valdo Williams and Sadik Hakim—two bebop pianists recently arrived from New York City through Canada's open-door immigration policy—to replace Wade. Wilkinson's place was taken by Al Jennings, Billy Graham, and Kenny Edmonds. Nobody replaced Girard—nobody could—and when the violinist quit, never again to hold a steady, full-time job as a musician, the Metcalf band was reduced to a sextet with a conventional three-horn front line.

"Even though they left Metcalf, he forgave them," said May Oliver. "He didn't get mad at them. People'd say, 'I don't believe these guys—after all you've done for them!' And he'd say, 'No, no, no. They wanna do their own thing, good—go ahead. I'm not mad at them.' He just replaced them, and life went on."

Life on the bandstand couldn't have gone on as smoothly for Metcalf as it had before. His International Band's repertoire had been committed to memory and polished by three-and-a-half years of nightly playing. With only Metcalf, King, and Watanabe providing continuity with the past, and the character of the front line irretrievably altered by the departure of Girard, the quality of the band's music inevitably suffered as the remaining chairs rotated among a pool of other musicians. Moreover, the band had lost the luxury of a steady engagement and was moving from club to club. It even returned to the Café St. Michel for a brief engagement, probably during the house band's week off. Metcalf was offered a job with his band for the summer of 1950 at Chateau Blanc, a resort hotel on Missisquoi Bay near the American border, but he declined the offer and handed the engagement to Johnson. Then, in late September or early October, Metcalf secured a long-term engagement for his band back at the Café St. Michel, scene of his greatest Montreal triumphs. The return to glory was short-lived.[19]

During the band's first week off, on the afternoon of 13 November 1950, Metcalf, King, and Winestone set off by car for Ottawa to attend a concert by Louis Armstrong. The RCMP, possibly tipped off by an anonymous telephone call, stopped the car near Dorion, Quebec, found several marijuana joints, and arrested the three musicians. That night,

One of several later versions of the International Band, probably taken during a brief return engagement to the Café St. Michel in late 1949: Al King (bass); Louis Metcalf (trumpet, vocals); Willy Girard (violin); Butch Watanabe (trombone); Al Jennings (drums); Benny Winestone (clarinet, tenor saxophone); Sadik Hakim (piano, posing with guitar). *Courtesy of Sadik Hakim. John Gilmore Jazz History Collection, Concordia University Archives.*

police raided Sadik Hakim's apartment in Montreal and arrested him for possession of marijuana as well.

Ten days later the four musicians went to trial. They pleaded guilty and the proceedings were brief. A newspaper reported their lawyer's attempt to offer mitigating circumstances to the judge before sentencing:

> Myer Gross, defence lawyer, said that his clients were almost compelled to smoke "reefers" to satisfy their patrons and fans, who were constantly demanding lively music.
>
> The judge replied that this was certainly no excuse, and recommended that Mr. Gross's clients smoke "good cigars, as you do."[20]

The musicians were sentenced to six months in prison plus fines of two hundred dollars each, a typical sentence for possession of marijuana at the time. King was handed an additional six-month concurrent sentence for possession of a pipe with which to smoke marijuana. The four were expelled from the musicians' union in Montreal in December. How much time they spent in prison is not known.[21] Winestone probably left town after he was released from prison: it was several years before he was reported working again in Montreal. Metcalf, King, and Hakim were apparently deported to the United States as a result of their convictions. Metcalf never returned to Montreal. He remained in the United States, leading various bands, until his death in New York City in 1981. Hakim eventually returned to Montreal in 1966 and remained in Canada for nearly a decade, working in clubs and on radio, recording two albums, and making an important contribution to the Montreal jazz scene of the late 1960s. King was never heard of again.

"To be truthful, Metcalf was a misfit in the band, and yet he was the leader." Wilkinson's appraisal of the man who helped to make him the most talked about jazz drummer in Montreal in the late 1940s points to the heart of the paradox surrounding Louis Metcalf's four years at the head of the city's first bebop band.

Metcalf was not a bebop musician by training or by temperament, and despite his openness to bebop he never became as fluent in the new idiom as the musicians who grew up playing it.[22] He was not alone in this shortcoming: none of the jazz musicians who had been raised on swing ever succeeded in fully making the transition to a pure bebop style, so radically different was bebop's phrasing.[23] And yet Metcalf—a musician who had been active in the higher circles of jazz since its infancy in the 1920s—organized, promoted, and held together, by the sheer strength of his will and professional expertise, the first bebop band in Montreal.

He did so partly by remaining true to the professional ethos of his generation: that jazz musicians were, above all, entertainers who must reach out to their audiences. This pragmatic philosophy showed up in Metcalf's congenial stage presence and in the careful path he trod between the precipices of pure entertainment on the one side, and pure jazz on the other—the first fatal to the creative spirit, the second fatal to nightclubs. Metcalf's manner and leadership earned him occasional scorn from his sidemen, who dubbed him "Mister Business" behind his back, but the fruit of his philosophy, aided by his public profile, was undeniable: the Metcalf band's engagement at the St. Michel was the closest thing to a steady *jazz* job Montreal musicians had ever known. It wasn't until the early 1980s that more than a handful of Montreal jazz musicians could speak of earning a decent living for an extended period of time playing pure jazz in the city's nightclubs.

138

If there was a lesson to be learned from Metcalf's experiences in Montreal, it was that show business could survive without jazz, but jazz—even the best the city had to offer—could not survive without show business. Such was the context in which jazz musicians lived and created. Metcalf accepted this as a fact of life. A diplomat rather than a revolutionary, he chose to work within the system to gain greater recognition for jazz. He accomplished this by demonstrating that his band could do the job which nightclub managers, entertainers, and audiences expected of it—and then go one step further and actually draw crowds night after night by playing a new and challenging style of jazz.

By all previous standards of the Montreal nightclub industry, a band which featured music no one could dance to should have failed after a few weeks in Montreal. Yet the Metcalf band not only survived, it flourished, winning audiences over to jazz and setting new standards of performance and repertoire for local jazz musicians to aspire to. Metcalf was aware of his status as a leader in the local jazz community as early as 1947, when he told *Down Beat*: "I'm showing Canadians that they have a host of fine musicians—jazz men as well as symphonic—right in their own back yard."[24]

The first bebop record made in Canada. *Courtesy of Herb Johnson. John Gilmore Jazz History Collection, Concordia University Archives.*

Though Metcalf's enthusiasm for Canada had soured by the time he was ushered back to the United States in police custody, the seeds which he had sown in Montreal were quick to germinate. Shortly after Metcalf's trial, Wilkinson gathered together those alumni of the International Band who hadn't been arrested—Girard, Johnson, Wade, and Watanabe. He brought in Allan Wellman to take Metcalf's place and Bob Rudd to replace King, then added Freddie Nichols on baritone sax. The resulting eight-piece band, which Wilkinson called his "boptet," worked for a few months at the Café St. Michel. It disbanded when Wilkinson's drug-related health problems prevented him from carrying on. Before it disappeared, however, the boptet recorded a single 78 r.p.m. record in Montreal in 1950, for an independent Toronto label called Monogram. This was the first bebop record made in Canada, a testimony to Metcalf's influence on the Montreal jazz community.[25]

CHAPTER SIX

Steep Wade

The last show was over at the Café St. Michel but the musicians hadn't left the stand. They weren't about to. Ordering whiskeys at the bar were several members of a touring band from the United States, thirsty for adventure after their work uptown; unwrapping his instrument offstage was the band's swaggering young bassist. It was the kind of occasion Steep Wade rose to.

As the visitor hugged his wooden bass into the spot vacated by Al King, Steep and drummer Wilkie Wilkinson locked eyes. Like a catcher calling a pitch, Steep gave Wilkie a thumbs up: take this man *upstairs*!

Without a word being spoken, Wilkie slashed out at his ride cymbal, setting a blistering tempo. Breaths caught in throats around the bandstand; ears cocked expectantly towards Steep, waiting for him to call the tune. He let Wilkie measure eight bars, grunted "G" at the band, then began punching out the chords to the last eight bars of "How High the Moon," a pop tune the beboppers had plundered for its chord progression to create an anthem of the new age called "Ornithology." Had the bassist heard it?

He had. By the time Steep was through the turnaround and back to the beginning of the tune, the bassist was spelling out the chords with a note placed resolutely on every beat. The horns jumped in with the bebop melody, Steep plugged the gaps, and Herb Johnson ran off with the first solo. By the time he'd spoken his mind and relinquished the soapbox to Butch Watanabe, the strain of the tempo was showing on the bassist. Wilkie's ride cymbal wouldn't let up; Steep's chords fed each successive soloist with new ideas and nudged them on to yet more choruses.

"Get up there, man!" Steep shouted as the bassist's pulse slackened momentarily, threatening to drag down the tempo. Sweat was raining from his brow under the hot lights. Chorus after chorus burned by under his fingers. Now it was Steep's turn to solo, and he feasted on three full choruses as the horns prodded him on with a riff.

Back into the turnaround again, Steep feinted he was ready for the horns to replay the melody, then at the last moment barked "bass!" under his breath and pulled Wilkie up short. The guest was on his own for sixteen headlong bars. Caught unprepared, his fingers screaming for relief, he played it safe and continued walking through the chord progression rather than venturing a solo around the beat and risk losing his way. In seconds the band was on top of him, waving the "Ornithology" banner one last time. Steep improvised an ending and Wilkie sealed it with a crash. They had been making music at four beats a second for more than seven minutes, and the bassist alone had been forced to play every one of them. He was already on his way to the bar for a drink when Herb caught his breath and, eyes popping, turned to Steep and Wilkie: "God *damn*, man!"

Grinning, Steep looked around for another bassist.

The legend of Steep Wade is brimming with stories such as this:[1] stories that have been stewed and seasoned and served up time and again in the decades since his death. The stories have matured with the years, embellished and transformed like a bebopper's version of "How High the Moon." It hardly matters any more who was there the afternoon American jazz saxophonist Wardell Gray tracked Steep to his room in the St. Antoine district and dragged him out of bed, insisting they jam together; nor how many times Steep tossed a piano-tuner's business card over the counter in a blind pig, commanding the manager to "fix that box!" Legend is a savoury blend of fiction and fact, the two complementing one another like the pig's feet and rice that Steep's mother served up at the family table for her wild boy and his musician friends.

Grinning with devilment one minute, cantankerous the next, Steep Wade remained to his sudden and shocking end a quasi-mystical figure of a man: gentle in his bulk, oftentimes withdrawn, at all times fiercely devoted to jazz. He was revered by his juniors, respected by his peers, and immortalized by legend as a musician around whom the Montreal jazz scene revolved during the late 1940s, when his playing was at its peak.

Wade's was the kind of life, and music, on which legends grow. There is a skeleton of fact—dates, and places, and a few minutes of obscure recordings[2]—but the flesh is all anecdote. There are as many stories about Steep Wade as there are musicians who remember him: as many stories about his punishing indulgence in drink and drugs as about the thousand-and-one-nights he burdened the piano bench at the Café St. Michel with his overstuffed frame and entranced attentive listeners. And yet, when all of the anecdotes have been plucked of hyperbole and scoured clean of contradiction, one overriding fact remains: decades after his death, jazz musicians—that breed of artist which rarely agrees among itself on the merits of any single player—have continued universally to praise Steep Wade's piano playing. For that reason alone, his stature as one of the leading musicians of Canadian jazz cannot be seriously doubted. Strip away half of the adulation and a great musician still remains.

"Steep Wade was a true jazz piano player—a great one," remembered Art Roberts, who as a teenager pestered Wade for piano lessons. "Charlie Parker came to town for two or three days and he was jamming privately in the black community. He told Steep Wade, he said, 'Steep, you should come to New York. You're the best feed man in the business.' By that he meant the best 'comper,' the best accompanist for a jazz soloist. And really, Steep was that great.... He comped like Bud Powell—punchy—a hard bop style.... We had Oscar Peterson in town at the same time, but Oscar was more of a soloist. Most people preferred Steep's accompaniment, though Steep was a wonderful soloist too."

Peterson, seven-and-a-half years younger than Wade, has been quoted as saying:

> Steep Wade was my favorite pianist. He had one thing—I know because I was very close to him—he had the same sense of time as Nat Cole: impeccable. He could not sit down at the piano unless it swung. If I learned nothing else from him, that's one thing I learned from Steep.... Technically he was not a great pianist, but he had a way of playing things, of making them work musically, of making them *his* statement. You could always recognize Steep.[3]

Wray Downes, who abandoned a career as a classical concert pianist to play jazz, has said of Wade: "He just petrified me, because in my book, had he lived I don't think there would have been an Oscar.... He was a demon on the piano."[4]

Whoever tagged Harold Gordon Pemberton Wade with the nickname "Steep" had a caricaturist's eye. His was a mountainous brow, rising steeply from kind, sleepy eyes to a ridge of skull at the summit of his six-foot-one-or-two frame. Steep was born in Montreal in 1918 and raised just west of the nightlife corner of Mountain and St. Antoine, in the heart of the city's black community. His parents had come to Canada from the British West Indies: Jack Wade, his father, was from Monserrat Island, and worked for the railway; his mother, Alberta Pemberton, came from neighbouring Nevis Island. She was a strong-willed, progressive, community-minded woman, with seemingly inexhaustible reserves

143

of energy when it came to organizing women's groups, social functions, and amateur concerts at the neighbourhood Union United Church. Her open-house policy for Steep and his friends was equally legendary in the community: even after he left home and moved into a nearby rooming-house, Steep and an entourage of nightclub performers and musicians would frequently drop in at the Wade home in the afternoons, to impro-vise jazz around the player piano in the parlor, then descend on his mother's home-cooking. If his mother knew about the darker side of Steep's lifestyle, her support for her son remained unwavering: she never turned him away. From time to time he would even return to the family home to sleep.

Neither of Steep's parents was particularly musical, but they paid for violin lessons for his younger sister Caroline and whatever piano lessons Steep may have been persuaded to take as a child.[5] He preferred to learn the piano in his own way, studying the movement of the keys as he pumped a piano roll through the instrument, and picking out other tunes he liked by ear. In some fashion he learned to read music. When he was about eleven or twelve, he accompanied his sister in amateur recitals at the Universal Negro Improvement Association hall.

Sometime in his early childhood, Steep also began teaching himself how to play the alto saxophone. His childhood friends were Hugh and George Sealey: they were learning to play the clarinet and saxophone. The three boys practised together. When they reached their early teens they began playing their horns with the older black musicians at Rockhead's Paradise. This was Steep's first taste of the jazz life, and it may have been at the encouragement of the older musicians that he began taking the piano more seriously, buying method books and prac-tising his sight-reading with an eye on a full-time job in a nightclub band.

Steep was not a successful student. It took him nine years to complete seven grades at the local Royal Arthur Elementary School. By the time he graduated to Strathearn High School, an imposing building uptown on Jeanne Mance Street, Steep was already fifteen and playing saxo-phone, and occasionally piano, in the downtown nightclubs. Bored in the classroom, he failed twice to pass the first half-year of grade eight, despite high marks in typing and arithmetic. In January 1934 — sixteen and headstrong—Steep quit school, determined to become a profession-al musician.[6]

In the four remaining years of his adolescence, Steep established him-self as a valuable member of Montreal's black music community. He joined the Clef Club, the city's black musicians' union, and he played alto saxophone in small bands at the Terminal club, where he probably worked under Myron Sutton's leadership. When Sutton landed an engagement for his large group, the Canadian Ambassadors, at the

A young Steep Wade (centre) playing alto saxophone with Myron Sutton's Canadian Ambassadors at the Silver Slipper in Toronto, September 1938. Other band members: Benny Montgomery (trumpet); Willie Wade (drums); Frank Johnson (trombone); Brad Moxley (piano; standing without instrument); Mynie Sutton (alto saxophone, left); Lloyd Duncan (tenor saxophone); Clyde Duncan (bass). *Photo by W. H. James. Myron Sutton Collection, Concordia University Archives.*

Montmartre cabaret in the east end, he asked Steep to join the band. It was to be the Ambassadors' last blaze of glory. Steep, still only nineteen, found himself working in one of the city's most popular nightclubs as a member of the city's hottest black band. He travelled with the Canadian Ambassadors to Toronto, Hamilton, and Windsor the following year, and probably served out the band's bitter finale at Connie's Inn during the winter of 1938-39. When the town's tastes turned to white shows, the Ambassadors broke up, leaving Steep and the other members to go it alone.

He wasn't neglecting the piano. By the late 1930s Steep had begun taking occasional jobs playing "the box," as he derisively called the instrument on which his reputation stands. Throughout the Second World War he managed to avoid military service. According to some

Steep Wade at the piano, surrounded by other members of Jimmy Jones's racially mixed sextet during an engagement at Standish Hall in Hull, Quebec, summer 1943. Left to right: Mark Weinberg (drums); unknown (bass); Herb Johnson (tenor saxophone); Wade; Harry Maxham (alto saxophone); Jimmy Jones (trumpet). *Photo courtesy of Harry Maxham. John Gilmore Jazz History Collection, Concordia University Archives.*

stories, he was drafted but rejected by the military when he admitted to smoking marijuana. Whatever the reason for his exemption, Steep worked steadily throughout the war, on both saxophone and piano, while many other musicians were absent from the scene, serving in military bands or on active duty.

Steep was a homebody, and the St. Antoine district was his home. He ate there, drank there, jammed there, and slept there; it took some convincing even to get him to venture uptown. In the summer of 1943 he worked what was to be his last, long-term engagement outside of Montreal, with trumpeter Jimmy Jones's mixed quintet. The band was booked for the summer at Standish Hall in Hull, near Ottawa, and Steep was playing piano in a rhythm section that included drummer Mark Weinberg and a bassist picked up in Ottawa. "We were an overnight hit," said alto saxophonist Harry Maxham, recalling how the band opened the engagement with some sixty frenzied choruses of "Lady Be Good" which sent the youthful audience into ecstasy.

The band's reputation reached the Ottawa offices of the National Film Board, a newly created, government-funded studio which was then turning out wartime propaganda films. A producer invited the Jones band to record the sound-track for a three-minute animated film called *Stitch and Save*. The film was intended to encourage citizens to recycle old clothes into new fashions, thereby freeing cotton for military uniforms. In the final product, a crudely drawn scissors and needle dance across the screen, snipping and sewing trousers and coats, to the accompaniment of a pastiche of jazz styles and moods. There was, however, considerable irony in Steep's participation in the film: he was a zoot-suiter, one of the fashionably rebellious young men and women who flaunted wartime conservation efforts by sporting blatantly oversized clothes.

Back in Montreal, Steep continued working with the Jimmy Jones band until the end of the war, though there were times when Jones's stomach ulcers were hurting so much that the band was left idle. Yet Steep was seldom without a job somewhere. He worked for a while in a sextet led by Willie Wade. And through the winter of 1945-46 he played behind shows at the Café St. Michel in a band led by saxophonist Lloyd Duncan, who had come to Montreal with the original Canadian Ambassadors. It was a four-horn group, with Allan Wellman on trumpet, Bill Kersey on tenor sax, and Lloyd and Steep both playing altos. And it was a typical seven-night-a-week engagement. But rather than working six weeks straight and taking the seventh week off, as most nightclub bands did, Duncan let his sidemen take off one night a week each.

The policy depended for its success on the versatility of Duncan's musicians. The horn players sent a substitute when they could find one; when none was available, the front line simply closed ranks and improvised new harmony parts. A drummer was indispensable, however, and Wilkie Wilkinson only got a break when he could find a capable replacement. When bassist Jack Kostenuck was off, the band looked to pianist Arthur Davis to play bass lines and stronger chords with his left hand. And when Davis himself wanted a break, Steep left his horn in its case and slipped behind the piano. The management allowed this musical chairs to go on from Sunday to Thursday nights, but insisted that Lloyd Duncan and his Seven Sharp Swingsters be in full attendance on weekends.

The engagement was a turning point in Steep's life. He became friends with Wilkinson, who had been travelling back and forth to New York City and was bristling with excitement about the jam sessions he had witnessed there involving young black musicians looking for a way out of the strait-jacket of swing. Steep was harbouring his own frustrations with the swing-based nightclub music he had been playing all his life, and Wilkinson's enthusiasm was catching. When the first bebop records arrived in Montreal, the pair quickly became disciples of the new music and its cool ethic. With Steep on piano, they experimented with the new music at jam sessions, adapting their instrumental styles and conception of rhythm to the demands of bebop. For a while, Kostenuck jammed with them, but he soon began drifting, leaving town to work on carnivals and taking work uptown during his stopovers in Montreal.

The engagement with Duncan's Seven Sharp Swingsters was a turning point in another way as well: when it was over, Steep put his saxophone aside and concentrated exclusively on piano. He and Wilkinson quit the Swingsters in early 1946 and went across the street to Rockhead's Paradise, to work in another show band. But Steep was becoming increasingly reluctant to compromise his devotion to jazz by working long hours playing music for shows. Like the New York beboppers they emulated, Steep and Wilkie were scorning the musician's role as entertainer.

Steep flirted twice with the music of the big swing bands around this time, but both affairs were brief. He subbed for Oscar Peterson in Johnny Holmes's orchestra but, according to Holmes, Steep simply "didn't fit in." He lasted longer as pianist in Maynard Ferguson's big band, around 1945. Steep was the only black in the band. When Ferguson accepted a booking at a dance hall in Toronto, Steep left. "He swore he'd never do another commercial job after that one," Wilkinson said. "Steep was extremely temperamental. This is why he never took a commercial gig. He didn't care if he starved—and he went hungry a few days, you better believe it! But he always managed to stay on the corner after that."

For the next three-and-a-half years, Steep did manage to stay on the corner of Mountain and St. Antoine, thanks to the success of Louis Metcalf's band at the Café St. Michel. The American trumpeter had arrived in town at the right moment for Steep and Wilkinson. The pair had just quit Duncan's Swingsters and moved across the street to Rockhead's Paradise, but they were finding the music there no less constricting than what they'd left behind. Metcalf didn't have to ask twice whether they were interested in forming a band with a modern orientation: of the six local musicians that began rehearsing with Metcalf in early 1946, Wade and Wilkinson were the most strongly committed to bebop.

Steep was the first Montreal pianist to master bebop, and for the next seven years—all that remained of his life—he was the city's high priest of the new music. The long residency with Metcalf at the Café St. Michel were Steep's years of glory. In the vernacular of the street, he "lived" on

148

the corner: holding court in the afternoons at Rockhead's tavern, at night on the bandstand at the Café St. Michel, and in the early hours of the morning at jam sessions at the Snake Pit or Aldo's. He kept a room at the nearby Orgen rooming-house where many of the entertainers stayed, and he ate in local restaurants, or at his mother's table. He bought Chinese lottery tickets regularly, and swapped jokes and gossip at a neighbourhood barbershop. He was, in essence, a man of habit, set in his ways before he was thirty. He was also hooked.

At some point during their tenure with Metcalf, Steep and Wilkinson both became addicted to heroin. Use of the narcotic was almost *de rigueur* among hard-core beboppers in the United States, and in their determination to align themselves wholeheartedly with the jazz revolution, it was only natural that Steep and Wilkie should try the drug and embrace the bebop lifestyle. Older musicians had long been consuming liberal quantities of marijuana and alcohol. Steep continued in the tradition even after adding heroin to his daily diet. Herb Johnson remembered that "one of the first things Steep always done when he come on the job — and he'd always be early—was order a double whiskey and a beer chaser."

How Steep managed to support his lifestyle and drug habit on a nightclub musician's salary is a mystery. He was frequently overdrawn on his pay from Metcalf and ran up long bar bills. Yet he was never known to resort to crime. Certainly Steep's charisma carried him a long way: the waiters at Rockhead's tavern regularly furnished him with free beer because he attracted such a large entourage, and he was always charming meals and drinks from friends and hangers-on. Many local pianists would have gladly paid Steep for piano lessons, but only the most persistent succeeded in pinning him down. An eighteen-year-old Art Roberts was one of them. Though Steep never kept an appointment with his pupil, Roberts managed to wring half a dozen lessons out of Steep at five dollars a throw:

> It was when you could catch him and when you could find him. I'd go to his house first, and if he wasn't there I'd look in the clubs or at the tavern at Rockhead's. Then you'd have to convince him to give you a lesson. He wanted the money but he didn't want to waste the time....
>
> The lessons were basically "You play, Steep, and I'll watch." Steep played a polychord: he played an F7 in his left hand and a G Major triad in his right hand—a very modern sound at that time. He hit it, and I said "Wow! What's that?!"
>
> "That's an F7."
>
> "What's the G chord doing on top?"
>
> "It *sounds* good."

> That was all the theory explanation he gave me. Other times he'd play a beautiful line and I'd stop him.
>
> "What was *that*?!"
>
> "You mean this?" And he'd play something completely different.
>
> I eventually just let him play and I watched. I found out he was so spontaneous he couldn't repeat a line.

Steep's inventiveness at the piano was a source of wonderment to his peers as well as his juniors. He turned heads on the bandstand with his unexpected substitutions of new chords for those commonly associated with a tune. His fat voicings, rich with dissonant colour and scattered with rhythmic ingenuity over the middle range of the keyboard, suggested new directions for soloists to develop their improvised melodies. He was indispensable yet unobtrusive, the supreme achievement of all great accompanists. Visiting jazzmen delighted in playing with him and wondered aloud why he had not claimed his place among the inner circle of beboppers in New York City. Wilkinson explained:

> Dizzy Gillespie tried to talk to him. I don't know how many people tried to talk to him. But you couldn't get Steep out of this town with a crowbar.... He had no illusions of grandeur about going to New York. No, he didn't want to be great, or make a name for himself. He wasn't interested in notoriety. Just give him a box and a place to play all his personal feelings that he wanted to get out of him.

At least two other factors kept Steep in Montreal: racism and his addiction. Steep knew that racial discrimination was worse in the United States than in Montreal: touring musicians continually reminded him of the severity of life there for blacks. Nor was Steep one to endure racism in silence. Insults quickly roused him to a fighting fury. Seen in this light, the St. Antoine district was more than just a home for Steep: it was his refuge, from a white world that caused him pain.

Even if Steep had wanted to move to New York City, the legal problems would have been almost insurmountable. U.S. Immigration routinely barred Canadian musicians from entering the country to work. Steep's drug addiction could only have exacerbated the problems. As an addict, he was under surveillance by the Royal Canadian Mounted Police, who would probably have tipped off American authorities had he tried to cross the border. Entering the United States illegally would not have been difficult, but musicians required a special permit issued by the police to work legally in nightclubs in New York City. Known addicts were routinely denied a permit, forcing them to go underground or leave the city.

A candid glimpse of Steep Wade at the piano, autographed by Wade to Wilkie Wilkinson. *Photo courtesy of Mark "Wilkie" Wilkinson. John Gilmore Jazz History Collection, Concordia University Archives.*

Ultimately, heroin made Steep, and Wilkinson, prisoners of Montreal. The simple act of travelling was a frightening prospect for the two musicians. Their physical and mental well-being depended on daily meetings with a pusher, and their incomes were too low to allow them to stockpile sufficient quantities of the drug to see them through an extended journey. Locating a supplier in a strange city was both risky and uncertain. Wilkinson recalled one occasion, probably after the Metcalf band had broken up, when he and Steep were talked into travelling to Ontario to accompany singer Phyllis Marshall for a month. It was probably Steep's last journey out of Montreal.

> The money was good, and I was in debt. So I talked Steep into going up with me; I don't remember who the bass player was. We worked two weeks in Hamilton, and we managed to cop there, then we had to go to Toronto for another two weeks. At first we were lucky, we managed to cop, but then the supply ran out. I don't know how we made those last few nights. Oh, man, were we ever sick. The night we finished Steep couldn't even wait for the fast train to get out of there. He took the milk run at seven o'clock in the morning, and I was right behind him. We had to get back to Montreal.

Thereafter, Steep let the world come to him. It was an adoring world, for the most part, but he greeted it with a casualness that could border on self-deprecation. "There were some nights," Wilkinson said, "that Steep would play some phenomenal changes with his left hand. Then he'd slap his hand and say, 'Stop that!'" Nonchalant about his own talents, Steep had little patience for mediocrity in his fellow musicians. He delighted in cutting overconfident musicians down to size, and he railed against imposters. Wilkinson continued:

> Steep was very outspoken. He had no qualms about telling a rhythm-section player. He would just walk off the stand. He had *no* qualms, he'd just tell 'em: "Man, you ain't makin' it. Forget it!" And you'd better let Steep know who's going to be sitting in—and he'd better be able to play—or Steep wouldn't talk to you for the rest of the night.
>
> He had a beautiful soul, a *beautiful* soul, but he was murder on drummers. Oh, man, was he murder on drummers. If a drummer was laggin' or something, Steep would say, "Come on, man! What's the matter with you, man? Get up there! I ain't haulin' all this weight myself!"

On 28 July 1949, Steep walked down the aisle of the Union United Church with Johaunias Baker, a show girl from the United States who preferred to be called by her stage name, Jo-Hann Baker. The newlyweds took up residence at the Orgen rooming-house: Steep expected life would continue much as it had before. The following month, however, Steep lost his throne at the Café St. Michel. Louis Metcalf took the band to a club in the east end. The musicians were discouraged; some members quit. Steep—dispirited, in poor health, or lured briefly to other jobs—apparently shared the piano bench in Metcalf's band with Sadik Hakim and Valdo Williams for almost a year. In June 1950 he handed Metcalf his notice to quit.[7]

The musicians had begun noticing a change in Steep. His health was deteriorating as his consumption of heroin and alcohol grew more punishing. According to Wilkinson, Steep never tried to overcome his addiction. There was, in any case, nowhere to turn for help: addicts avoided hospitals because they feared the doctors would turn them over to the police. Near the end of 1950, Steep enjoyed a brief return to glory at the Café St. Michel in a "boptet" formed by Wilkinson on the ruins of the Metcalf band. But Wilkinson's own drug-related health problems soon forced him to leave, and the band fell apart. An era was ending at the corner; the Café St. Michel had ceased to be the focal point of the city's jazz community. Sometime in the early 1950s, Wilkinson committed himself to the state-run narcotics rehabilitation hospital in Lexington,

Kentucky. Three-and-a-half months later he returned to Montreal, cured of his addiction but eschewing the jazz life.

The last three years of Steep's life are almost a blank. He lived with his wife in the rooming-house and hung out on the corner, but no one remembers him working much. In fact, there is little evidence of him working anywhere other than three months at a nightclub called Rand's, deep in the east end of the city. Art Roberts was working an equally nondescript job nearby. During breaks he would run over to Rand's to hear Steep play:

> It was a commercial band, playing for shows and strippers. But the chords Steep played behind those singers—and sometimes he didn't even play the melody line on top—they had to be *good* singers to stay in tune, because he played jazz all the time. No compromise! His eyes would be squinting shut as he was about to hit an altered chord, because he knew it was a dissonant chord, but he played it anyway.

In February 1953, Steep took part in one of Montreal's most memorable jam sessions. Charlie Parker was in town, the guest of a local musicians' organization called the Jazz Workshop. The Workshop arranged for Parker to perform first on a CBC television program, accompanied by a rhythm section which included Montreal pianist Paul Bley, one of the cofounders of the organization. Two days later, on a Saturday afternoon, jazz fans and musicians flocked to the Chez Paree nightclub to hear Parker in person. The jam session concert was staged by the Workshop itself, one of a series it ran at the large uptown club to raise money for the Workshop's activities and to give local musicians an opportunity to play with jazz musicians from the United States.

The afternoon began without Parker: local musicians jammed for two hours before the saxophonist finally arrived. By the time Parker was ready to take the stand, so many local players wanted to play with him that the Workshop decided to change the rhythm section midway through the concert. Valdo Williams was first at the piano; Steep took the last half. Keith White, the other Workshop cofounder, hired a local amateur sound recorder named Bert Joss to tape the concert by tapping the wiring of the club's public address system. White and Joss endured Parker's displeasure to capture five tunes on tape — among them Steep accompanying Parker on "Embraceable You" and "Now's The Time." Years later, White's edited version of the tape found its way into the hands of an American record producer, and Steep's chordal accompaniment for the master saxophonist of bebop appeared on one track of a bootleg Charlie Parker album.[8]

Ten months after the Parker concert, Steep died. He was thirty-five.

Jazz history is too riddled with drug-related deaths—including Parker's, two years later—to make Steep's exceptional in any way. He died alone, at the rooming-house, early one Sunday morning in December 1953. Jo-Hann returned home at nine to find him in bed, lifeless. The coroner later ruled that Steep Wade's death had been sudden, and due to natural causes, and that no one was to blame.[9] On the street, the verdict was heroin.

INTERLUDE TWO

Wilkie Wilkinson Speaks

A bright, comfortable apartment on the seventh floor of a high-rise, just off the neon and traffic of east-end St. Catherine Street. He is sixty.

I never went anywhere without Steep. If he didn't seek me out in the daytime, I could always find him sitting in the tavern, Rockhead's tavern, bullshitting with some entertainers, somebody like Redd Foxx. We had no real set time to get up in the morning, unless Metcalf had called a rehearsal—and he usually called rehearsals two or three times a week. They were rough. You can imagine, now, if you had worked the whole night and then you had gone out and had a session to maybe five, six in the morning, until—well, you'd come out and the sun would be hitting you in the eyes. You wouldn't go to bed before eight, because invariably you went and had something to eat before you turned in. So Metcalf would call a rehearsal for two, and it was always a couple of hours. If there wasn't a rehearsal, I would sleep till about three in the afternoon, three-thirty, and I would practise for a couple of hours. I'd have maybe a Danish and some coffee while I was setting up my practice pad and my chair and my method book.

For breakfast sometimes we'd go to the Chinaman, or else we'd go up to Peel and find some restaurant, just for the walk. We used to go to Dominion Square and sit in the park sometimes. There was a cafeteria on the corner of Peel and St. Catherine called the Harmony Lunch, we'd go in there and get something to eat. Or else there was the old Northeastern, the "one-arm" place with the little tables, where you'd get a plate of beans and coffee. Best thing on their menu was toast, beans, and coffee—that was twenty-five, thirty cents. Our pay at the St. Michel was forty-five, fifty dollars a week, and that was considered good money.

After breakfast I'd go back to my room and practise, or sometimes I'd go into the club to practise—nobody there but the guy cleaning up and

155

the old cook in the back. I'd practise for at least a couple of hours, that was a necessity. You never neglected that, even though you were working. I can't emphasize it too strongly: when you lived it, you lived it! There was nothing else in life existed for you, especially when you knew you had to keep improving. Nothing stands still, you either go forwards or backwards.

Most of the show people would show up on the corner about four o'clock, seeing if there was any action. That was the only opportunity they had to meet other show people from the other clubs. Rockhead's tavern was the gathering spot for all the black musicians. We'd be sitting there with, say, four or five musicians from a band that was in town, and we'd think nothing of going over to the St. Michel and blowing for a couple of hours. For supper we'd stay on the corner. There was a restaurant just up the street from Rockhead's—no white clients except for me and a few other musicians that used to play on the corner. They served great biscuits. Or, Steep's mother was a good cook, we'd go over there for some peas and rice and trotters....

The jazz life takes a toll on an awful lot of musicians. The competition is so keen, it puts an awful strain on you. The majority of your waking hours you are applying your trade in one way or another, either practising or sitting in. You don't let any opportunity go by. Your entire life is monopolized by jazz. Nothing else concerns you. It really takes over to that extent.

You have to eat, sleep jazz—that's what it amounts to. And there are periods you go through of frustration. Marital problems get into it because of the hours you keep. If you can cope with them, fine. My problem was I couldn't cope with them; I didn't know where to draw the line. It's pathetic in some respects, because I don't feel that I really reached my potential before I started going downhill.

You feel that you are getting into a rut, that you haven't advanced in the past few months. You feel you were playing better two months ago than you are now—why? why? And then you get to saying, maybe I'm not practising enough. You're competing with yourself. You take such pride in what you're doing—I don't think there's anything in this world that will equal it. And you say to yourself that you've got to be the best, or forget it, knowing quite well that no matter how well you play there's always that one guy that will walk up the stairs and blow you right out of the establishment. It's happened to me: Max Roach, Philly Joe Jones—I stood in awe. I remember one night Ray Brown wanted to sit it. I just couldn't visualize myself playing with Ray Brown. I just tightened all up. And it was Ray that leaned over to me and said, "Come on, man, loosen up. I know you can make it. Don't worry about it." Just from what he said, I said to myself, "Ya, he's just a bass player—let's go!"

I was never impressed by anyone telling me how well I played. I was the one that had to be satisfied, and I never was. You feel that you do your best work under the influence of drugs or alcohol, but that's a fallacy. As a matter of fact, I think you do your worst, though I didn't know that at the time. I think it's more insecurity than anything else that gets musicians into it—insecurity about not being able to make it, the insecurity of whether the gig is going to close this week, or whether you've got another gig to go to. See, the whole thing in my day was to keep yourself employed and be able to do what you're doing without bastardizing your trade by having to commercialize it and go out and play bar mitzvahs and hotel gigs. This is the reason why I stayed on that corner for so many years. I started to really deteriorate when I had a house full of kids and I *had* to go out and play gigs. You think you're a good jazz musician—not the best, but a good one—and you have to go out and play polkas and waltzes and every damn thing. A gig like that, it was like pulling up sidewalks with my bare hands. Of course you feel you're bastardizing your profession, because basically you want to be a good musician. But the scene was so limited in this town. It was limited to one area, really, which was the corner. If you didn't work on the corner, you didn't play jazz.

I remember I took a small group into the Latin Quarter and after the first couple of nights the manager came to me and he said, "You play some dance music. The people are here to dance." And I said, "No, man, we're playing jazz. I told you I was bringing in a jazz group." "Well," he said, "I have to give you your notice." I said, "Fine"—and we went out swinging. We worked out our two-week notice, but we went out swinging. This town has always been a bad town for jazz, if you wanna make some bread, because the people won't patronize a jazz joint on a consistent basis.

It's easy to understand why musicians get so frustrated—when you work so hard at something and you know you're not getting anywhere. Even though the monetary factor was not that important to you, you could use the bucks. I was still supporting my family, though I was often short. I would sometimes come home, but the majority of times I'd either stay with Steep, or I'd stay at the Orgen rooming-house—that's *negro* spelt backwards. That's where all the entertainers stayed from the St. Michel.

There are some times you get so despondent, because you are working so hard and nobody seems to understand. People will sit around the bandstand and tell jokes, talking—they're not really listening to the music. It's pretty frustrating. Here you are up there doing your best and it's not being appreciated at all. So you gotta get frustrated. But then again, without them I don't get any pay on Sunday night. So what you do, you build up a protection screen against these people, and what you're doing is really playing for yourself and the band. You don't care about the people, what they think and what they don't think. That's the only way you can stay alive and play jazz.

Sometimes, after coming off the stand, we'd go upstairs and blow a little smoke. We did up. You gotta understand—in those days we worked long hours, and there was no such thing as a day off. The whole attic at the St. Michel was the dressing room. I've seen as many as twenty musicians up there, all huddled in little groups, everybody doin' up. The owner, he'd call upstairs, "I wish you wouldn't smoke up there, because it's coming down into the club!" And in those days, even if you got caught with only one joint, you were gone for six months. There was no fine, nothing. If The Man [the police] busted you, you didn't even get a chance to say "good morning, judge." It was automatically six months.

The other musicians, they resented the jazz musician because he was a breed unto his own. He was a kook. They turned their noses up at a jazz musician. The jazz musicians themselves were very clannish. There's one thing you could say about jazz musicians—if you didn't make it, they didn't play with you. There was nothing hypocritical about it. A guy got up on the bandstand, he either made it or he didn't. And if he didn't make it, that was it. He'd come off the bandstand fast....

I don't think you could mention one great jazz musician who was working in that era who hadn't visited that corner. You name it—any great jazz musician that worked Montreal made it down there. I could ream off so many names. Wardell Gray used to get Steep and I out of bed to jam in the afternoons. Lester Young—he didn't even have a gig in Montreal and one time he came up here and spent a couple of weeks on holiday, just sitting in and playing sessions. The name Café St. Michel had become notorious all over the United States among musicians: "You go up to Montreal, there's only one place to go—hit that corner! Go down there and blow! Blow after hours!" There was always some place to blow: Aldo's up the street, or the Snake Pit under the Café St. Michel, or some blind pig. The place was loaded with blind pigs during the Duplessis era. We were never stuck for anywhere to blow after hours, because these guys that run the blind pigs were getting free music. Old Steep used to put the kitty-pot out there on the piano. 'Course, Steep loved it because your glass was never empty. He loved his whiskey.

That corner never closed. The Snake Pit was open during the daytime; so was Rockhead's tavern. There was gambling, too, upstairs on the corner. There was always a card game, and of course the barbotte[1] joints were going then. And right on the corner you could play the Chinese lottery tickets, it was like the numbers racket in New York. It was cheap, then, a quarter, and you could hit for two thou', three thou', four thou', six thou'—depending on what was in the bank and how many spots you hit. I never won, but I used to play....

Later, when I got strung out on The Heavy [heroin], we used to make it down to the east end of Montreal, around The Main. That was the only place to cop. Or The Man [the pusher] would make a trip down to the corner. We'd have a certain number to call, we'd call it, he'd come by in the streetcar and drop it off.

The Man [the police] knew me, knew I was a user. He lived in the St. Michel. He went to bed with me and he got up with me, even knew what kind of toothpaste I used. I'd go outside my home and he'd be sitting there in his car, waiting to see where I was going to cop. I've been hassled—chased through Eaton's one day: I lost him through the side door, jumped in a cab, and gone. I went through some pretty bad scenes, but I was never busted. A certain amount of kindness and a lot of luck. I was trying to keep a family and keep a habit, too, so I had to move my ass. That's why I was doing studio work and working the clubs at the same time. I was never home. I can't understand why this woman is still with me today, because my first love was my drums.

I eventually completely broke down. I just couldn't work any more. It seems jazz and dope were completely synonymous for me. I couldn't get any help up here, so I had to go to Lexington. And I vowed that I would never get strung out again, so I had to leave the jazz scene.

I haven't any regrets. I could die tomorrow and I haven't any regrets. I would never have been able to progress to the extent that I did as a jazz musician had I not been exposed to that atmosphere and that element—never! Had I stayed uptown as a white musician, working commercially, there's no way I could have made it. The jazz life for me in Montreal was the best period in my life —the *best* period in my life. I've never had anything that I've had such a love for; I guess I never will. And if I live to be eighty I will still be listening to jazz, because jazz will be with me till I die.

Edited excerpts from interview with Mark "Wilkie" Wilkinson in Montreal, 7 September 1982.

CHAPTER SEVEN

Show Biz and Jazz

Show biz. The era is gone, but images remain. Neon signs beckoning in the night: the Montmartre and the El Morocco; the Downbeat, the Esquire, and the Savoy; Rockhead's Paradise, the Tic-Toc, the All-American. Long bars upholstered in pleated red leather, and expanses of mirror reflecting bottles and customers' intrigues. Thematic decors and costumes evoking Hawaii or Harlem, Cuba or the Creole South. Masters of ceremony like Johnny Gardner and Nipsy Russell, warming up audiences packed knee-to-knee around tiny tables with jokes or a song. And then—the show: Perhaps a juggler. Or a fire swallower. Or a contortionist with a name like Rubberneck Holmes. Perhaps a concert singer, billed as "Naomi Webb, the human violin," to dip into the light classics. Certainly a comedian, and with luck a rising star like Redd Foxx or Jimmy Durante. Legions of singers and vocal groups: Alberta Hunter, Sammy Davis Jr., Tony Bennett, Sarah Vaughan; Le Double Six de Paris, the Delta Rhythm Boys, the Ink Spots, the Golden Gate Quartet. And the dancers: "eye-filling exotic dancers" with names like Lady Trindida, Francis Yum-Yum, and Venus Halloway; dancers who teased the imagination with smiles and winks and swirls of feathers and veils; "apache" dance teams feigning a lovers' quarrel, tossing each other over their shoulders and cascading across the hardwood, only to collide in a forgiving embrace; precision tap-dance teams—Dutch and Dutchy, Stump and Stumpy, Tip, Tap and Toe, the Kit-Kats; and, in the biggest clubs, a finale: a high-heeled, high-kicking chorus line.

This was show biz—the work place of Montreal's jazz musicians, from the budding of the nightclub industry in the 1920s to its suffocation four decades later under the onslaught of television, rock music, strip shows, and a new mayor's vision of a city without vice. For as long as the good times lasted, the musicians worked. Their music crossed all barriers of class, race, and language. From the small, neighbourhood clubs where local MCs and singers held the stage, to the fancy spots fea-

Show entertainers pose with house bandleader Herb Johnson (far left) and club manager Albert Lean (far right) at the Belmar, 1951. In the centre is American bandleader Count Basie, who was making a social visit to the nightclub after a performance elsewhere in the city. *Photo by Geraldine Carpenter Studio, courtesy of Herb Johnson. John Gilmore Jazz History Collection, Concordia University Archives.*

A show dancer at Rockhead's Paradise. *Photo by Emile of Montreal, courtesy of Walter Bacon. John Gilmore Jazz History Collection, Concordia University Archives.*

Moke and Poke, a comedy acrobatic team. *Photo by James Kreigsmann, courtesy of Walter Bacon. John Gilmore Jazz History Collection, Concordia University Archives.*

turing top acts from the United States, live music propelled live entertainment all over town.

The scale of Montreal's nightclub industry during its peak in the late 1940s and early 1950s was staggering. Musicians swear there were literally hundreds of clubs in the city offering some kind of show. The biggest of these clubs were entertainment factories, labour intensive yet enormously profitable. The Bellevue Casino was one such operation. Three stories tall, with a lounge on the ground floor, a spacious cabaret on the second, and a mezzanine overlooking the stage on the third, it employed ninety-seven permanent staff, spent eight to ten thousand dollars a week on entertainment, and grossed more than a million-and-a-half dollars a year. An average of fourteen hundred people attended the club on weekday nights, and more than two thousand on Saturdays. Its attraction was hard to resist: a customer could enjoy a beer and a show featuring top American acts for less than two dollars. The Bellevue was big business, but it was far from unique: one journalist counted close to two dozen other Montreal clubs operating in the same league in 1951.[1]

Most of the city's nightclubs employed two bands, one to provide music for the shows and the twenty minutes of social dancing that followed, another to provide light background music while the show band rested and new customers settled in. The show bands were occasionally as small as a trio, but most employed four to six musicians, sometimes more. Trumpets and saxophones dominated the front line, with drums and a piano or guitar behind. Few club owners could be convinced to hire a bassist: they rarely understood the instrument's importance in the harmonic and rhythmic foundation of the music, and would sooner have paid for another horn than for an instrument which no one but the musicians seemed to hear anyway. The relief bands were smaller, seldom larger than a trio. Bass players, in quieter company here, often accompanied an accordion, guitar, vibraphone, or piano. Duos were common, while some clubs made do with a solo pianist during intermissions.

The music played by Montreal show bands reflected the city's embrace of both French and American cultures. Clubs in the francophone working-class neighbourhoods east of the city centre regularly featured francophone entertainers; most were local but some were imported from France. The music for these shows courted more the French music-hall tradition than the swing of American show biz, though singers sometimes drew songs from the American pop music repertoire and sang them in English. Not suprisingly, most of the musicians who worked in these clubs were themselves francophone. Musicians who were drawn to jazz, however, aspired to a job in a nightclub in the centre of the city. There the shows featured American acts and music written by American arrangers in the jazz idiom.

While the uptown clubs on or near St. Catherine Street West offered musicians the highest salaries and the most prestige, jazz often bubbled closest to the surface in the clubs which featured black shows. It was in these clubs that most of the city's black musicians found work, but here too could be found those white musicians who loved jazz and enjoyed playing for black entertainers. Many of the so-called black clubs were located in that part of the city centre known as the east end, around the corner of St. Catherine and The Main. But for most Montrealers, and especially for black visitors to the city who were justifiably wary of the reception they might receive uptown, the corner of Mountain and St. Antoine was synonymous with black show biz. The corner's fame rested on two clubs facing each other across Mountain Street—Rockhead's Paradise on the south-east corner, and the Café St. Michel on the west side a few doors down. Saxophonist Herb Johnson:

> I played in practically every club in the city of Montreal since I came here in 1935, and I tell you—you *knew* you were in show biz when you were working at Rockhead's Paradise or the Café St. Michel. It was like transporting yourself to Harlem.

The Café St. Michel was the less formal of the two, and while it featured leading black entertainers from the United States just as its rival did, the club's fame rests on the long residency it offered Louis Metcalf's International Band during the late 1940s. Rockhead's Paradise, on the other hand, became famous not for its bands but for the consistently high quality of its shows and the hospitality of its owner, whose name and manner became so intimately linked with the club that it was widely referred to as simply Rockhead's.

Rufus Nathaniel Rockhead was born into a proud community of fugitive slaves and their offspring in Jamaica, near the end of the nineteenth century. As a young man he sailed to Canada, where he joined the army and fought in the First World War. Returning from Europe, he settled in Montreal, ran a shoeshine stand for a while, then went to work as a railway porter. During eight years on the Montreal-Chicago run, Rockhead smuggled bootleg liquor into Al Capone's empire, a popular and lucrative sideline for many porters as long as Prohibition lasted in the United States. One day, as his train approached Montreal, word reached the porters that the police were waiting for Rockhead at Windsor Station. He slipped off the train at a suburban station and went into hiding until the heat blew over.

Rockhead's career as a porter had abruptly ended, but with abundant savings from eight years of smuggling he was ready to set himself up in business. Rockhead began lobbying for a liquor permit; city and provincial authorities didn't look kindly upon blacks owning bars, and it took him two years to obtain a permit. In 1928 he bought a three-storey, red-brick building on the corner of Mountain and St. Antoine. A tavern and lunch counter shared the ground floor; the second floor was a dining room; and on top was a fifteen-room hotel. Rockhead converted the lunch counter into a long, narrow cocktail bar and the dining room into a beverage room; the hotel continued to do a brisk business with prostitutes and their clients.

When the Depression struck, Rockhead tried to ease the hardship for the local black community by hiring as many staff as he could afford to, even when there was little work to be done. He also organized amateur shows in the beverage room, offering a few dollars and bottles of wine and beer for prizes. Three years after he bought the building, Rockhead began importing professional black entertainers from the United States. He hung a red-neon sign on the wall outside proclaiming Paradise. When the room could no longer hold the crowds, he knocked down the room dividers on the third floor, cut a large oval hole in the floor overlooking the stage below, and transformed his modest establishment into a two-story nightclub with seating for four hundred. One bedroom on the third floor was left intact, a tiny closet of a room behind the checkroom that became the club owner's second home.

Rockhead's day began with an egg-nog for breakfast at home with his wife and three children. It was the only meal he ate with his family. By ten-thirty or eleven he was at the club, attending to business and helping out behind the counter in the tavern. From four to eight every afternoon he slept in his tiny room on the third floor, then dressed, ate whatever the club's chef was preparing that day, tucked a red flower into the lapel of his suit jacket, and assumed his position at the top of the stairs. There he remained until closing time the next morning, greeting every guest personally. "He didn't come to the door without that flower," recalled his son Kenny. "It would have been like coming to the door undressed."[2]

"Good evening, Mr. Rockhead," the men addressed him as they entered the club. To the women he was simply "Rufus." So popular did his red flower become with the ladies that he began buying dozens of them every morning on his way to work—roses if he could get them, carnations otherwise—and offering them to women at the door. He was a gracious, sober host and became widely respected in the black community, whose interests he took to heart. On special occasions he organized matinée shows for the neighbourhood children, serving them sandwiches and soft drinks. At Christmas he mounted a special family show. And when local youths such as Hugh and George Sealey began to show promise as musicians, he convinced their fathers to let them play alongside older musicians at the club on weekends—and assumed personal responsibility for seeing them home after the show.

Allan Wellman's band at Rockhead's Paradise in the early 1950s: Wellman (trumpet); George Sealey (alto saxophone); Leroy Mason (tenor saxophone); William Spotswood (piano); Walter Bacon (drums). *Photo by Emile of Montreal, courtesy of Leroy Mason. John Gilmore Jazz History Collection, Concordia University Archives.*

Rockhead was as meticulous about his shows as he was about his dress. If he didn't personally approve of an act, it didn't appear on his stage, no matter how far it had travelled for the booking. Saxophonist Vern Isaac watched Rockhead in action from his place in the show band:

> Rockhead had some of the best shows in Canada. He would "censor" his show. He'd be there at rehearsals, watching, but he wouldn't say anything. That night, opening night, he'd be there, watching. And after the first show, he'd point to someone and say, "Mr. So-and-So, you're not good enough to be on my stage."
>
> And they'd say, "But what about my contract?!"
>
> "I'll pay it. But every time that show hits, I want to see you sitting here looking at it."
>
> He pulled some hell-fine singers off. They weren't good enough to be on his stage. And every night of the week there was a line-up waiting to get in, because he *always* had a good show.

Nor did Rockhead neglect the music. He demanded professionalism from his house bands; in return he provided respect and steady employment to the musicians he liked best—among them trumpeter Allan

American jazz celebrities Louis Armstrong and Cozy Cole sit in with Allan Wellman's band during a social visit to Rockhead's Paradise in the early 1950s. On stage are: Wellman (without instrument); Armstrong (trumpet); Cole (drums); Vern Isaac (alto saxophone); Leroy Mason (tenor saxophone); Valdo Williams (piano). The club's master of ceremonies, Marsellis Wilson, is seated at bottom left, smoking. *Courtesy of Vern Isaac. John Gilmore Jazz History Collection, Concordia University Archives.*

Wellman, who led the house band for years, and drummer Willie Wade. The show dancers loved Wade's loud, driving beat, and Rockhead loved a hard-working dancer. He insisted that only black musicians could provide the right musical feel for his all-black shows. With rare exception Rockhead enforced a black-only policy on his club's bandstand,[3] though he hired mixed bands to play in the cocktail lounge downstairs. Drummer Dennis Brown was one of the white musicians who coveted the chance to play for Rockhead's shows:

> I knew Mr. Rockhead for many, many years. And I would walk into the club, first when Willie Wade was playing drums with Allan Wellman's band. And Mr. Rockhead would say, "Hello, Dennis."
>
> And I'd always say, "Good evening, Mr. Rockhead. How are you?"
>
> He used to continue, "I hear you're coming along pretty well on the drums."
>
> And I'd say, "I'm trying, Mr. Rockhead."

And he'd invariably throw in the next line: "Yes, they tell me you're pretty good, but no white drummer can play my shows."

Ironically, Rockhead's was no different from the other black clubs in town in its reliance on white clientele for the bulk of its business. Though Rockhead's was loved by black residents and tourists, and played host to such black celebrities as prize fighter Joe Louis, jazz star Louis Armstrong, and the Harlem Globetrotters basketball team, it depended on a steady stream of whites up the stairs to keep the gears of Paradise well oiled. There was no shortage of business, both from a public that appreciated the talents of black entertainers and musicians, and from that crowd of ostentatious, well-heeled spenders for whom the disparaging term *slumming* was first coined. Tired of the more reserved atmosphere of the uptown hotels and clubs, and fortified with good whiskey and champagne, the slummers would descend to the corner for the late show at Rockhead's or the Café St. Michel. Always respectful, Rockhead ushered them into Paradise—in stark contrast to many white club owners uptown who made black patrons feel distinctly unwelcome, if they didn't refuse them entry altogether.[4]

Uptown at the El Morocco, a short, athletic man with horn-rimmed glasses and a biting sense of humour was leading the show band. Maury Kaye was the quintessential white Montreal jazz musician of the 1950s. Born Morris David Kronick, he endured the kind of classical music training befitting the son of a synagogue choirmaster. Then, in his thirteenth year, destiny called in the form of a teenage dance band with a summer engagement at a Laurentian resort—but no piano player. Kaye was adopted, and quickly intoxicated by his first taste of popular music. When the engagement ended, he immediately began finding work for himself in other dance bands around Montreal, while continuing his music studies at McGill University's conservatory for another two years.

At nineteen, and by now sporting the name Maury Kaye, which an older musician had bestowed upon him, the pianist formed his own quartet and held down a job as house bandleader at the Esquire for eight months. The following year he was engaged to open a small club on Closse Street in the shadow of the Forum, the city's hockey arena. When business picked up and the El Morocco expanded into one of Montreal's largest and most prestigious nightclubs in 1952,[5] Kaye enlarged his house band from a trio to a septet; for special shows he would occasionally augment the group with as many as eight additional musicians. During the seven years Kaye was resident at the El Morocco, he earned the respect of entertainers and musicians—as a prolific writer of exciting arrangements, as a commanding and spirited bandleader, and as an

One of several versions of **Maury Kaye**'s septet from the El Morocco, at the Black Orchid room above Dunn's. Saxophones left to right: John Kelsey (tenor); Bob Roby (alto); Leo Perron (baritone); others: Kaye (piano), Fred McHugh (bass), Walter Batagello (trumpet), Paul Lafortune (drums). *Photo by O'Neil of Montreal, courtesy of Hal Gaylor. John Gilmore Jazz History Collection, Concordia University Archives.*

absorbing bebop-styled soloist on piano. Adding to his appeal was his versatility: he had taught himself to play trumpet, valve trombone, and french horn, all of them well enough to use on the job.

The boys in Kaye's band went to work every night in the uniform of their profession, what musicians still refer to as a B-flat suit. The boss at the El Morocco demanded it be dark blue, accented with a thin red tie. The band looked, behaved, and performed irreproachably—if you were willing to overlook their socks. The boss wasn't. He cringed every time the spotlight swept the bandstand and revealed fourteen socks of a variety of colours, some of them not even matching the one on the other foot. He implored Kaye to make his boys wear black socks, and Kaye dutifully passed on the instructions. But night after night the checks, stripes, and colours flashed in the spotlight beneath the pressed and matching suit trousers of the seated musicians. One night, the musicians arrived for work to find a polished metal railing installed around the bandstand, at calf-height. Hanging from the rail was a short velvet curtain. The musicians' socks were never mentioned again.

A less successful nightclub manager might not have cared what colour socks his musicians wore, or if he did he might have fired the lot of them in exasperation. The best clubs, however, knew that the success of their shows depended greatly on the quality of their show bands, and that entertainers performed best with musicians they respected and felt they could rely on. Kaye's band, stocked with local jazz musicians such as trumpeter Guido Basso, alto saxophonist Bob Roby, and bassist Fred McHugh, was one of the best Montreal had to offer. Kaye recalled:

> A lot of acts would come up to Montreal when they had new music—written, say, by somebody like Nelson Riddle—and they wanted to hear how it sounded. They would come up and work for less money than they would normally get in New York to break in the new music, because our band played it right the first time.... Not that the people down in the States couldn't play it correctly. But our attitude was a lot healthier. We were happy to get somebody with good music, whereas down in the States it was, you know, "Ah, it's just another act!"

This combination of professional attitude and musical skill, displayed by several generations of Montreal musicians, helped make the city a popular destination among touring nightclub performers. Musicians such as Kaye were proud of the fact that they were among the most highly regarded in North America for playing shows. At the same time, the city was known for the high expectations of its audiences: Montrealers were used to seeing the best acts in the world, and they didn't hesitate to express their disappointment. New York booking agents, aware of the city's reputation, sent new acts to Montreal on trial runs. "If you got a half-assed reception here," said pianist Roland Lavallée, "you'd be big time in the United States." May Oliver, who helped manage Louis Metcalf during his stay at the Café St. Michel, corroborated:

> In North America, two cities were best for shows—New York, of course, and Montreal. As far as prestige for an entertainer, New York was the place. But they knew that audiences in Montreal were quite discriminating. Not cruel in any way, but if you could do well in Montreal you *knew* you were gonna be a smash in New York. A lot of people said that, both musicians and entertainers.[6]

So vibrant was Montreal's show scene in the golden decade after the Second World War that finding work was seldom a problem for musicians who were able and willing to play shows. Jobs were so plentiful that the musicians juggled them until they found the one, or more, that fit their tastes and abilities. Under such conditions, recalled Herb Johnson, "you could either quit or be fired, and find yourself on some-one else's bandstand the following night."

"If you didn't like one place," said Bob Roby, "all you had to do was go jam some place and you'd end up with another job very quickly. Or you let the guys know you were available and you got a job right away. You were never out of work. The choice was always there. There were so many clubs."

Roland Lavallée elaborated:

> If you wanted to, you could play three different jobs a day, seven days a week. You had a lot of clubs with music in the afternoons. I used to play the Copa Cabana from two to six in the afternoon. I'd go home for supper, then I'd go and play at the Algiers from nine or ten o'clock at night till three or four in the morning. From there I used to go and play from about four in the morning till about eight or nine o'clock in a blind pig, a classy blind pig, with trios. We'd play jazz and requests.
>
> Going home? We didn't know what that meant. We went home when the sun was up, at eight or nine in the morning, then sleep four or five hours, wash, and back on the job at two in the afternoon. But you know, we were young and strong, and we were having fun. We didn't have to do it, but we wanted to do it.
>
> Musicians used to be like one big family. How many times, if a musician didn't feel well on the job, the other piano player [in the alternating band] would say, "Go home, man, I'll finish your night, and some other time you finish my night." So you'd do the whole night—seven hours non-stop — and when there's a drum solo you'd run to the piss-house for a pee and a cigarette and then run back.

The music, especially those well-crafted arrangements carried by headline acts from New York, was frequently challenging, at least until constant repetition dulled its novelty. The musicians were expected to read it faultlessly after a single rehearsal. When a band lacked a particular instrument for which there was an important line of music in the arrangement, the musicians played it anyway, transposing at sight: in this way a saxophonist might also play parts written for a flute or oboe, while a bassist might fill in for a missing trombone or cello. Particular challenges awaited drummers, for whom music was frequently not provided by the performer. They were nevertheless expected to anticipate, and react to, every change in tempo and dynamics, and to highlight a performer's movements with appropriate splashes of colour and rhythm. Dennis Brown explained:

MONTH	DAY	DESCRIPTION	RECEIVED	PAID OUT	
		TOTALS BROUGHT FORWARD	1 493 02	230 98	1 262 73
Août	3 au 9	St Michel	81 62	11 50	69 58
9 Août		Reçu 2% de Vacance	29.86		29.86
10-16		St Michel	81 62	11.50	69 58
17-24		"	81 62	11.50	69 58
24	31	St Michel	81 62	11 50	69 58
Septembre 53					
1 = 7		St Michel	81 62	11 50	69 58
7-13		St Michel	81 62	11 50	69 58
14-20		"	81 62	11 50	69 58
21	27	St Michel	81 62	11 50	69 58
Oct	8	Radio Sherbrooke			20.00
"	10	Clay Ermite			16.00
"	11	Session Latin Quarter			10.00
30	30	Butch Carpentersville	15.00		15.00
31	31	Butch Vallefield	20.00		20.00
Nov	11	Beaver Club			11.00
Nov	14	Mc Gill			13.00
Nov	19	Beaver			11.00
"	20	St Jean			15.00
"	26	Butch			25.00
"	27	Beaver			11.00
"	28	Joe Christi	15.00		15.00
	29	Quartier Latin			9.00
Dec	1	Savoy Café			11.00
Dec	2	St Jean			22.0
"	4	Palestre National			14.00
	5	Cavendish café			15.
		TOTALS CARRIED FORWARD			

A page from Roland Lavallée's engagement book from 1953, showing a steady engagement at the Café St. Michel followed by a succession of one-night jobs for as little as $9.00 a night. *Courtesy of Roland Lavallée. John Gilmore Jazz History Collection, Concordia University Archives.*

You caught punch lines on comedians' jokes, jugglers, a dancer's kick—everything that moved you accented it, pointed it up. And all this had to happen while you still knew where you were in the context of the music. You still had to swing, or, if you were playing Latin or Afro, you still had to maintain that feel.

Drummers often made up their own cue cards for an act. Brown continued:

I'd note the order of tunes, the possible changes, the possible insertions, tempos—like "walk four," or "easy swing." For a dancer's routine, one with many changes of tempo, I'd draw a little picture of a pose, a position in their dance. I'd draw them on my cue sheets so when they hit a certain pose I'd know to make an abrupt change of tempo and mood. I played for so many dancers that I could pick up their roots, whether they were West Indian, or Cuban, or straight American, and vary the rhythm and feeling accordingly. Like, I could get into a calypso thing, or a Cuban thing, or a shake-dancer straight-Harlem thing. And in the black clubs, it would range from blues to old-time tap-dancers, Afro-Cuban dancers, or jazz dancers from, say, the Palladium in New York. We had a whole range of experience.

Some performers, usually the smaller names, arrived in town without any written music. They simply outlined their act verbally to the band at rehearsal, and left the rest to the musicians. Saxophonist Leroy Mason explained:

Each musician would have a cue sheet. It would say things like: "16 bars of 'I Got Rhythm,' segue into 'How High the Moon,' segue into 'Black and Tan Fantasy.'" We wouldn't write out the changes; we got to know them. Segue means going from one tune to another without a break. If the tempo changed, the drummer would give a cue. There was no pause, unless you paused to give the artist a chance to take a bow. *That's* show business!

On stage with nothing but a cue sheet before them, the musicians improvised arrangements as the show unfolded. They did so by drawing from an unwritten reservoir of musical phrases, harmonies, and conventions which were familiar to all musicians who had learned to play jazz by ear. One musician might play a short phrase, or riff, as a background to a dance or song; the other horns would immediately join in, usually in harmony. Or, the horns might play soft, sustained harmony behind a singer's ballad, weaving through the chord progression confident in their understanding of what harmony notes each instrument would play next. "They would just look at each other and—bam!—it was there," said Dennis Brown. "And the next show, they'd do those same riffs. They'd remember them, note for note."

"One of the differences between the music scene in the 1950s and the music scene today," recounted trumpeter Jack Long in 1983, "is that in those days it was almost unheard of for a musician to expect to make a living playing jazz." He continued:

> We played what we felt we *had* to play to make a living. There seemed to be much more stress on making a living in those days. We prided ourselves on being *musicians*. A lot of us prided ourselves on being able to play a variety of different types of music. We were, for the most part, quite adequate readers. Some of us had quite varied types of experience in other types of playing, even a bit of legit playing. But what we were *really* interested in was jazz. Jazz was what everything else revolved around.... It was our *raison d'être* in the music business. But it was not what we did for a living, or ever hoped to do for a living. The only exception to this was probably some of the rhythm players—piano players, a few guitar players, bass players, drummers—who, by working on gigs where they played light jazz that had a fairly commercial appeal, had jobs which you could really call jazz jobs. As far as the horn players, it was just about unthought of, *unheard* of, that you could play jazz for a living.[7]

The conflict between life and art was never far below the surface. The bottom line, as Maury Kaye spelled it out shortly before his death in 1983, was that "if you wanted to call a jazz musician a musician who plays nothing but jazz for a living, there was no such animal." There were, however, many talented musicians who accepted the necessity of working within the commercial context of show business but who nevertheless retained a strong allegiance to jazz. Where a nightclub gave the musicians some freedom in determining the music, they played tunes favoured by jazz musicians and tailored them to the requirements of the job and the audience's expectations. When a club permitted the musicians less leeway, they communicated to one another on stage in a kind of secret, communal language, weaving their jazz ideas inconspicuously into the fabric of the popular music: a chord substitution here, a rhythmic variation there, and perhaps a quote from a jazz composition or famous solo. "As long as we cut the show, fine," said drummer Billy Barwick. "But sometimes you'd get a little flak from the club owner, like, 'Hey! There's a little too much jazz in there, and we don't want it.'"

The dance sets at the end of the shows offered the greatest latitude in repertoire and improvisation. Pianist Stan Patrick:

> I guess we learned very early from the older guys that if you play the melody down once, and people recognize it, after that you can do whatever you want to, as long as they don't feel you're trying to show them that you're far above them. Give them a little

taste of something they're familiar with and you can go wherever you want with it.

Some musicians, applying this philosophy more liberally than others, believed that all the public needed to dance to was a familiar rhythm. Saxophonist and valve trombonist Paul "Boogie" Gaudet led a quartet of Montreal jazz musicians for three consecutive summers during the mid-1950s at a resort near Grandmère. Their job was to provide dance music for the vacationers:

> During the days we'd memorize jazz tunes from records—
> Clifford Brown, Parker, Miles, Dizzy—then we'd play them on
> the gig. We might have to play them a little slower for the
> dancers, but the dancers never complained. They'd say, "Play a
> jitterbug," so we'd play "A Night in Tunisia." The tempo was
> right. We'd try not to make the tunes too long so they didn't die
> of exhaustion on the floor. For a mambo we'd do, maybe,
> "Bernie's Tune," or "Manteca." The people were satisfied. They
> could dance to it. And we were playing what we wanted. We had
> a chance to blow, and over fifty percent of our tunes were jazz
> tunes.

Montreal's jazz community was healthier and more cohesive in the ten or fifteen years after the end of the Second World War than at any other time in the city's history. This vitality was largely attributable to the prosperity of the city's nightclubs and the popularity of stage shows. Show business stimulated the jazz community both directly and indirectly. The abundance of work for musicians was directly responsible for the size and stability of the jazz community. More musicians came to the city than left it: musicians were in demand, esteemed for their skills, and well-paid. They had the money to live well, buy instruments and records, travel to New York City for inspiration, and hang out at clubs with their fellow musicians after the night's work was done.

At the same time, the nature of show work—the nightly repetition of exacting music, and the frequent antipathy of club owners to jazz—indirectly stimulated the jazz community by creating a pool of frustrated musical creativity in search of an outlet. This creativity could find only partial release on the job; the lid came off later, in the hours before dawn, when the musicians gathered informally to play for the sheer pleasure of playing, sharing their musical ideas without fear of censure. Saxophonist Leroy Mason:

> Any musician that loves to play, he loves to jam. Because working
> a job, playing shows, was frustrating. Jamming gives a guy a
> chance to let out his frustrations. You can imagine, playing the
> same thing three or four times a night, seven nights a week, for

174

A gathering of some members of the Montreal jazz community after a concert, in 1956. Left to right: Steve Garrick (piano), Arlene Smith (vocals), Abby Smollen (non-musician, member of Emanon Jazz Society), Bob Schilling (bass), Billy Graham (drums), Maury Kaye (trumpet), Jack Rider (tenor saxophone), Saul Sherman (trumpet), Freddie Nichols (alto saxophone), John Kelsey (baritone saxophone). Squatting: Guido Basso (trumpet). *Photo by O'Neil of Montreal, courtesy of Bill Graham and Jack Rider. John Gilmore Jazz History Collection, Concordia University Archives.*

two weeks—and maybe three or four weeks if the act was held over. After playing those shows, you gotta do something! We didn't wanna go home, so we'd go to jam sessions till seven or eight in the morning. That was the life of musicians—and that broke up a lot of marriages.

There was no shortage of places for the musicians to gather. Many clubs remained open all night; some literally never closed. A few, like the Latin Quarter, scheduled jam sessions on Sunday afternoons to attract more business. But most of the jam sessions were unorganized and unadvertised; the word simply got around, and the musicians showed up. Clarinetist Al Baculis:

If you were a jazz pianist and you had a gig, you might say to the boss, "Do you mind if some of my buddies drop in around one-thirty and we'll play to about four or five?"

The owner, if he wanted to stay open, he'd say, "Sure, invite them over."

"We'll be playing jazz...."

"Oh, that's OK kid, just don't play the jazz in the best part of the night. You know I'm trying to make a living here."

Bassist Fred McHugh:

> Every night you would go somewhere. The clubs were open twenty-four hours. We used to play in the Black Magic Room of the Chez Paree on Stanley Street. We used to get out of there at nine o'clock in the morning. The regular band would finish at four. It was open to musicians to jam, and all the night people would come by—taxi drivers, waiters, hookers, and dancers. The place would be jammed till nine every morning, and everybody'd be playing....

Every jazz musician active in Montreal during the 1950s at some time or other jammed at Aldo's, the spot favoured by Steep Wade and his entourage. "Aldo's was *the* place," said saxophonist Frank Costi, whose ten-piece dance band at the Palais d'Or employed some of the city's top jazz musicians and their arrangements during the early 1950s. "If you weren't seen at Aldo's there was something wrong: 'How come you didn't show up last night?'—you know. *Everything* went on there. And they had a great chef. You could eat Chinese food at six o'clock in the morning. It never closed. It was open twenty-four hours a day."

Though unpaid jamming was prohibited by the union on the grounds that club owners were profiting from the music and should be paying the musicians, the sessions were irrepressible—a spontaneous reaffirmation of the jazz musician's calling. The jam sessions also served as clearing houses for work and proving grounds for younger musicians and new arrivals in town. Pianist Stan Patrick remembered his initiation to the ranks of the city's professional musicians at a jam session:

> There were two things in your initiation. One was something way up tempo, the other was a very slow ballad. You could more or less bluff your way on the up-tempo thing, but on the ballad everybody heard every note. They also deliberately changed keys. That's what Vern Isaac did to me—made me play the blues through every key, and then through the minor ones.

Boogie Gaudet was twenty-five when he moved to Montreal in 1953 from his native New Brunswick. Though determined to make a career for himself in music, he was unknown to the local musicians and therefore had no immediate hope of being offered work in a club band. To

176

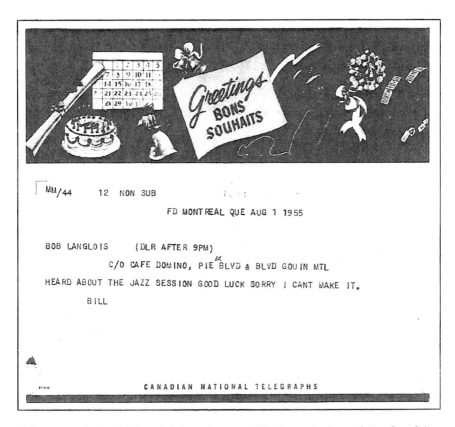

Telegram to pianist Bob Langlois from drummer Bill Martucci congratulating Langlois for organizing a jazz night at the Café Domino, where he was leading the house band. *Courtesy of Bob Langlois. John Gilmore Jazz History Collection, Concordia University Archives.*

survive the transition period, he took day jobs in a steel mill and a candy factory; to demonstrate his skills to the local musicians, he played at every jam session he could find.

> I remember once I had gone to the Bal Taborin, it was a Sunday night, and the piano player was Bob Langlois. I jammed all night, and all of a sudden, around six o'clock, I put my horn in my case and got ready to leave. So Bob says, "Where are you going? You're not leaving now!" I said, "Ya, it's six o'clock. I gotta go to work—I start at seven." I did that a lot. That's how I made my connections.

Some musicians took the initiative to create their own opportunities to play jazz. Private jam sessions were organized in practice studios and at musicians' residences. A rooming-house at 1476 Crescent Street, run by a woman sympathetic to jazz musicians, became famous within the jazz community for its afternoon jam sessions around the piano in bassist Bob Schilling's room.[8] Musicians also tried to convince club owners to hire bands to play jazz exclusively. They rarely succeeded; when they did, the jazz engagement was usually short-lived. Club owners knew they could attract more customers and earn higher profits with stage shows than with jazz.

At the same time, the nightclubs were competing for the jazz fan's money with large concert venues which regularly brought popular American jazz musicians to Montreal. During six months in mid-1952, for example, the Seville theatre on St. Catherine Street West brought in Louis Armstrong and his All-Stars, Lionel Hampton's big band, and the Stan Kenton orchestra; the Ideal Beach dance pavilion featured the big bands of Buddy Rich and Lionel Hampton; and the Forum staged several jazz concerts, including one featuring singer Billy Eckstine, pianist George Shearing's combo, and the Count Basie big band. There was no shortage of jazz in Montreal, but the musicians being paid to perform it were mostly from the United States; local musicians were left to play for free at jam sessions. The city's jazz community was too small to provide consistent revenue for a nightclub on a scale matching that generated by stage shows. Not suprisingly, club owners never sought out musicians to play jazz: it was only through persistent initiative that musicians created jazz work for themselves in Montreal.

One of those who succeeded, briefly, was Maury Kaye. He craved the opportunity to show the local jazz community what his septet was capable of, given the opportunity to play Kaye's own jazz arrangements unrestricted by the El Morocco's show policy. He found his chance in early 1958 at a club above Dunn's delicatessen on St. Catherine Street West, in the heart of the uptown nightclub district. Every night, Kaye's septet taxied over to Dunn's after the last show at the El Morocco and played jazz until dawn in the club. Kaye invited local poets, including Irving Layton and Leonard Cohen, to read from their work on stage, with the band playing jazz behind them.

The after-hours engagement lasted only a few months. A couple of years later, in 1960, Kaye convinced Dunn's to take another, even greater, chance on jazz. His band was hired to play jazz during regular club hours. The gamble didn't pay off, however, and Dunn's let the musicians go after two months. Though short-lived, the second engagement at Dunn's was a source of immense pride and satisfaction for the musicians in Kaye's band. Bob Roby was one of them:

> It was a dream. We played jazz every night. I used to tell my wife,
> "Pinch me—I don't believe I'm alive, because I'm going to be

playing jazz tonight!" And every night it would be the same routine. I kept telling my wife, "Pinch me! I want to realize that tonight I'm going to a gig and I'm not going to be playing shows, I'm actually going to be playing jazz the whole night—and good jazz!" That was so unusual, to get paid for just playing jazz.

Knowing how short-lived a jazz job was likely to be, musicians faced a tough decision: should they give up a steady, well-paying job in a show band for the satisfaction of a tenuous jazz job? The answer depended as much on the personal responsibilities of individual musicians as on their devotion to jazz. Single men without financial responsibilities were less hesitant to take the leap and endure the inevitable drop in income that accompanied the pursuit of jazz: show work paid salaries fixed by the union, while jazz work frequently offered musicians nothing more than a percentage of the receipts at the door. Drummer Billy Barwick:

> That was our biggest headache: "I wanna play jazz but I can't give up this money." Really, that was a headache. Guys would get depressed about it. They'd lose their ability at stretching out and playing jazz because they were confined to playing shows. Your heart is in jazz, and you wanna go out and do it. But you're afraid of giving up that steady job, because that job's gonna last indefinitely. So you just try to get a little jazz influence into playing the shows, and jam afterwards—and lose a lot of sleep.

Maury Kaye:

> The show-business industry swallowed up the musicians into steady-paying gigs. The show-business industry was big, there was work for everybody. If you could read a few notes and play your horn half-assed and in tune, you got a job. And *that* was security. It took you off the streets. So individual endeavour got sublimated so that people could go to sleep with a full belly and a warm bed.

One dream helped sustain Montreal jazz musicians: the dream of going to New York. The jazz capital of the world glowed like the sun, just over the horizon; music radiated from it—on the radio late at night, on the latest records, and in the person of leading jazz musicians passing through town. A chance to work in New York would make the years of practice, struggle, and anonymity in Montreal worthwhile. Few Canadians were ever given the chance: U.S. Immigration blocked them at every turn. But the success of Oscar Peterson and Maynard Ferguson in the United States, and the occasional slipping through the immigration net by other Montrealers, kept hope alive in the hearts of many local jazz

179

Paul Bley in Montreal. *Photo courtesy of Paul Bley. John Gilmore Jazz History Collection,* *Concordia University Archives.*

musicians. Billy Barwick:

> New York was Mecca. We *all* thought of going to New York, one day. That's why we practised so hard and wanted to play all the time and stayed up for days. Our dream was to go to New York.

Maury Kaye:

> New York was the goal, the prize. If you could get to New York and get a job, you could become a "jazz musician." If you didn't get there you were never gonna be one. You had to get that stamp on your hind quarters: "Trained in New York."

If the musicians couldn't go to New York, a taste of New York could always be brought to Montreal. That was one of the premises behind the most ambitious initiative of Montreal jazz musicians during the 1950s. The Jazz Workshop was founded in 1952 by pianists Paul Bley and Keith White. White was working as a musician at night while studying sciences during the day at Sir George Williams College; Bley was studying composition and conducting at the Juilliard School of Music in New York City and commuting back to his native Montreal on holidays to work. Unlike the several jazz societies and record collectors' groups which sprang up in Montreal in the decade after the Second World War, and which catered almost exclusively to non-musicians, the Jazz Workshop was created by and for musicians. The Workshop organized occasional Saturday afternoon jazz concerts at the Chez Paree, where White was working. Members played for free, the Workshop collected money at the door, and the club profited at the bar; in this way, the organization built up a fund to finance its activities. It used the money to rent a room over a bar near the corner of Mountain and Dorchester where members could meet, rehearse, and jam at any time of the day or night. And it paid jazz musicians to travel up from New York City, to play with members at the Chez Paree concerts and to jam at the Workshop's room afterwards.

A second, related initiative began with a few words of encouragement from some touring American musicians. Woody Herman's big band was appearing at the Chez Paree. Leading the relief band at the club was a local pianist and Jazz Workshop member named Steve Garrick. One night Garrick showed up with an arrangement he'd written for the Herman band. Impressed with his writing, several members of the Herman band encouraged the pianist to form his own big band in Montreal. Garrick recognized that the city would not support a professional jazz orchestra on a full-time basis. Instead, in about 1954, he proposed to the Jazz Workshop that Montreal musicians form a cooperative big band to rehearse, and occasionally perform, members' compositions and arrangements. The band would have no leader: whoever showed up at rehearsal with an arrangement for the band would lead the musicians through that particular piece of music.

The Workshop jumped on the idea, and the musicians began writing and rehearsing. Garrick, a self-taught arranger, proved to be the most prolific writer, and as the musicians became accustomed to his leadership, the seventeen- or eighteen-piece band gradually evolved from a cooperative unit into the Steve Garrick Orchestra. Garrick organized weekly rehearsals for the band at the Downbeat club, the Legion hall on Mountain Street, or wherever else he could obtain a room for free on a Saturday afternoon. There was no fixed membership to the band, but Garrick's leadership and writing gave the musicians an identity around which to rally.

Local jazz fans in turn supported the Jazz Workshop and the Garrick band through a remarkably successful organization called the Emanon Jazz Society: its name ("no name" spelt backwards) was taken from the title of a Dizzy Gillespie composition and reflected the membership's commitment to the modern jazz of the beboppers. At its peak in the early 1950s, the Emanon was drawing up to 350 people to some of its

Pianist Steve Garrick leads his jazz orchestra in a concert at the Legion hall on Mountain Street. Left to right, saxophones: Jack Rider (tenor), Lorn Lang (tenor), Dave Saxe (alto), Tony Amor (alto), unidentified (baritone); trombones: Maury Kaye , Gordie Marsh, unidentified, unidentified; trumpets: Al Kane, Jack Long, Roger Hufford, Guido Basso; others: Hal Gaylor (bass), Dennis Lacroix (drums). *Photo courtesy of Hal Gaylor. John Gilmore Jazz History Collection, Concordia University Archives.*

events, which included lecture demonstrations by local musicians, talks by visiting American musicians, record presentations, and organized jam sessions; musicians were given honourary memberships in the private organization to circumvent union rules against jamming in public. At the same time, the Emanon published a newsletter and, through flyers and calls to radio stations and newspapers, vigorously publicized local jazz events, including the Jazz Workshop concerts. On several occasions the Emanon itself organized jazz concerts. One, held at the Legion hall in June 1955, featured Garrick's eighteen-piece band and two smaller groups drawn largely from the personnel of the orchestra—an octet led by Maury Kaye on valve trombone, and a quintet led by drummer Billy Graham.

The Jazz Workshop was the first of these local initiatives to die. It faded from the scene about 1954, weakened by internal disputes over finances and direction, and cast adrift by its founders: Bley moved to

182

New York City to work, while White opted to pursue a non-musical career after realizing he could never earn a living playing jazz.[9] Garrick's orchestra and the Emanon Jazz Society hung on until the latter half of the decade. Garrick began spending an increasing amount of time in New York City after 1956, and his orchestra gradually dissolved. By 1960 he had settled in New York and effectively abandoned jazz to pursue writing for film and television, record producing, and other commercial work. The gradual demise of the Emanon, sometime after 1956, was further evidence that an era of vitality and cohesion in the Montreal jazz community was coming to an end. Broader social, political, and cultural forces were already at work eroding the traditional foundations of jazz in Montreal.

CHAPTER EIGHT

The 1950s and the Decline of Show Biz

Daybreak on 26 October 1954 was like any other Tuesday morning in Montreal. The bars were open. Taxis were dropping men at the front doors of brothels and gambling dens. And jazz musicians were jamming in the clubs while the night people partied around them. Only one thing set this particular Tuesday morning apart: the topic of conversation.

Montreal had a new mayor. Throughout the previous day, voters had crushed into polling stations to register their outrage at what a recently concluded judicial inquiry had confirmed: that police and municipal authorities had for years been profiting from and protecting organized crime and vice. Now, as dawn broke, taxi drivers were drifting into the all-night spots bearing the first edition of the morning newspapers like a guilty verdict from the electorate. "Drapeau Goes in on a Landslide," the *Gazette* headlined: "'Clean Up City Hall' Campaign Swamps All 8 Rivals."

The election of Jean Drapeau sent shock waves through the city. The thirty-eight-year-old balding lawyer with the heavy, dark-rimmed glasses and weak moustache had announced his candidacy only eighteen days before polling day, vowing to rid the city of vice and corruption. It was the first real challenge to the city's entrenched criminal underworld since organized crime had seeped into Montreal from the United States during the 1920s. The underworld and its collaborators met Drapeau's challenge with their full arsenal of electoral tactics, including payoffs, ballot-rigging, intimidation, and outright violence; four men armed with baseball bats demolished Drapeau's campaign headquarters on polling day. It was the roughest election in the city's history,[1] but the public's thirst for the moral vision Drapeau offered was stronger than his adversaries' muscle. When the ballots were counted, so overwhelming was Drapeau's victory that all eight other candidates for mayor's office lost their deposits.

A new era in the city's history was clearly beginning; a golden era for

Montreal jazz and show biz was beginning to come to an end. The rise of Drapeau and the rebirth of civic morality enjoyed exuberant media and public attention; in contrast, the slow death of traditional show biz and the depression of the city's jazz community was widely ignored. Nevertheless, the two historical trends were deeply entwined. Nightclubs were an integral part of the world of vice and organized crime which had corrupted city hall and the police. Drapeau swept to power on a promise to rid Montreal of vice and corruption. To that end, he unleashed and pursued a two-pronged cleanup campaign, driving suspect officials from office while simultaneously driving vice from public view. The campaign was not explicitly calculated to undermine the economy of the nightclubs, but inevitably it had that effect. The nightclubs lost clientele and revenues; traditional show biz faded; the entertainers and musicians lost work. In this respect, the policies of Jean Drapeau directly and gravely damaged the health and spirit of the city's jazz community.

The mayor alone was not to blame, however. Other factors coinciding with his rise to power contributed to the demise of show biz and jazz. The economy was in recession and unemployment was rising: people weren't spending as much on entertainment. The arrival of television meant they didn't have to; instead of going out to nightclubs, they could stay at home with their friends or children. A lengthy battle between the unions representing musicians and entertainers forced the cancellation of many shows, and the temporary closure of some nightclubs. Finally, a new sound was sweeping the world—rock and roll. Jazz was being displaced as the music of popular entertainment and dance. Alone, each of these factors was harmful; together they were devastating. Yet of all the factors which contributed to the shrinking of the nightclub job market for jazz musicians, none was so easily fixed in time and memory as the stunning arrival of a young, new mayor. Not suprisingly, then, jazz musicians who watched their way of life change for the worse in Montreal point to the election of Jean Drapeau as the beginning of the end.

The vice which Drapeau set out to eradicate had been proliferating in Montreal since Prohibition, when organized crime syndicates from the United States moved into Montreal to take control of the lucrative liquor-smuggling trade. At the same time, the city's population was swelling with immigrants from Europe and new arrivals from the countryside, providing a rapidly expanding market for vice, especially prostitution and gambling. Horse-racing tracks sprang up—there were five operating in the suburbs of Montreal in 1928[2]—and the harbour became an important point of entry for contraband narcotics, much of it destined for the United States. By the end of the decade, gangs of criminals had built the foundations for a massive vice industry in Montreal. This in turn was stimulating nightlife and generating work for musicians and entertainers.

Organized crime and vice expanded rapidly in Montreal through the 1930s and 1940s.[3] In the vernacular of the street, the city was "wide open," known across the continent as "The Paris of North America." Any illicit pleasure could be purchased at any time of the day or night. There were an estimated seventy-five to one hundred permanent brothels in the city, the larger ones employing upwards of a dozen women on each of two or three shifts.[4] Some used loudspeakers to solicit business; others seated naked prostitutes at the windows. Gambling, likewise, went on around the clock. Locations ranged from lavish mansions such as the Mount Royal Bridge Club, where the wealthy played roulette and banker's craps while sipping free champagne, to the converted homes in working-class districts that served only soft drinks and cigarettes to people playing a popular dice game called barbotte.[5] As many as two hundred gambling houses were running at any time; the greatest concentrations were found around Peel and St. Catherine, and around St. Denis and Mount Royal. The biggest gambling houses turned profits of up to four hundred dollars an hour.

That was only part of the organized gambling industry in Montreal. Five hundred slot machines—"one-armed bandits" they were called—could be found throughout the city and the Laurentian resort area; each one pulled in an average of one hundred dollars a week. There were illegal lotteries on baseball and hockey games, and a numbers game run by members of the Chinese community. For those who liked to play the horses, more than fifty neighbourhood betting parlours had direct telephone and teletype links to a central betting service at 10 Ontario Street East, which was in turn plugged into a continent-wide bookmaking network. Montreal was one of the busiest centres on the network, and when authorities in the United States put the heat on bookmaking in that country, Montreal became headquarters for all of North America.

The scale of organized crime in Montreal created what amounted to a parallel economy. In the late 1940s, authorities estimated that illegal gambling and betting alone were raking in $100 million a year for the underworld—$40 million more than the city's tax revenue. About twelve thousand people were believed to be directly employed by the various rackets in Montreal. Countless others—including jazz musicians, entertainers, and nightclub staff—benefited indirectly from the wealth generated by vice.[6]

Among those who profited directly from vice were many police officers, municipal and provincial politicians, and public employees. The gangsters delivered cash, alcohol, and other goods and services to the authorities through full-time underworld employees called "edge men."

186

In return, the authorities performed an elaborately contrived show for the public, pretending to hunt down criminals and bring them to justice. In reality, they were doing nothing to stop the marketing of vice, or to protect its victims.

Collaboration between the authorities and the underworld was blatant and systematic. The police notified the owners of brothels, gambling dens, and blind pigs before staging a raid. Arriving at the scene, they made no attempt to identify the real owner; instead, a minor employee was allowed to volunteer for arrest, plead guilty, pay a small fine, and immediately return to work. (Prostitutes who served this function in brothels were called "straw women.") Serving as a stand-in became a kind of underworld career: some stand-ins amassed hundreds of convictions without ever going to jail. The underworld always posted their bail and paid their fines. When customers were inadvertantly caught in a raid, police accepted bail for them on the spot and almost never embarrassed them with a court appearance. Found-ins were never fingerprinted or photographed. Roulette wheels, telephones, and other equipment essential to the operations were never confiscated. And business was rarely interrupted for more than a few minutes.

When a judge ordered that a gambling den or brothel be padlocked, police graciously slapped locks on side entrances, closets, bedrooms, even fake doors nailed to walls just for this purpose. When a real entrance was padlocked, police conveniently overlooked the fact that another adjacent door led to the same vice. The owners of brothels and gambling dens showed their appreciation by routinely changing the street numbers above their doors to avoid embarrassing the police with a long list of raids at the same address.

While all this was going on in clear public view, city hall was boasting to the press and public that the police were raiding and closing down hundreds of illegal establishments. In fact, city hall was channelling one-hundred-dollar-a-month bribes to journalists to persuade them to overlook the obvious, and issuing permits for snack bars at horse-betting parlours. No one was fooled by the elaborate charade, and many were content to see it continue.

Previous attempts to curtail Montreal's vice and nightlife had produced no lasting results. In 1941, for example, the provincial Liberal government which replaced Duplessis's Union nationale for one term during the Second World War restricted the number of liquor permits available in Montreal; issuing these permits was a provincial jurisdiction. The city's drinkers, however, were hardly inconvenienced. Some bars and nightclubs were forced to close, but business continued uninterrupted at the underworld's blind pigs. It was the musicians and other nightclub employees who suffered most from this attempt at reform: the Clef Club saw ten of its twenty member musicians thrown out of work due to the tighter liquor laws.[7] The closure of Montreal's brothels during the last year of the war, a measure taken only at the insistence of the armed forces, was equally ineffective. City hall and the police continued to tolerate all other forms of organized vice, from gambling and bootlegging to narcotics trafficking and extortion. When the war ended in 1945, the brothels reopened, the nightclubs blossomed, and the golden era of jazz and show biz began.

The bubble, however, was about to burst. Throughout the war, a quiet young lawyer named Pacifique Roy Plante had been earning his living as an obscure city attorney, helping to prepare prosecution cases for morality trials. Detecting a pattern of police complicity in vice rackets, "Pax" Plante appealed to the city's police chief to let him unofficially run the morality squad. The chief—already under pressure to open an inquiry into a recent gangland slaying, and planning to retire soon anyway—agreed. It was 1945. The war had just ended, and public displeasure with vice was mounting, fueled in part by the sudden reappearance of brothels. Under Plante's unofficial leadership—in title he was still only a legal advisor to the police and prosecutors—the morality squad swept down on brothels, bookmaking operations, and even church bingo games.

Plante's biggest coup brought the notorious Harry Ship to justice: the city's richest gangster and the owner of both the Tic-Toc nightclub and the Mount Royal Bridge Club was sent to prison for six months. The public clamour for a thorough housecleaning mounted. In 1946, religious groups presented a petition demanding a public inquiry into organized crime and corruption. A new police chief was appointed, and Plante was made his assistant, legalizing the power he in fact already exercised. The raids and prosecutions continued, but tensions grew between Plante and the new chief. Eight months later Plante was fired without warning, ostensibly for insubordination; in fact, he had refused to censure a fellow police officer on false charges.

Disillusioned, Plante floundered, looking for a new direction and flirting briefly with the idea of entering politics. Le Devoir, the city's most respected French-language newspaper, persuaded him to collaborate with journalist Gérard Pelletier in writing a series of articles exposing police complicity in organized crime. To fend off any lawsuits that might arise in connection with the articles, Le Devoir hired a young lawyer named Jean Drapeau. Plante's revelations were published over three months during the winter of 1949-50. Public outrage mounted with each article. When the series was published later as a book, it quickly sold out.[8]

Largely in response to the series in Le Devoir, a popular reform movement calling itself the Montreal Public Morality Committee was formed in 1950. The group hired Plante and Drapeau to present a massive legal petition to Quebec Superior Court demanding a public inquiry into organized crime and corruption. Faced with thousands of allegations against sixty-two members of the Montreal city council and police force, and offered a list of more than one thousand potential witnesses, the court promptly ordered an inquiry.

The judge appointed to head the commission was Justice François Caron, a dynamic man who had gained a reputation for rooting out corruption as head of a similar investigation in Hull. Caron swung quickly into action: he suspended officials under suspicion, including Albert Langlois, the police chief who had fired Plante; and he hired Drapeau and Plante as his special assistants, in effect making them co-prosecutors. Both lawyers were given police protection.

Caron took two-and-a-half years, including ten months of public hearings, to complete his investigation. Yet despite the pressure he brought to bear on police and city hall, Montreal remained wide open. Many brothels were temporarily closed, but barbotte games simply moved to the suburbs, out of the grasp of city police. Bars and night-clubs continued to ignore legal closing hours. The underworld's empire was not fundamentally shaken. Moreover, thanks to an even tougher inquiry into organized crime being conducted simultaneously by the U.S. Senate, hundreds of gangsters moved clandestinely from the United States into Montreal. Among them was Carmen Galente, right-hand man to the leader of one of the largest Mafia families in the United States. He arrived in Montreal a few months after Caron wound up his inquiry in the spring of 1953.

The wait began. Caron was faced with the awesome task of sifting through four thousand files, one thousand exhibits, and the testimony of almost four hundred witnesses. He worked in solitude for eighteen months. Finally, on 8 October 1954, Caron entered a crowded Montreal courtroom and delivered a judgement that took him four-and-a-half hours to read. It was a scathing indictment of the police and city hall. "What emerged," summarized one journalist, "was a picture of mink-coated, $30,000-a-year bawdy-house madams driving Cadillacs, gambling joints raking in fortunes under the eyes of corrupt police officers, and city councillors pretending they knew nothing about conditions that were common knowledge."[9]

Caron's judgement ordered that Chief Langlois and nineteen other police officers be fired. The politicians, however, were left at the mercy of the electorate. It was seventeen days before the city elections. On the eve of Caron's historic reading of the judgement, one of his special assistants assembled the press and declared he was running for mayor.

Pacifique "Pax" Plante (left) and Jean Drapeau assisted Justice François Caron in investigating organized crime and corruption in Montreal. Public outrage over the commission's findings swept Drapeau into power as the city's mayor. *Public Archives of Canada, PA-144559.*

Drapeau claimed the backing of a new reform movement called the Civic Action League, which had been quietly preparing an assault on city hall. The man who had helped to expose vice and corruption in Montreal was vowing to clean it up.

Drapeau took office in November 1954. Less than two weeks later, a union battle which had inflicted heavy damage on the nightclub industry in Montreal came to an end. The battle had been raging since the beginning of the year. The American Federation of Musicians (AFM) had been trying to force nightclub show acts to abandon the American Guild of Variety Artists (AGVA) and become auxiliary members of the musicians' union. In this way, the AFM hoped to attain full control over nightclub entertainment. To pursue this goal, the union had instructed its musicians not to play for nightclub performers who didn't hold AFM cards. Caught in the middle, the nightclubs had been forced to cancel shows where acts wouldn't join the AFM. Some clubs had simply closed their doors. Others had hired name bands from the United States to perform as feature attractions. Still others had reduced the size of their house bands in an effort to cut expenses.

Ultimately, nothing was achieved by the battle between the two American unions, which had been fought largely in Canada. A truce was called; the unions agreed to resume the status quo and refrain from raiding each other's memberships; the nightclubs were free to resume featuring stage shows. But club owners were bitter, and wary. Their business had been badly hurt by the ten-month battle.[10] Now Montreal's new mayor was beating at their door.

Prostitution, gambling, and corruption were the enemies Drapeau had sworn to eradicate, but only the naive could have believed that Montreal's nightclubs would be untouched by his cleanup campaign. Common wisdom linked many of them to the underworld, and in the public's eye nightclubs were both symbols of, and gateways to, the racy world of vice. Drapeau claimed he had no desire to kill Montreal nightlife; he only wanted to see the nightclubs operating within the law.[11] His first goal was to prevent prostitutes from working out of the city's bars and nightclubs. Soon after Drapeau took office, the word went out to club owners to evict the prostitutes or face police action.[12] The warning was obeyed: by the end of November, there were hardly any prostitutes to be found in Montreal bars and clubs. As the prostitutes left, so did the business they attracted.

Drapeau turned his attention next to gambling. For this assault he needed strong police action. The biggest obstacle was Albert Langlois. The police chief had responded to Justice Caron's firing order by immediately lodging an appeal with Quebec Superior Court against Caron's judgement. As a result, Langlois could not be fired until the court heard his appeal. He could, however, be suspended a second time. One of Drapeau's first acts in office was to do just that. Langlois's assistant, Tom Leggett, became acting police chief pending the outcome of Langlois's appeal. The move left Leggett's office vacant. Drapeau filled it with Plante, appointing him assistant chief of police in charge of morality. The two lawyers quickly went on the attack.

Montreal police raid a gambling establishment at 1236 Crescent Street on 10 September 1955. Such spectacular raids were part of Mayor Jean Drapeau's campaign to drive vice out of the city. *Photo by M. T. Johnson, Montreal Star Collection, Public Archives of Canada, PA-167071.*

City hall stopped paying bribes to journalists[13] and the police department began giving reporters, not the criminals, advance warning of its raids. The vice squad staged spectacular raids on barbotte joints, horse-betting parlours, slot machine locations, and brothels. Criminals and found-ins were arrested and brought to trial; several American gangsters were deported. Drapeau banned lotteries, even for charitable causes.[14] By early January 1955, there was almost no gambling to be found in Montreal.[15] A few weeks later the city and provincial police forces launched a joint campaign of raids on blind pigs.[16]

The impact of this climate on the nightclubs was devastating. With all the newspaper coverage of raids and arrests, people were afraid to go out to nightclubs for fear of being caught up in a raid for prostitutes or gangsters. By mid-February 1955, business was so poor that nightclubs all over the city were cancelling late shows and closing as early as 1:00 a.m.[17] What role the police had in this move to early closing is not known. They may have begun enforcing the provincial law on closing hours which the bars and nightclubs had been openly ignoring for years; or the fear of attracting police attention, combined with poor business, may have been enough to convince club owners to close their doors early. Regardless, the impact was the same: as nightclub profits fell, owners cut costs by reducing their entertainment expenses. Musicians worked less, and earned less; some lost their jobs. Saxophonist Boogie Gaudet:

> After Drapeau came to power, the clubs began closing earlier. Instead of doing three shows a night, we were doing two. We weren't doing any Sundays. And our salary was cut by maybe two-thirds. I remember weeks when we were getting fifty dollars each a week.

Pianist Art Roberts was working at the American Spaghetti House on St. Catherine Street near The Main when the axe fell:

> Our hours were from midnight to 5:00 am. A lot of musicians used to come in after work to eat, have a few beers, and listen to the band. We were working there for a couple of months and it was going really well, and then, after Jean Drapeau got into power, the strict closing times were enforced all over town. And that was it. We stayed open one more week, working from nine till two, but from nine to midnight it was pretty quiet. Then the boss came up to us and said, "I'm sorry, we're out of business."

The nightclubs were feeling the pressure from other quarters besides the police. The underworld was in turmoil. Drapeau's cleanup campaign was slashing criminal revenues and creating power vacuums as prominent gangsters were arrested, deported, or driven into hiding. Fighting escalated among rival gangs. The underworld's battles took place largely out of public view, but in a single week during the summer of 1955, gangs wrecked both the Montmartre and the All-American nightclubs.[18] Meanwhile, the underworld continued to extort regular payments from nightclubs not directly owned or controlled by the gangsters.

A third party—the provincial government—controlled the key to a nightclub's survival: its liquor permit. Montreal city hall had declared war on corruption, but in Quebec City the Duplessis government was still wallowing in it. Club owners were expected to contribute to the Union nationale's coffers in return for the privilege of keeping their liquor permits. The degree to which Montreal club owners continued to be at the mercy of Duplessis after Drapeau came to power is demonstrated by the fate of Rockhead's Paradise, the city's most famous black nightclub.

Rufus Rockhead had first run afoul of Duplessis in 1937, a year after the premier came to power in Quebec. "All the licences for Negroes, Jews, and Chinese were cancelled at the same time," Rockhead told a journalist more than thirty-five years later. "Ah, he gave us hell, Duplessis, but I got my liquor licence back eventually. You know Quebec: I got somebody to start working on it, know what I mean? A friend of the liquor commissioner's."[19]

It wasn't as easy the next time. Early one morning in the spring of 1953,[20] police swooped into Rockhead's Paradise, confiscated ten thousand dollars worth of liquor stocks, and padlocked the doors of the nightclub and its street-level cocktail lounge. Once again Rockhead found his liquor permit revoked, ostensibly for serving alcohol after the legal closing hour. That much was true, but Drapeau had yet to be elected and every other bar and club in Montreal was flaunting the law with equal abandon.

Rockhead later claimed the action was triggered by his refusal to acquiesce to a demand from someone in a position of power in Quebec City—he never disclosed who—for a forty thousand dollar payoff. "I offered them twenty thousand dollars, but they said no."[21] Rockhead made fifteen trips to Quebec City to try to get his liquor permit back, but to no avail; according to his son Kenny, on one occasion Rockhead took fifty thousand dollars in cash to a Duplessis aide, but the gift was refused.[22]

The reason for the closure of Rockhead's Paradise will probably always remain a mystery. One clue, however, may be the fact that Rockhead was an open supporter of the provincial Liberal party. Nineteen fifty-two was an election year in Quebec. Frank Hanley—an independent member of the legislature who was close to Duplessis, and a long-serving city councillor—held the riding of Saint-Anne's in which Rockhead's Paradise was situated. In the adjacent riding of Saint-Henri—where the club owner had lived until 1950 and where he continued to meet his contact for political pay-offs—the Union nationale lost to the Liberals. Moreover, the defeated Union nationale incumbent was no ordinary backbencher, but a minister without portfolio in Duplessis's cabinet.[23]

Whatever the reason for Duplessis's tough action, Rockhead was left with serious financial problems. Though Duplessis probably believed he was being lenient with Rockhead in allowing the tavern attached to his nightclub to remain open, the closure of the club and cocktail lounge for nine years coincided with the peak of show biz in Montreal. Rockhead claimed he never recovered the ten thousand dollars worth of liquor confiscated by the police. To make matters worse, he had recently invested one hundred thousand dollars in renovating the club and installing air conditioning. There were bills and bank loans waiting to be paid; the building still had to be heated and the property taxes paid. "I sold three properties—a big apartment building and two duplexes—to keep the place going," he said.[24]

For the rest of the decade, Rockhead struggled to hold on to his nightclub. He managed to survive, on the earnings from his tavern and the occasional rental of the club for a private social function. Then, in quick succession, Duplessis and his successor Paul Sauvé died, and the Union nationale lost power to the Liberals in June 1960. Two years later Rockhead got his liquor permit back. By then, however, the kind of show biz that Rockhead's Paradise had been famous for was on the wane in Montreal. The St. Antoine district was suffering from urban decay, and the once-famous corner of Mountain and St. Antoine was no longer a popular centre for nightlife. Rockhead, by now in his sixties, handed management of the club over to his son Kenny, who began importing soul, Motown, and rhythm and blues bands from the United States in an attempt to capture a younger clientele. The new entertainment policy revived the club, but Rockhead's Paradise never regained the glory it had known in the years before its enforced silence.

In 1975, Rufus Rockhead suffered a stroke. Two years later Kenny sold the club to Roué Doudou Boicel, a younger black entrepreneur who irreverently tore the neon Paradise sign off the outside wall and moved his popular Rising Sun jazz and blues club from its original home on St. Catherine Street West down to the corner.[25] But Boicel had misjudged: the recycled Paradise ran up heavy debts, and the Rising Sun eventually moved back to its original uptown location. Rockhead himself didn't live long enough to see the famous red-brick building abandoned: he died in a war veteran's hospital in 1981, widely mourned by the city's black community and the musicians who spoke proudly of having worked in his club.[26]

Drapeau's cleanup campaign was only in its second year when it received a stunning blow from an unexpected quarter. Quebec Superior Court overturned Caron's decision that Montreal's police chief had been corrupt—and ordered Langlois reinstated in his old job. Drapeau had no choice but to comply. Plante relinquished his post at the head of the morality squad, from where he had effectively been running the force, and went to work codifying bylaws for the city's legal department, severing his ties with the police for the last time.

The opponents of Drapeau's cleanup campaign were elated. With Plante off their backs, the gangsters regrouped. Duplessis, at the peak of his power, masterminded a huge opposition campaign to unseat Drapeau at the next municipal election. Sarto Fournier was put up to run for mayor: his speeches promised an "open but honest" city administration. As voting day drew closer, musicians and other nightclub employees received a solemn lecture from representatives of the underworld: if they reelected Drapeau, they'd never work again.

In October 1957, Fournier defeated Drapeau. Montreal was open again for vice.

> I got one rule: I'm hired to play. Because if I don't play, I don't live. And I don't see anything when I play, except those keys.

Pianist Billy Horne's attitude was typical of the pragmatic philosophy of musicians who made their living in Montreal's nightclubs during the 1950s. Economic necessity brought them into close association with the underworld and the corruption it engendered. Relaxing between shows in the kitchen, the musicians observed money changing hands. They saw bottles being passed out the back door to uniformed policemen lounging in patrol cars in the alley. They witnessed the intimidation and the beatings by which underworld discipline was maintained. And from their vantage point on stage, they watched as customers were cheated, robbed, and sometimes beaten. On occasion they even witnessed the business meetings of the underworld bosses, held at clubs during the afternoons while the musicians rehearsed the shows. Through it all, the musicians remained silent. Their livelihood, if not their lives, depended on an outward show of indifference. Saxophonist Vern Isaac:

> You sit on the stage, man, and you see things go on that you think should not go on, but people pay it no mind. You see girls picking pockets. Or they smash somebody's brains in. You don't see nothin'. You just sit there, playing.

Drummer Dennis Brown:

> You were there to play music. So you came in to work, you played, you minded your business, you said *ciao*, and you left. You weren't there to interfere with anything.

Violence in the nightclubs became increasingly commonplace as the decade progressed. The Caron probe and the Drapeau cleanup campaign had kicked sand into the well-oiled machinery of vice, upsetting the balance of power and destabilizing the underworld economy. When Plante was ousted and Drapeau defeated, the city underwent another tumultuous upheaval. The underworld and its collaborators scrambled to fill the vacuum. Territories were redefined. Dormant rackets were revived. And muscles were again flexed, with savagery. If the musicians feigned indifference to the violence they witnessed, the customers, they noticed, were equally reluctant to speak out. Drummer Bill Martucci:

196

I saw some pretty bad fights. People would sit around and not do anything, because they knew it usually involved gangs. I saw one cat, they beat him, and he was on the floor; then they picked up one of those metal tavern tables and started clobbering him with it—and nobody moved, including myself. I said, "For Chrissakes, they're gonna kill the guy!" The phone's right there, you know, but nobody made a move. You make a move to help, and it's your ass. That happened right in the clubs, in front of hundreds of people.

Vern Isaac:

I played for [the gangsters] at a place we called the Bucket of Blood. That wasn't the real name of the club, but that's what we called it. And they killed one guy while I was sitting there at a table. Just shot him—bang!—and swept up the blood. He disappeared.

For as long as the underworld had ruled the night, the standing order for musicians working in Montreal clubs had always been: if trouble breaks out, play louder. Only when shots were fired did the musicians take cover. But as soon as the fighting ended, they were expected to be back at their instruments, restarting the show, and distracting the customers. The scene that bassist Hal Gaylor witnessed at the Chez Paree a year or two before Drapeau came to power was typical of the musicians' working environment:

I remember one night [singer] Connie Boswell was on the bandstand. I was working in the relief band, so I was hanging out on the balcony watching the show. I saw a ruckus and I saw this guy go down. And then I saw people screaming and jumping and tables and chairs going, and then I realized somebody had been stabbed. There was about a thirty-second cleanup. That was all it took, because the people knew what to do. They got the guy away, they got rid of the knife, they got the blood cleaned up, and they got the body out and into a cab—and it didn't stop the show!

Most of the underworld leaders were known to the musicians, at least by sight. When one showed up at a club, usually late at night with an entourage of bodyguards and women in tow, the musicians were prepared for anything to happen. Gaylor continued:

Frank Petrulla would come into the Chez Paree, and in one breast pocket would be the fifties, in the other the hundreds. He'd give Nick the doorman a hundred, and Nick would make sure nobody else came in. He'd pass the word, the cheques would come, and people would be asked to leave. And then he would invite the show, the quartet, four waiters, and three busboys to stay. "Open your champagne and put your steaks on!" He'd pay for everything. He would dance by the band, and if he didn't drop a hundred dollars every time he came by it was unusual. We would walk out of there with sometimes six to eight hundred dollars, in one hundred dollar bills. Two hundred dollars apiece! That happened often, and not only at the Chez Paree. Of course, we'd play whatever he wanted.

Another local underworld boss had a reputation for erratic behaviour if he became sentimental and drunk at the same time. Pianist Keith White remembered the night the gangster came into the Chez Paree late, slapped a hundred dollars on the piano, and began requesting tunes. As the man became progressively drunker and his requests increasingly sentimental, the musicians began eyeing the exits. When the first tears began to roll down the gangster's cheeks, the musicians grabbed their instruments and fled to a taxi which the head waiter had kept waiting for them in the alley. Reporting for work the next night, the musicians learned that the expected had indeed happened: the gangster, his eyes filled with tears, had peppered the club with bullets.

However distasteful the musicians may have found the power and methods of the gangsters, they realized that with the underworld in control, nightlife in Montreal was thriving. "You can say what you like," pianist Joe Sealy summed up, "but there was a lot of work for everybody when they were running things."

Bandleader Maury Kaye concurred:

The town was generating money like a printing machine. It was very healthy in terms of economy, commerce. I don't know about spiritually or morally, but who cares? Everybody was happy and everybody was making a lot of bread, and nobody was hurting. The fifties was a very healthy time in the city.

A job in a gangster-controlled nightclub had real advantages for the musicians, not the least of which was the security of knowing they'd be paid at the end of the week. Pianist Stan Patrick:

A lot of the legit club owners had excuses, like "We don't got any bread, it was a bad week." But with [the gangsters] it was *cash*.

The musicians also felt safe with the gangsters around, despite the violence of their environment. Art Roberts:

The mob looked after the musicians. They took care of them. There was one club on St. Catherine Street that was Mafia-controlled. A musician was working there and was standing outside. An irate customer thought he'd gotten overcharged and he was berating the musician on the street, saying, "You're all a bunch of crooks!" He was gonna beat the musician up. The doorman saw it, went over, sent the musician inside. The club owner said to him, "You're not the crooks, we're the crooks. Don't worry. We take care of you."

With Drapeau out of power, the political climate in Montreal favoured a resurgence of the nightclub industry and a return to full employment for the musicians. The clubs and musicians certainly fared better after Drapeau's defeat, but other forces had in the meantime begun undermining the market for the traditional, multi-act stage shows which jazz musicians had relied upon to earn their livings. New technology was transforming the entertainment industry, and a new youth music was fast becoming popular. By the end of the 1950s, musicians would be caught up in a dizzying evolution of the entertainment industry over which they had little control—and which would ultimately leave many of them by the wayside.

Television was probably the single, most destructive agent in the collapse of the traditional nightclub entertainment package of singer, dancer, comedian, and acrobat—and the subsequent rise of strip shows. Television became widely available at the beginning of the 1950s. By the end of 1954 there were more than three hundred thousand TV sets in Quebec alone, and the number was growing by almost thirty thousand a month.[27] People were no longer obliged to leave home to be entertained visually. Television variety shows such as Ed Sullivan's—available in Montreal—featured the same kinds of performers, and often the very same acts, that appeared in nightclubs and vaudeville theatres. For couples moving to the suburbs, television offered a novel alternative to the cost and inconvenience of going out for a night's entertainment. As the new medium gained steadily in popularity, attendance, especially by couples, declined at live entertainment venues.

The impact of television was readily apparent at Montreal's vaudeville theatres, which had continued to draw large audiences into the early 1950s with a popular entertainment package of feature films and live stage shows, mainly by Quebec performers. Television decimated the vaudeville industry. A weekly TV series called "Les Plouffes," launched in 1953 by the French network of the Canadian Broadcasting Corporation, is credited with singlehandedly draining vaudeville halls on Wednesday nights, when it was broadcast.[28] In the same year, the city's largest vaudeville theatre, formerly called the Gayety, reopened as Radio-Cité with a cast of thirty performers and a large pit orchestra.

Almost thirty-five hundred people packed the St. Catherine Street theatre every day at the beginning. Two years later it closed, drained of an audience by television.[29]

At the same time that television was luring people away from the nightclubs and vaudeville theatres, it was pushing up the cost of staging a show. Once performers had tasted the prestige and high pay that accompanied a television appearance, they began demanding more money for live appearances as well. Those who were receiving regular calls to perform on television became reluctant to accept club or theatre bookings away from the main urban broadcasting centres, for fear of missing a call; thus top American entertainers who had once appeared regularly in Montreal as part of a tour of the northeastern club circuit preferred to remain in New York City. Ultimately, television productions became too grandiose and costly for the smaller clubs and theatres to emulate: the kinds of shows that had once been commonplace in nightclubs across the continent could thereafter be seen live in only a few large hotels and concert halls.

The other major challenge to traditional nightclub shows came from a new style of popular music whose impact upon the entertainment world proved to be as tumultuous, and enduring, as jazz's had been four decades before. Rock music burst into the public's consciousness in 1955 with a hit recording by Bill Haley and the Comets called "Rock Around the Clock." The following year, Elvis Presley became a household name, in part due to his television appearances. Like the white jazz of the 1910s and 1920s, rock brought with it new styles of social dancing, a new youth aesthetic, and a new kind of band. Rock's unrelenting, heavy-handed beat spurned the subtlety and sophistication of the swing and Latin rhythms which had until then been the basis of nightclub and dance-hall music, not to mention jazz. Equally devastating to the nightclub musicians was rock's adulation of the electric guitar, loudly amplified. The older musicians scorned the new music's simplicity and crudeness but were powerless to arrest its onslaught. The nightclubs, already losing audiences to television, began to rethink their entertainment policies. Rock acts began appearing in some nightclub revues as early as 1954. By 1956 the Esquire had abandoned traditional shows entirely and begun importing rock bands from the United States. By 1960, rock audiences were filling the Forum to see such stars of the new music as Chubby Checker, Bo Diddley, and Bobby Rydell. Those clubs which didn't go over to rock reduced the size of their shows and bands, and looked to blatant sexual exhibition to recover lost clientele.

The rise of strip shows during the 1950s was not a sudden aberration in show biz, but rather the culmination of decades of erotic entertainment in nightclubs. What changed was the emphasis: from partial nudity and provocative dancing as one act in an evening of varied entertainment, to blatant exhibition and provocation as the main attraction. In the first three decades of the century, burlesque theatres and cabarets had used chorus lines of high-kicking young women to fire up audiences. During the 1920s and 1930s, many small clubs, including the Terminal, employed show girls whose job included "working the tables." At a designated point in the show, while the band improvised, members of the audience would be invited to place folded bills overhanging the edge of their tables. The women would dance from customer to customer, lifting their skirts and pinching the money off the tables between their upper thighs. By the 1940s nightclub shows included elaborately costumed "shake dancers" who offered audiences glimpses of thigh and breast between swirls of plumes, tassels, and veils.

Well into the 1950s, the women who entertained on nightclub stages understood, if only intuitively, that an appeal to their audience's imagination was more powerful than an appeal solely to their eyes. Even as the acts became more *risqué*, they remained strongly based on the skills of the women as dancers, and strongly spiced with humour. For this reason, the routines of the shake dancers and other erotic acts were rarely perceived as offensive by women, who continued to make up a significant proportion of nightclub audiences. But even as traditional show biz was at its height in Montreal, a subtle, at first imperceptible, change was taking place in the role of nudity on stage. Appeals to the eyes of the audience began to replace appeals to its imagination; costumes became more important than talent, the body more important than the dance. A new word was coined to describe the new breed of show dancer: "exotic."

By the end of the 1950s, nightclubs were hiring exotic dancers to strip down to "pasties" and "G-strings" as an intermission act between the feature show. The role of the relief bands changed as a result, from providing light background music during intermission, to playing whatever music the dancers requested for their act. Some of the erotic dancers remained worthy of the show business tradition. Dennis Brown:

> These were the dancers that came up from New York City with three thousand dollars worth of costumes for one show—some of the big names out of Strip City and Minsky's. The *real* dancers. But then there were the ones who, you know—they couldn't get a job at Woolworth's and thought stripping was glamorous. *That* was another category: the "walkers" we called them.

With television offering inexpensive, family entertainment at home, and with blatant exhibition of the female body becoming an increasingly predominant ingredient of nightclub shows, the composition of nightclub audiences underwent a noticeable change. Women stayed away, and unaccompanied men became the majority.[30] Strippers were seemingly an effective, and inexpensive, way of attracting them. The strippers commanded less prestige, and so demanded less money, than leading stage performers, who were raising their fees under the influence of television. Equally important to nightclubs trying to cut back on expenses, the strippers demanded less sophisticated music—and required smaller bands.

The deathknell for traditional, multi-act show biz had sounded. By the early 1960s, clubs were switching exclusively to strip shows. The Chez Paree—which had previously featured some of the biggest names in show biz—became the model of the new breed of entertainment factory: it worked several dozen strippers on two floors, providing nonstop striptease from early afternoon through to the following morning. Many of the strippers were doubling as prostitutes under the control of the gangsters.

The standard band employed to play behind strippers in Montreal nightclubs was a trio—tenor saxophone or trumpet, piano, and drums. Club owners still weren't hiring bass players; if they had money to spend on another musician, they wanted another horn on stage. The piano players of the day, like many of their predecessors in show biz, developed strong left-hand techniques playing forceful stride or boogie-woogie figures, or sometimes a walking, single-note bass line in imitation of the absent bass. "I had a helluva left hand when I was working in Montreal," pianist Joe Sealy recalled twenty years later at his home in Toronto. "Most of the commercial gigs I did had no bass player. *I* was the bass player, walking with my left hand."

The strippers made few musical demands upon the musicians. They wanted only a steady, shuffling rhythm, a gutteral running commentary on their sex appeal from the horns, and plenty of punches from the drummer to highlight their bumps and grinds. A few of the big-name strippers imported from the United States brought written music with them for the band; but, as Sealy parodied, most of the girls would simply say, "You play 'Harlem Nocturne,' and when I take off my top you play 'Night Train.'" Those two tunes, together with "Honky Tonk," were staples of the strip-band repertoire, and the musicians played them again and again in the course of a day's work.

Bored by the limited musical requirements of the strippers and the absence of any challenging arrangements to play, the musicians retreated into jazz and used the opportunity to improvise at length. For several winters during the late 1950s, Boogie Gaudet led a quartet of jazz musicians as a relief band in Montreal strip clubs:

202

By November 1960, the Chez Paree had abandoned traditional nightclub entertainment in favour of non-stop strip shows. *Photo by Gar Lunny, Montreal Star Collection, Public Archives of Canada, PA-167070.*

When we played for strippers at Vic's or at the French Casino, they'd ask us to do blues. So maybe we'd do "Honky Tonk" or "Night Train," which were sort of jazz/rhythm and blues tunes. They'd always leave it up to us: "Play whatever you want as long as we know when you start and when you stop." So I would tell the girls, "The boss told me *you* have to do four minutes and *you* have to do eight minutes...."—because each girl didn't get paid the same: the girls that closed the show did more tunes and earned more money than the girls that opened the show. So I'd tell 'em, "As long as we're blowing, then keep dancing. When you hear the theme again, you know it's your last chorus." If one girl wanted a cha-cha, we'd do a tune in a cha-cha beat, but we'd blow to our heart's content between the theme and the last chorus. The drummer would have to follow her. If she'd do bumps and grinds, he'd have to catch her. And some of them would want drum solos.... We had a tight jazz group because we'd also play jam sessions together, and maybe a jazz concert thing on our days off. But we worked long hours. At Vic's, we started at eight o'clock and went right till five o'clock in the morning [alternating

203

with a show band]. I was clearing about $165 a week as leader;
the guys were getting about $110.

At some nightclubs, bands were allowed to play a tune of their own
choice alone on stage between each stripper. Dennis Brown remembered
one such job at the New Orleans in the mid-1950s, when strippers were
just beginning to infiltrate the nightclubs:

> At the New Orleans it was one dancer, one band number, one
> dancer, one band number. Now the dancers were mostly jazz and
> Afro-Cuban dancers, so we were still playing jazz, but with their
> requirements. The next number we could play whatever we
> wanted. And this was six or seven nights a week. You really felt
> like a pro, you were in shape, and we could play some fast tem-
> pos—"Air Mail Special," "Cherokee," "Billy's Bounce," "Move."
> And the dancers often wanted things like "Night in Tunisia" or
> "Manteca."

Such enthusiasm for work at a strip club became increasingly rare as
the years passed and the formula coagulated through constant repetition. Though the work paid well, was in plentiful supply, and allowed
the musicians to improvise at length within the confines of the strippers'
requirements, the biggest challenge was fending off boredom and cyni-
cism. The strip clubs—especially "the cheap places where," as drummer
Norm Villeneuve put it, "you get the ten, fifteen dollar broads walking
around the stage, looking like they're ready to retire"—had neither the
warmth, the glamour, nor the prestige of the nightclubs in the era of
quality show biz. They were hardly the atmosphere in which to create
joyous and sophisticated music; in fact, the music seemed hardly to matter any more. From there it was only a short step in the minds of club
owners to doing away with the musicians altogether.

INTERLUDE THREE

Roland Lavallée Speaks

The door opens after the second ring. Roland Lavallée coughs a welcome from the top of the stairs, shirtless. The pianist, a forty-year veteran of Montreal nightclubs, has just risen, late, after a night's work. The television is glowing in the kitchen. He stuffs tea bags into a beaker of boiling water, lights a cigarette, and pulls on a shirt. Outside, the winter daylight is fading.

I witnessed some things.... The Chez Paree was plush. Sixty girls dancing there. An elevator to go to the second floor. Bouncers all over the place. They were making their own champagne in the back—how? They used to take an empty champagne bottle, fill it up with ginger ale, put in a colouring to make it rosy, and there was a kid in the back, just filing down the corks so they'd fit; and they'd recap 'em.

There was no tables for two, so if you're a businessman sitting there with another guy, two chicks come over and sit with you and start to talk with you. And the bucket of champagne arrives—and you didn't offer them anything! It's just ginger ale. The waiter pours the drink for the two girls and puts the bottle in the bucket on the floor. When the girl bends down to pour herself another drink, she fills her glass and pours the rest in the bucket. So out of a big bottle they had maybe two little glasses each, because these girls were sick of drinking ginger ale. And then the waiter brings you the bill.

And you'd say, "I don't know these girls. I didn't offer them any champagne."

"Oh, well, sir, they're sitting with you. I assumed they were your girl friends."

"No, I refuse to pay."

"Well, if you don't want to pay the bill you'd better go upstairs and talk to the manager in his office."

You'd go. And they'd beat the shit out of you until you were unconscious. They'd rob you of your rings, your watch, your wallet, everything. And then the *police* would take you into the lane, put you in the car, and dump you four or five blocks away. That I saw every week, year 'round....

There were four bands working at the Chez Paree. Sixty dancers. They'd give you sex, anything you wanted, right at the table. All the girls were hookers. That club was a beauty. They never stopped dancing, four bands rolling, two upstairs, two down, and the Black Magic Room next door—that's where we played jazz. In the club we played for strippers. It was rough, but the musicians were so respected by the Mafia. The best people to work for were the guys in the racket....

I saw fights, killings. I once saw a guy with a knife a foot long. They're arguing at the table next to my piano, a little, white baby grand piano. All of a sudden this guy stands up and—phuuuuuutt!—right through his body with the knife, and the blood flew onto my piano. I had to clean it off the piano. And then, ten minutes later you don't hear nothing about it. The police don't come, nothing.

Every policeman in the city was on the payroll. We used to see them come and get their pay every Saturday. The chief of each station was getting about four hundred dollars a week, the rest were getting anywhere from one to three hundred. They paid off the vice squad investigators to let the girls operate. They'd come and arrest two girls, take them in front of the judge, they'd plead guilty, and the police would bring them right back to the club. It was just to make it look like they were doing their job....

Private parties? I played for the Mafia's private parties, and for the law's private parties—the judges and the lawyers. It was just piano alone, usually in a small hotel, maybe in St. Thérèse. They'd tell me: "Be blind, be deaf, and don't talk." And for one night they'd pay me one hundred and fifty to two hundred dollars. And all I had to do was play a little background music while they were drinking and switching wives. They used to have key parties. All the wives would put the room keys in a basket and pull one out. Then they'd go up to the room and no matter what man was there they'd screw—these were the lawyers and the judges. With the Mafia, it was business. They'd talk business, strictly private, in rooms above the clubs....

When you'd hear a shot in a club, it would scare the hell out of everybody, because you never knew where the next shot would be from. You gotta duck, man, and get out fast.... Once I had a quartet at the Chez Paree and the boss says to me—he was very nervous—he says, "Roland, as soon as you've finished tonight, tell your boys to pack up your instruments and get out fast. Don't stall, because there'll be trouble tonight." So as soon as we finished, we got out. And I sat in my car across the street in a parking lot and waited. There was four police cars there, and about fifteen guys went inside the club. They were from the east-end

Roland Lavallée at the Algiers, circa 1950, with Al King (bass) and Ron Wetmore (tenor saxophone). *Photo courtesy of Roland Lavallée. John Gilmore Jazz History Collection, Concordia University Archives.*

Mafia. They demolished the place. Holes in the walls with axes. Smashed mirrors. Carpets ripped up. And I saw them walk out and say to the police, "OK, good night, everything's fine, good night boys." And *then* the police went in. The owners of the club had left by the back door. They didn't lay charges. It was a gang conflict. They rebuilt the club. We were off for about three weeks, but we still got paid. No problem. I'd go in every week and get my cheque. Then they opened up again, just like before.... Musicians, we were always protected. I don't know of one musician who was ever hurt. They used to tell us in advance, "Don't go on the bandstand now, you're through for the night, leave!" You don't ask questions, you just leave. The next day you find out what happened....

They paid the girls a basic salary, which was about a hundred and twenty-five dollars. That was as a supposed dancer. Now, she has to peddle her ass. At this time, they owned their own houses on MacKay Street, just for that purpose. The girls would pick up a customer, jump in a taxi, go to the rooms, do their business, and be back in an hour. Now, *half* of that money went to the club. She's told what to charge. And if she tries to lie or anything, she ends up with two broken legs, or in a cement block in the St. Lawrence. I knew some girls—twenty-two, twenty-five years old; I knew them well—they found them in the river. When Drapeau came to clean up the town, it was time! A human life meant nothing to those guys....

I voted for Drapeau. I didn't tell *them*! But I had just had a little baby and I said to myself, "I don't want him growing up in this type of world." Drapeau killed the town, in a way. But I still agree with what he did, because god knows where it would have led. There was murder. In one year, eleven men that I knew were murdered—bar men, guys in the Mafia, racketeers, guys that ran the prostitution. We knew them all, because they were with us every night.... For the night side of it, yes, I wish those days were still here. But it was too rough. And another thing—there was so many gambling joints, card games, barbotte games. Man, they were all over the place. So if you weren't careful you lost all the money you made. How many waiters do I know—good friends of mine—they made a fortune and ended up selling their suits for twenty, twenty-five bucks so they could go and gamble. Gambling, then, was twenty-four hours a day. Bread men, milk men, delivery men—they'd leave their truck at the door and spend ten to fifteen minutes, drop two dollars, ten dollars—by the end of their run they're broke! Many musicians got in debt. And those Shylocks, they used to lend you money at fifteen or twenty percent interest per *month*. So you paid the interest all the time, and there was no end to it. So you used to gamble more to try to pay off these cats, 'cause if you don't pay—[he slams his fist into the palm of his hand]—don't try to run away!....

Sometimes I tell my son stories. And he says, "Oh, Dad, it couldn't have been like that. No place in the world could be like that!" But it was. Ask any musician my age that was around....

Edited excerpts from interviews with Roland Lavallée in Montreal, 16 December, 1982 and 26 January 1983.

CHAPTER NINE:

The 1960s: End of an Era

St. Dominique above Sherbrooke, in 1961, was a narrow, easily over-looked street of working-class housing, a kind of back alley to the textile factories, supermarkets, and European import stores of bustling St. Lawrence Blvd. It lay at the threshold of a cosmopolitan neighbourhood of European immigrants and working-class Québécois. This was not a district of nightclubs and nightlife, but of front-yard vegetable gardens, taverns, poultry markets, and small convenience stores. In a third-floor loft above a St. Dominique Street garage, however, there was evidence that a cultural revolution was germinating. Young Québécois artists, intellectuals, and students gathered at night to discuss politics and art, to play chess, to write poetry, and to applaud the *chansonniers* among them. They wore berets and smoked French tobacco, badges of a newly awakened pride in their French heritage. They called their loft Le Mas, a word for a farm or house in the south of France.

The jazz musicians, too, congregated at Le Mas. They climbed the stairs late on Friday and Saturday nights after the *chansonniers* had finished performing. Some drove through the night from out-of-town engagements to reach the loft before the jam sessions ended. The horn players stood in line to solo. Through the fall and winter of 1961-62, Le Mas provided jazz musicians with a desperately needed place to meet and to create in Montreal. It also provided them, inadvertently, with their first sustained, intimate exposure to the intellectual, political, and cultural fervour that transformed Quebec society during the 1960s.

The decade began with two historic elections in the space of four months. Duplessis, Quebec's conservative patriarch, had died suddenly of a brain haemorrhage in the fall of 1959. His Union nationale empire quickly crumbled. In June 1960, Quebec voters turned out in huge numbers to elect a progressive and outward-looking Liberal government headed by a skilled orator named Jean Lesage. So profound was the modernization program which Lesage unleashed on the province's economy, education system, and culture that soon after he took office, journalists dubbed the new era dawning in Quebec the Quiet Revolution.

Under Lesage, the stranglehold of the Catholic church over the province was quickly broken, opening the doors to new ideas and a permissive morality. At the same time, nationalism flowered—not the parochial, reactionary nationalism of Duplessis's day which had stifled change, but a nationalism based in a radical rethinking of history and a radical reappraisal of social goals. Pride in the French language and French culture stimulated new links with France and an intellectual and cultural renaissance at home. Finally, political discontent over the economic exploitation of the province by English Canada and American companies coalesced into a movement for political independence that rapidly accelerated as the decade progressed.

Montreal was Quebec's metropolis, and it became the main stage for the manifestations of social and political change that swept the province. But other currents were buffeting the city as well. As the decade began, Montreal was enduring another crime wave under Mayor Sarto Fournier's "open but honest" administration. Vice was again rampant, and visible. The populace, realizing how fragile Drapeau's victory over organized crime and corruption had been, looked to him again for salvation. In October 1960, four months after Lesage came to power, Drapeau was reelected mayor of Montreal with two-thirds of the popular vote. This time, his reform team also captured two-thirds of the city council seats, ensuring Drapeau a strong political base from which to operate. The mayor would hold power uninterrupted until his retirement twenty-six years later.

Back at the helm, Drapeau immediately relaunched his cleanup campaign. He appointed a new police chief and sent the force out to close down the brothels, gambling dens, and blind pigs that had sprung up during his absence. He brought in a senior police officer from Scotland Yard and another from Paris to study the organization of Montreal's police force; based on their advice, sweeping changes were made to minimize corruption, including subdividing the morality squad into four sections with overlapping territories so that the sections policed each other as well as the city. At the same time, Lesage was reorganizing the provincial police force to root out endemic corruption there.[1]

The hardest blow to Montreal nightlife, however, was the city's decision to strictly enforce a law prohibiting the serving of alcohol after 2:00 a.m. Nightclubs were forced to close early; again the musicians suffered. The injury was not only monetary, however: no longer could the musicians meet and play jazz in the clubs after work. Early-closing drove Montreal's jazz musicians out of their traditional, late-night environment in search of a new milieu in which to create. They found it in the city's coffee-houses.[2]

American baritone saxophonist Pepper Adams performs as a guest soloist at the Little Vienna restaurant in 1960 or 1961, accompanied by Keith White (piano) and Stan Zadak (bass). *Courtesy of Keith White. John Gilmore Jazz History Collection, Concordia University Archives.*

Le Mas was one of the most active jazz coffee-houses in the city, but it was not the first on the scene. The idea of performing jazz in a small room without alcohol had first been explored by a Montreal restaurateur, even before the jazz community had needed an alternative to the nightclubs. The owner of the Little Vienna restaurant, one Mr. Nash, was a jazz fan. In November 1958 he began hiring a trio of local musicians to play jazz on weekends. The Little Vienna was ideally situated on Stanley Street in central Montreal, a few steps from the back door of Sir George Williams College. Student jazz societies were popular at universities and colleges in Montreal at the time, and Sir George Williams had the most active;[3] several younger jazz musicians, including pianists Joe Sealy and Stan Patrick, were studying there. The Little Vienna became a hang-out for members of the Sir George Williams jazz society. They faithfully attended the weekend sessions and frequently sat in with the house trio.

Most of the city's jazz musicians played at the Little Vienna at some time. The formula—no alcohol, modest prices for coffee and food, and some of the most exciting live jazz in the city—proved so successful that in March 1960 Nash began importing American jazz musicians to perform with the house trio. The fans and musicians revelled in the music of such guests as Jackie McLean, Pepper Adams, and J. R. Monterose. But Nash had overestimated the ability of his limited-capacity restaurant and weekends-only jazz policy to generate the money needed to pay for the imported musicians. In the spring of 1961 he abandoned live jazz entirely. By that time, however, Nash's idea had caught on at coffee-houses around the city.

Coffee-houses had first become popular in the United States during the 1950s. Informal and inexpensive, they sprang up around universities, serving as meeting places for students and performance centres for folk musicians. In Montreal, two coffee-houses began presenting jazz in December 1960, two months after Drapeau was reelected. Le Grenier, on Crescent Street, adopted a jazz policy on Monday and Tuesday nights, devoting the rest of the week to folk music. Another coffee house, on the same street as the Little Vienna, was more ambitious: it called itself the Chabada Jazz Club and presented jazz nightly. The following month saw the opening of the Kasavubu Jazz Club, a coffee-house located on the ground floor of a private home several kilometres west of the city centre. It, too, presented jazz nightly, and was quickly dubbed the Musicians' Workshop. Complementing these night spots was a coffee-house on St. Catherine Street West called Circle A, which began presenting jazz on Saturday and Sunday afternoons.

This sudden flowering of new opportunities to play jazz was heartening to the community, but it quickly became apparent that the coffee-houses offered no more stability than the nightclubs had. The lower profit margins of nonalcoholic drinks and a mainly student clientele made the coffee-houses tenuous enterprises. Those located in residential neighbourhoods were harassed by complaints about noise. Others were closed by police raids aimed at stopping illicit drug and alcohol consumption on the premises. The optimism sparked by the appearance of jazz coffee-houses in the winter following Drapeau's reelection was short-lived. In March 1961 the Chabada Jazz Club closed and the Circle A abandoned jazz. A few weeks later the Little Vienna restaurant ended its jazz policy. Len Dobbin, then Montreal correspondent to the Toronto-based jazz magazine *Coda,* summarized the mood of the community in a report published in April: "The whole scene seems to be in a sad state, with many fine musicians without a place to play."[4] A few months later the Musicians' Workshop also closed.

Throughout the 1960s, coffee-houses featuring jazz came and went in Montreal. There was Le Op, on Park Avenue in the student ghetto east of McGill University. And there was a string of coffee-houses near Sir George Williams, which had since become a university: the Place, the Bamboo Cage, and the Seven Steps, all on Stanley Street; Café Bizarre on Bishop Street; and the Jazz Gallery on Mountain Street. The musicians gravitated towards the more bohemian and spirited coffee-houses. At Le Mas, the atmosphere was more evocative of Paris than of a North American folk house: the debates and the *chansons* echoed in French, and the jazz musicians rubbed shoulders with the young intellectuals and artists of the Quiet Revolution.

When Le Mas closed in the spring of 1962 following a police raid for alcohol and drugs, the after-hours jazz scene in Montreal shifted to an equally bohemian coffee-house called L'Enfer—literally, "hell." Jazz was heard there almost every night, beginning long before the clubs closed. The owner hired young, apprentice jazz musicians—at minimal pay—to perform until the older musicians arrived from their jobs in the night-clubs. Occasionally an out-of-work professional would drop in before two o'clock and conduct an informal workshop for the apprentices on stage, but it was the after-hours sessions that drew the biggest crowds. Entire American bands would join in, fresh from an engagement elsewhere in town, and the music rarely stopped before dawn. Complaints from neighbours pursued L'Enfer from its first home near Bishop and Dorchester to a loft on Ontario Street near Bleury. Police raids for alcohol and drugs were common. Finally, in July 1963, police closed L'Enfer for good.

Drapeau's renewed cleanup campaign was changing the face of nighttime Montreal. Organized crime was withdrawing from visible rackets such as prostitution, gambling, and blind pigs. It was not, however, retreating from the city. The gangsters quickly expanded their less visible activities such as narcotics smuggling, lotteries, and protection rackets. A month after Drapeau was reelected, a gang smashed the Chez Paree nightclub when its owner refused to pay money to a new protection ring. The Chez Paree reopened, but other clubs were not as resistant to the combined impact of Drapeau's policies and the continuing onslaught of television and rock music.

The nightclubs could only survive by cutting costs. By the middle of the 1960s, strip shows had become commonplace and club bands had shrunk to four musicians. The arrival of tape recorders and sound systems on the popular marketplace presented clubs with a way to reduce expenses even further. Some strip clubs began replacing their bands with recorded music as early as 1965. By 1968, the city's three major strip emporiums—the Chez Paree, the All-American, and the Metropole —had switched to recorded music, eliminating at least fifty jobs for musicians. How many more jobs were lost to tape recorders in small bars and clubs throughout the city is impossible to estimate, but the impact of the new technology was devastating. There were simply not enough jobs to go around any more. Full employment in the nightclubs—always a key factor in the cohesiveness of the city's jazz community—had become a thing of the past.

Some musicians found alternative work in small combos in restaurants and hotel lounges; others set off on extended tours as accompanists for popular singers. Some took club work in Trois-Rivières,[5] or played in rock or rhythm and blues bands in hotels in outlying regions of the province; a few abandoned music altogether as a livelihood. For those with the right skills and personal temperament, however, there was another option: the studios.

Musicians first began obtaining regular studio work in Montreal during the 1950s, when CBC radio and television formed orchestras for their variety shows. Nick Ayoub, Al Baculis, Yvan Landry, and Tony Romandini were among the first of the city's jazz musicians to abandon the nightclubs during the late 1950s and earn their livings principally in the studios. As television grew rapidly in popularity and the recording industry in Montreal boomed during the early 1960s, the demand for instrumentalists, composers, arrangers, and copyists increased. By the middle of the decade, almost a dozen more Montreal jazz musicians had gone into the studios.[6]

The studios offered good wages, but they could not accommodate all of the underemployed musicians in the city. Tragically, many excellent musicians were not suited to the demands of studio work, with its impersonal, highly technical environment, split-second timing, and early morning calls. The work was stressful and the musical compromises

214

Montreal jazz musicians in the studio for a CBC broadcast,
circa 1963. Seated: Oliver Jones (piano); standing left to right:
Norm Villeneuve (drums), Bob Rudd (bass), Bruce Yates
(guitar). *Photo by Ed Bermingham Inc., courtesy of Ed Bermingham.*
John Gilmore Jazz History Collection, Concordia University
Archives.

A quintet led by tenor saxophonist Nick Ayoub performs
before an audience at L'Hermitage hall during a taping for the
CBC radio program "Jazz en liberté," December 1965: Al
Penfold (trumpet, valve trombone), Cisco Normand (drums),
Don Habib (bass), Art Roberts (piano). *Photo courtesy of Al*
Penfold. John Gilmore Jazz History Collection, Concordia
University Archives.

were often dispiriting. Moreover, the studios demanded an ability to sight-read styles of music—including rock and "legit," or classically phrased, music—which many nightclub musicians were not practised at playing. Not suprisingly, the studio orchestras were dominated by younger musicians. They, far more than their elders, were likely to be comfortable with the latest styles of popular music, to play more than one instrument, and to have formal training and diverse ensemble experience. Thus, the generation of musicians who had grown up on bebop captured the most rapidly expanding job market of the 1960s. In so doing, they insulated themselves from the economic hardships caused by the decline of live performance work in the city.

In part through the presence of jazz musicians in the studios, jazz music found an outlet there. It was, of course, a more tightly controlled jazz than could be performed live, for it had to conform to the rigid schedule of a radio or television program. Jamming was out of the question, and composition and arrangement were emphasized over extended improvisation. The producers, with few exceptions, had little specialized knowledge of jazz, or even an awareness of the city's best jazz soloists; nevertheless they determined who and what was broadcast as the best of Montreal jazz. As a result, some so-called jazz programs featured musicians with only a limited ability to play well in the idiom. This was due mainly to what writer Mark Miller has identified as the tendency of the CBC and the recording industry to look "more often to the studio than to the jazz world to find musicians for jazz broadcasts or recordings—in effect, casting from within their own ranks."[7] There were, fortunately, a few exceptions. Among them was trumpeter Herbie Spanier, who earned a tenuous living playing in hotels and clubs during the 1960s, but enjoyed considerable exposure on CBC.[8] Spanier was featured often on the weekly CBC radio program "Jazz en liberté," taped before an audience at L'Ermitage hall on Côte des Neiges beginning in 1965. Though the program featured mainly pick-up bands, it was respected by musicians and fans alike for consistently presenting many of Montreal's leading jazz musicians in a setting conducive to creative work. Meanwhile, the CBC was also taking the initiative to record many Montreal musicians playing jazz, though most of the bands were pick-up groups of studio musicians.

With rock becoming the music of entertainment and dance, and after-hours jamming confined to the coffee-houses, jazz had to survive on its own terms in the nightclubs if it was to survive there at all. This necessity gave rise to a new breed of nightclub in Montreal: the jazz club. The 1960s was the decade in which jazz musicians first began to be hired by Montreal nightclubs on a regular basis to perform unadulterated jazz, rather than show or dance music.

Previously, most of the jazz that had been performed by paid musicians in Montreal had been presented in theatres and other concert settings, and then almost exclusively by famous American musicians or bands. From the 1930s into the 1950s, theatres such as the Seville and the Loew's had featured jazz musicians of the calibre of Fats Waller, Coleman Hawkins, and Duke Ellington in their entertainment packages of feature films and live stage shows. Local entrepreneurs or groups had occasionally organized jazz concerts at His Majesty's theatre, the Forum, or other venues. And American impresario Norman Granz's touring Jazz at the Philharmonic concerts stopped regularly at the Forum from the late 1940s through the 1950s. The loss of most of these opportunities to hear jazz in Montreal by the beginning of the 1960s coincided with the end of after-hours jam sessions in the clubs and the growing presence of rock throughout the entertainment industry. The audience for jazz in Montreal, although not large, nonetheless represented a market waiting to be tapped.[9]

The initiative to feature jazz in Montreal nightclubs had always come from the local musicians and their fans. Successes had been few, and short-lived: club owners were quick to abandon jazz when they saw a bigger profit to be made elsewhere. The first attempt to book jazz musicians on a regular basis into Montreal nightclubs began in 1958 when a part-time bassist named John Cordell formed the Montreal Jazz Society. Unlike the earlier Emanon Jazz Society and Jazz Workshop, which had organized special events and jam sessions outside musicians' working hours, the Montreal Jazz Society set about presenting jazz in nightclubs during regular hours. The society began modestly. It convinced a succession of nightclub owners to hire a jazz trio for one night a week on the understanding that the society would fill the club with musicians eager to sit in and fans eager to listen. As the gatherings grew in size, the sessions moved from club to club, graduating from the east end of the city to the west end during the society's second year. As the confidence of club owners in the society grew, they began putting up extra money for guest soloists—occasionally a name musician from the United States, though more often a local horn player.

The guiding spirit of the Montreal Jazz Society's sessions for more than a year was René Thomas, a Belgian guitarist who had recently moved to Montreal with his family and his childhood friend, drummer José Bourguignon. Thomas had had his sights set on a jazz career in New York City when he first left Belgium in 1956. A brief visit to that city, however, had convinced him that American immigration barriers would be difficult to overcome and that the New York lifestyle would be harrowing for his family. Thomas had learned to speak English from the

René Thomas, with drummer George Braxton, at the Little Vienna restaurant, 1960 or 1961.
Photo by Keith White, courtesy of White. John Gilmore Jazz History Collection, Concordia University Archives.

American jazz musicians he had played with in Europe, and from the Hollywood westerns he remained a fan of all his life. His family, however, spoke only French. Montreal, where Thomas's sister Juliette already lived, seemed an ideal compromise—comfortable for his family, but close enough (seen from Europe, at least) to the New York jazz scene.

During the five years Thomas lived in Montreal, he visited the United States some fifteen to twenty times, staying for several weeks at a stretch. During these sojourns he worked and recorded with several important jazz musicians, including Toshiko Akiyoshi, J. R. Monterose, and Sonny Rollins. Rollins was an enthusiastic admirer of Thomas's playing, and he employed Thomas's solo talents on one side of a 1958 album; in the liner notes, Rollins is quoted as saying: "I know a Belgian guitar player that I like better than any of the Americans I've heard."[10] Immigration and union barriers probably prevented Thomas from recording more often in the United States; in Canada, he was ignored by record companies, though film-maker Guy Borremans employed him for a thirty-minute sound-track.

Thomas devoted his life to jazz, encouraged by his wife, Marie, who supported the family in Montreal. He practised at home for hours every

DoM   JULIETTE.

MIb SOL DO RÉ mélodie (main droite

accords
DO MIb SOL   SI MIb SOL   SIb MIb SOL   LA MIb SOL

MIb   SOL   DO   SdRÉ   DoRib
   mélodie

accords
FA LAb DO / MI LAb DO / MIb LAb DO / RÉ LAb DO/
mélodie DO SIb/   LAb   / LA SIb   / LAb SIb LAb/

mélodie   Rihent
    SOL SOL /   FA   / MIb   / RÉ
accords RÉ FA DO/ RÉ FA SI/ RÉ FA SI REFASI/

mélodie
   DO RE MIb / DO RE MI /

accords   DO majeur
Do MIb SOL/   DO MI SOL /

Guitarist René Thomas's original notation for his composition "Juliette," named for his sister who lived in Montreal. *Courtesy of Marie and Florence Thomas. John Gilmore Jazz History Collection, Concordia University Archives.*

day and sought no commercial work. Nor was he interested in learning to read or write music; instead he developed his own notation for sketching out his jazz compositions. Thomas was equally indifferent to the business side of his career: even after he returned to Belgium in 1961 and became an international jazz star, he continued to leave to his wife and his daughter Florence all of the practical work of managing his life, travels, and career. This freedom from financial and practical concerns was an important catalyst in Thomas's development as a jazz musician, especially in Montreal where it was virtually impossible to support a family while playing jazz exclusively. Other musicians in the city were obliged to seek commercial work; Thomas was free to play jazz all the time. He quickly became a central figure on the Montreal jazz scene, and one of a handful of non-studio jazz musicians to receive frequent exposure on radio and television. He led the rhythm sections for the Montreal Jazz Society steadily until April 1960, then spent much of his remaining time in the city leading the house band at the Little Vienna restaurant.

Thomas's departure from the Montreal Jazz Society coincided with a minor crisis in the organization. Cordell left the society during the summer of 1960, apparently amidst complaints from the musicians about his handling of affairs. Leadership passed to a non-musician named Hans Kunst and the society became more ambitious. During the winter of 1961-62, it booked jazz into several places on different nights of the week. By the following summer, it had moved its principal activities to La Tête de l'Art, a nightclub above a restaurant on Metcalfe Street in the centre of the city. Kunst and a drummer named Guy Lachapelle took over management of the club and began engaging American jazz musicians to perform with local rhythm sections four nights a week. In this way, in 1962, Montreal acquired its first true jazz club.

Thereafter, the Montreal Jazz Society served as little more than a banner for La Tête de l'Art's jazz policy. Organized jam sessions were abandoned. That winter Kunst and Lachapelle began booking complete American jazz bands into the club. The change in policy proved to be costly, however, and financial problems forced the club to close for a month during the spring of 1963. It reopened to bring in several more top American bands, including saxophonist John Coltrane's influential quartet, but soon abandoned the policy for good. The music was enthusiastically received by the local jazz community, but the financial costs of presenting top American bands on a regular basis was too high.

Nevertheless, La Tête de l'Art had demonstrated that there was an audience for pure jazz in Montreal nightclubs. Other clubs moved into the market. Those which restricted themselves to booking local musicians with only an occasional imported soloist fared the best. The Penthouse, on Peel Street, toyed with a jazz policy for most of the decade, sometimes nightly but more often on weekends only. Lindy's, a second-floor club at the corner of Park Avenue and St. Joseph Blvd. to the north of the city centre, managed an intermittent jazz policy for almost two years, using a local trio or quartet led by bassist Charlie Biddle. When Lindy's began importing American guest soloists in the spring of 1963, however, it quickly went under. Other venues also adopted intermittent jazz policies, among them Dunn's and the cocktail lounge at Rockhead's Paradise. Only one club surpassed the scale of La Tête de l'Art's jazz policy during the 1960s. The Casa Loma, on St. Catherine Street just east of The Main, was the leading nightclub in Montreal for popular Québécois entertainment. Its owner, Andy Cobetto, had helped launch the careers of some of the province's most popular singers, and the club had become famous among francophone audiences. Cobetto was accustomed to mounting extravagant shows. In this spirit, he decided to open a jazz club above the Casa Loma, in a large dance hall which had gone by the name of the Savoy Ballroom during the 1950s. The room was renovated, and quality lighting and sound equipment was installed. In December 1963 it opened as Le Jazz Hot.

The new club arrived on the scene as La Tête de l'Art was fading. Within two week's of Le Jazz Hot's opening, Cobetto drafted pianist Pierre Leduc from La Tête de l'Art to lead his house trio. From eight-thirty in the evening until closing, six or seven nights a week, live music never stopped at Le Jazz Hot. Leduc's trio alternated sets with the leading jazz artists of the day: John Coltrane's quartet; trumpeter Miles Davis; pianists Oscar Peterson, Bill Evans, and Thelonious Monk; saxophonists Sonny Rollins, Coleman Hawkins, and Cannonball Adderley; Art Blakey's Jazz Messenger's; and the big bands of Duke Ellington and Lionel Hampton. Some American bands stayed two weeks; some weeks featured double billings of two guest bands.[11]

The extravagance of this policy proved fatal. The jazz community was thrilled about the musicians Cobetto was importing, but attendance declined as ticket prices rose to meet the high salaries and travel expenses of the American bands. On 28 February 1965 Le Jazz Hot closed, only fourteen months after its birth. In a fitting epilogue, Cobetto reopened the club for one week in April to present the Duke Ellington Orchestra, then locked the doors for good.

Outliving all of the jazz nightclubs and coffee-houses of the 1960s was a basement room on St. Antoine Street with a distinctly modest approach to jazz. For one dollar, you could spend all night listening to live jazz. For another couple of dollars, you could eat a solid meal of "soul food"—chicken wings, black-eyed peas, and rice. The coffee was always steaming. And if you wanted something stronger, you needed only slip around the corner onto Aqueduct Street to a bar named Whitey's Hideaway.

The Black Bottom was to the 1960s what the Terminal club and the Clef Club had been to the 1930s and the Café St. Michel and Aldo's had been to the postwar golden years of Montreal nightlife. It served as a place for musicians, friends, and fans to meet after the night's work was done—a place to eat, talk, laugh, and play music together. All of the legendary meeting places favoured by jazz musicians in Montreal had been on, or near, St. Antoine Street, the main street of the city's black neighbourhood. The Black Bottom was the last club in this spirited tradition, and though it served no alcohol, everyone referred to it as a "club" just the same.[12]

Charlie Burke, a former railway employee, opened The Black Bottom in the fall of 1963 and hired a drummer named Charlie Duncan to form the house band. A transplanted American, Duncan had landed in Montreal a few years before with a touring trio, and decided to stay. The trio he formed for The Black Bottom underwent several personnel changes during its first few months. When legal problems prevented Duncan from continuing, leadership passed to the guitarist in the group. For the next four years—with only occasional time off to play elsewhere—Nelson Symonds remained at the head of The Black Bottom house band. It was his first job as a leader.

Symonds was from Nova Scotia. He had been raised in an extended family of musicians in the black community of Hammond's Plains, near Halifax. As a child he had absorbed by ear a rich dowry of popular songs and dance music from his uncles and cousins, many of whom played the banjo and guitar. The banjo was Symonds' first instrument, though he switched to guitar before leaving home. Like many of his generation, Symonds found his way to Montreal largely by accident. The route was circuitous: four years in Sudbury, Ontario, working in his uncle's garage and playing dances on the weekends; three years working for black carnival shows, wintering in the southern United States and summering in Quebec and Ontario. An offer to join a rhythm and blues band in Sherbrooke allowed Symonds to give up the carnival life; a tour of the province with some Montreal-based musicians, including Charlie Duncan, finally brought him to the big city in the winter of 1958-59.

Symonds worked his first jazz job in Montreal in 1959 as part of a band called the Stablemates—another rare example of musicians being hired by a nightclub to perform jazz. The all-black sextet, led by pianist Alfie Wade, worked six nights a week for nine months at a club called the Vieux Moulin, then broke up when no other engagements could be found for such a large band playing jazz. Symonds took a rhythm and blues job, then went to Milwaukee with some of the Stablemates and

The **Stablemates** pose for a publicity photo on the campus of McGill University, 1959. Left to right: Chet Christopher (alto saxophone), Alfie Wade (piano), Bob Rudd (bass), Nelson Symonds (guitar), Doug Richardson (tenor saxophone), Charlie Duncan (drums). *Photo by Chris Schon, courtesy of Doug Richardson. John Gilmore Jazz History Collection, Concordia University Archives.*

worked in a band with the American multi-reedist Roland Kirk. Returning to Montreal in the fall of 1960, Symonds began working in the jazz clubs that were opening around the city. Trio and quartet work became his favourite format.

Symonds' devotion to jazz quickly became legend in Montreal. He would practise at his rooming-house for hours every day; during his Black Bottom tenure, Symonds would sometimes put in six to eight hours a day alone, playing scales, learning chord progressions, and improvising. "If I wasn't single I wouldn't have been able to do it," he has said repeatedly. Symonds' simple lifestyle—no car, few possessions, a rented room—has allowed him to largely ignore the world of commercial music. He had much in common with René Thomas; yet, suprisingly, during all the years Thomas lived in Montreal, the two guitarists never sought each other out. Each admired the other's playing, but both were too shy to make the first approach. It wasn't until Thomas had returned to Europe and began visiting Montreal as a kind of returning hero that Symonds and he finally connected. They quickly became friends.

Symonds established a reputation for himself as a responsible but unassuming leader during his four years at The Black Bottom. Though union regulation entitled him to earn twice as much as his sidemen—and the scale for coffee-house work only gave him fifty-five dollars for three nights' work—he pooled his salary with the other members of the trio and split the money equally. "I don't think about money when I'm getting ready to play," Symonds told Mark Miller in 1979. "You have to make money in order to live, in order to survive, but you can't let it interfere with your playing or who you're going to play with."[13]

Symonds' trios[14] animated The Black Bottom from Thursday to Saturday. The music lasted until six in the morning; sometimes the musicians didn't stop until eight. When the club first opened, the band began work at 10:00 p.m., but after a few words from the union about overworking the musicians, starting time was set back to eleven. True to his calling, Symonds used the extra hour to listen to a set of music at another club before going to work himself.

On many nights you couldn't find a seat at The Black Bottom after eleven. The coffee-house crowd made up the first shift of spectators; after the nightclubs closed the musicians arrived. Many of the American musicians who worked at Le Jazz Hot went to The Black Bottom after work. Some would sit in with Symonds' trio; others would unwind, eat, and listen to the jamming. The place became so popular that Burke enlarged it. Other club owners in the city coveted The Black Bottom's success. Some tried to capitalize on its popularity: the nearby Café St. Michel, renamed the Harlem Paradise, hosted Saturday afternoon jam sessions in 1965, then as Soul City a few years later briefly imported funk/jazz musicians such as Les McCann. Neither venture lasted. The police were equally curious. "They couldn't believe the place was going that good just on coffee and food," said Symonds. One night they raided the club, sniffed everybody's cup, and took away a few customers who had spiked their coffee from private flasks. A minor public outcry followed, and thereafter The Black Bottom was left in peace.

The Montreal world's fair of 1967 was the culmination of Mayor Jean Drapeau's vision of a dynamic, world-class city. The exposition was the prize towards which the city raced in a bold modernization initiative which brought striking changes to the city in the heady years after Drapeau's 1960 reelection. Construction boomed: old buildings were erased from the urban landscape and replaced with high-rise office towers and a massive concert hall; tunnels were dug for a subway system modeled on the Paris *Métro*; and convoys of trucks hauling stone and earth from the countryside created two man-made islands in the St. Lawrence River, a site for the fair to which people from around the world flocked through the spring, summer, and fall of 1967.

In the years leading up to Expo 67, Montreal musicians had been hopeful that tourists flocking into the city for the world's fair would generate additional work in the nightclubs. The tourists came, but the nightclubs hardly prospered. The city promoted the fair as a complete tourist experience. On-site restaurants, theatres, free concerts, discothèques, beer gardens, and an enormous amusement park held people on the islands long after dark, leaving the city's indigenous nightlife in the shadows.

Focusing the spotlight on the Expo islands served two purposes at city hall. It brought much-needed revenue to the fair, easing some of the debt the city had run up in building the site. Equally important, it helped the city to put its best face forward to the world. The fair created an image of Montreal as clean, modern, efficient, and prosperous. The reality, for low-income Montrealers especially, was less impressive. Drapeau was enduring heavy criticism for spending so much money on Expo while pressing social problems—especially deteriorating housing —demanded urgent attention. For as long as the tourists were in town, however, nothing could be allowed to blemish the city's image. Before the fair opened, city crews were sent out to erect seven-foot-high, blue-and-white fences along major thoroughfares to hide the worst housing from the view of passing motorists.

In a variation of this policy, city hall cracked down on nightlife just before the fair opened. The mayor was sensitive about Montreal's reputation as a city of sin. While his cleanup campaign had driven vice from public view, organized crime remained endemic to the city, and one only had to scratch the surface to find most illicit distractions. Drapeau wanted to minimize the opportunities for tourists to be exposed to vice. Promoting wholesome nightlife on the Expo islands was one way of doing so, but city hall felt more drastic measures were required. Shortly before the fair opened, the city passed a new bylaw making it illegal for any nightclub employee or entertainer to drink, dance, mingle, or sit at the same table with a customer.[15] The law was intended mainly to discourage dancers from soliciting in the strip clubs, but it applied indiscriminately to anyone who worked anywhere alcohol was sold. Musicians and singers coming off the bandstand could not join friends or admirers in the audience for a drink or conversation. Married entertainers were afraid to join their spouses for fear of being arrested. The effect on the musicians was psychological rather than material: the bylaw did not limit their opportunities to work, but it humiliated them. Club owners and managers sent them to the kitchen or dressing room between sets, or advised them to meet their friends on the sidewalk outside.

To its credit, the city did include jazz in the panorama of musics presented at Expo 67. International jazz stars such as Duke Ellington, Sarah Vaughan, Thelonious Monk, and Dave Brubeck were imported from the United States for a series of concerts at the fair site. Large bands from Toronto were also showcased, including Phil Nimmons' nine-piece band and a twelve-piece band led by Ron Collier. Montreal musicians were confined mainly to working in trios, quartets, and quintets. A few of the city's established jazz players, including Nelson Symonds, worked regularly at the site, but in keeping with the fair's image as youth-conscious and forward-looking, many veteran Montreal jazz musicians were passed over in favour of young players and bands comprising mainly studio musicians. In one of the more loudly touted celebrations of Canadian jazz, Maynard Ferguson was brought to the fair to lead a big band of Montreal musicians for a live recording by the CBC. The nature of the event, however, dictated that all but one or two of the musicians chosen for the band would be experienced studio players. The CBC also taped its weekly "Jazz en liberté" program at the fair site throughout the summer, providing a more cosmopolitan audience for local musicians, though no additional work.

Many Montreal musicians found occasional employment of some kind at Expo 67, but the fair fell far short of most of their expectations. It did not reverse the steady erosion of their livelihood in the nightclubs, even for one summer. Worse, city hall had proved itself insensitive to their plight by drawing no distinction between musicians and other nightclub employees in its no-mixing bylaw. The musicians felt betrayed by the city and its mayor. Drummer Dennis Brown evoked the bitterness felt by many of the city's jazz musicians when, fifteen years later, he summed up the times with a vivid metaphor: "Expo cut the throat and let the blood out of the city." Indeed, the city seemed unwilling, or unable, to support any longer a stable community of jazz musicians with live performance work in its nightclubs.[16] Only the studio players were unaffected by the tragedy. For the rest, Expo 67 marked the onset of an era of frequent unemployment, profound disillusionment, and anxious searching for greener pastures that would continue well into the 1970s.

CHAPTER TEN

New Directions

In the wake of Expo 67, nothing seemed certain any more; everything was changing, rapidly. The bottom had fallen out of the job market for nightclub musicians. Those who hadn't found a place in the studios were struggling to make a living or talking about leaving town. Since the birth of jazz, Montreal had been drawing musicians from all over the continent with its employment opportunities; now it was sending some of its most talented jazz musicians into involuntary exile. Between 1967 and 1970, the city lost bassists Bob Rudd and Michel Donato; trumpeter Herbie Spanier; saxophonists Dougie Richardson, Alvin Pall, and Bill Holmes; drummer Walter Bacon; and pianists Sadik Hakim, Joe Sealy, and Linton Garner. Others would follow them into exile in the early 1970s: bassist Fred McHugh; drummers Claude Ranger and Norm Villeneuve. Toronto, a rapidly growing commercial centre with burgeoning radio, television, and recording studios, provided a haven for many; others migrated as far as Vancouver, California, and Florida.

Though underemployment was at the root of the crisis, the jazz community was no less traumatized by the realization that jazz's role in the cultural and commercial life of the city had changed, irrevocably. An era had ended. There was no going back, and there was no clear direction forward. Rock was everywhere. Swing and Latin rhythms had become old-fashioned, and bebop was on the defensive, taking shelter in a few specialty clubs and coffee-houses and seldom heard elsewhere in live performance. After-hours jamming in the nightclubs had become extinct.

Jazz, as the city had always known it, was losing its appeal to youth. Gone were most of the opportunities for young musicians to serve an apprenticeship working alongside their elders. Gone, too, was much of youth's respect for the traditions, discipline, and repertoire of jazz. Rock captivated the youth of the 1960s, including many aspiring musicians who in previous decades would have gravitated to jazz. Those who were still drawn to jazz were inspired less by bebop than by the searching, nakedly self-expressive music of American saxophonist John Coltrane, the most popular exponent of a controversial new musical phenomenon being called free jazz.

If the future of jazz in Montreal was unclear, one thing at least was certain: the city's jazz community would never be the same again. Where once there had been a sense that jazz musicians and fans of all ages shared a common allegiance to a music that no one, at least within the community, felt the need to define, by the beginning of the 1970s it was difficult to speak any longer of a single, homogeneous jazz community in Montreal. Instead, there were several smaller clans and cliques, delineated socially by workplace, age, lifestyle, and politics, and musically both by their openness to rock and free jazz, and by their allegiance —or lack of it—to bebop and the traditions of jazz. Among musicians and fans there was little consensus on either the boundaries of jazz, or what direction the music should be taking.

In retrospect, it is clear that jazz in Montreal, as it was elsewhere, was branching into three streams: a cautious mainstream; an experimental free jazz stream; and a popular, hybrid stream merging jazz with rock. The mainstream flowed out of bebop, though the older musicians were still playing the earlier swing style of jazz and the modernists had incorporated the modal approach. The latter was a harmonic innovation of the late 1950s in which modes, or scales, replaced a precise sequence of chords as the foundation for composition and improvisation. Most of Montreal's established jazz musicians kept to the mainstream, though their ranks grew thinner and their opportunities to work in public diminished after Expo 67. These were the musicians who, consciously or not, were struggling to keep alive the traditions of the city's jazz community—a nightclub employment base, a standard repertoire based on swing and Latin rhythms, an acoustic instrumentation, and creative exchanges among musicians through jam sessions and the long-established practice of guests "sitting in" with working bands.

The death of the original Black Bottom was a milestone in the decline of this tradition. The after-hours coffee-house survived Expo 67 with Nelson Symonds still leading the house band—only to fall victim to Mayor Jean Drapeau's vision of modernity in another way. Near the end of 1967 the city ordered The Black Bottom demolished to make way for a new expressway slicing through the St. Antoine district. The jazz community was devastated by the loss of its only after-hours room. Charlie Burke quickly reopened The Black Bottom near the harbour front, but as a nightclub this time. Though Burke attempted to revive the ambience of the original Black Bottom by serving coffee when the bar closed and staying open late, the club did not become popular as a meeting place for local jazz musicians. Its location, in an isolated district of the city with no nightclub tradition, discouraged casual dropping in. Symonds,

Members of Vic Vogel's big band pose for a publicity photo in the lobby of the CBC building shortly before their 1968 European tour. *Photo by Francis J. Menten, courtesy of Vic Vogel. John Gilmore Jazz History Collection, Concordia University Archives.* See page 305 for names of musicians.

dismayed, resigned as house bandleader a few months after The Black Bottom reopened. Thereafter, the club featured mainly bands from the United States, including many which played rock.

A string of Montreal nightclubs flirted with jazz during the late 1960s: the New Penelope, the Dream Lounge, the Playboy Club, Café Campus, Oliver's, the Winston Churchill Pub, the Downbeat, the Jazz Hut, Caesar's Palace, the Esquire. Only one offered local jazz musicians a stable home. Café La Bohème, a small nightclub on Guy Street just above St. Catherine Street West, adopted the novel policy of alternating sets of live jazz with recorded rock music for dancing. The resulting Jazztek—short for jazz discothèque—opened in December 1966 and provided a modest home for mainstream jazz into the next decade. It was there that Nelson Symonds went to work after leaving The Black Bottom; there that pianist Pierre Leduc led an explorative and widely respected quartet for two years in the late 1960s; and there that Montreal's longest-surviving big band was born.

Through the 1960s, saxophonist Lee Gagnon had been calling local musicians together to rehearse and occasionally perform jazz arrangements for a ten-piece band. Vic Vogel was a faithful member of Gagnon's band, playing trombone, tuba, and piano, and contributing many of the arrangements. In 1968, after Gagnon had abandoned the club scene and let his band lapse, Vogel began calling rehearsals for a full-size big band at Le Jazztek. With his reputation firmly established locally as a pianist and arranger, the thirty-three-year-old Vogel had little difficulty convincing many of the city's leading musicians to come out on Monday nights and rehearse his arrangements without pay. These rehearsal bands, first Gagnon's and then Vogel's, offered one of the few opportunities for studio and non-studio musicians to mingle and make music together. Vogel's big band worked little initially, but quickly became an important pillar of the mainstream jazz community in Montreal. By the mid-1970s it was performing concerts and club engagements, touring to Europe, and recording and broadcasting through the CBC. The band was still active, despite many personnel changes, in the late 1980s—a remarkable achievement seen against the backdrop of Montreal's jazz history. Vogel's tenacity is reminiscent of the energy and dedication exhibited by a long line of musicians who have served the city well. It is these qualities which would ensure mainstream jazz a voice in Montreal long after the disintegration of a homogeneous jazz community.

The second stream of jazz to emerge in Montreal was free jazz. Born in the United States, the controversial new music took years to find its own course in Montreal. When it did, shortly after the close of Expo 67, it diverged boldly from the mainstream and became a strident voice in the political arena.

Herbie Spanier. *John Gilmore Jazz History Collection, Concordia University Archives.*

Cisco Normand. *Photo by Al Penfold, courtesy of Penfold. John Gilmore Jazz History Collection, Concordia University Archives.*

In strictly musical terms, American free jazz was essentially a revolution in rhythm. Harmonically and melodically, the ground had been well prepared. The harmonic structures of bebop had begun breaking down in the latter half of the 1950s when musicians such as Miles Davis began using modes instead of chords as the basis for their music. Pianist Cecil Taylor, meanwhile, had begun using chords not as harmonic building blocks but as splashes of colour, much as the European impressionist composers had done. All that remained for the more explorative musicians of the free jazz era was to abandon tonality altogether.

Melodically, free jazz was essentially bebop and the blues taken to the extreme. Bebop's already jagged lines were exaggerated to the point of melodic discontinuity in free jazz, and punctuated with shrieks, squawks, and other near-vocal instrumental sounds reminiscent of the blues. Moreover, in abandoning a series of solos by individual musicians in favour of collective improvisation by several musicians, the free jazz players were reviving—however unconsciously—the concept of improvised polyphony which had formed the basis of early New Orleans jazz. Free jazz sounded radically different—and often chaotic—because the young musicians were at the same time rejecting the conventions and musical structures which had made early New Orleans jazz intelligible to listeners while providing a clear role for each instrument in the ensemble.

What was truly revolutionary about the new jazz was its abandonment of fundamental rhythmic conventions. A precise beat and metre, clearly delineated with bar lines in notated music, had been the basis for all form and structure in jazz since the birth of the music. It seemed inconceivable that jazz could be played without choruses of predetermined length based on strictly measured beats. The revolutionaries proved it could. As early as 1956 the American bassist Charles Mingus began puncturing the traditional fixed chorus structures of jazz by stretching chords and choruses over time almost at whim. By 1959 saxophonist Ornette Coleman was improvising solos which, though still tied to an identifiable beat, had only a loose relationship to the chorus structures and chords of his own compositions. In 1960 Coleman abandoned the foundations altogether in an album consisting of nonstop, collectively improvised music by eight musicians in which there was no allegiance to metre, tempo, bar lines, chords, or form. The landmark album was called, appropriately, *Free Jazz*.

The germ of Ornette Coleman's musical ideas reached Montreal concurrent with, if not a few months ahead of, his first, 1959 album. The carrier was Herbie Spanier. The itinerant, Saskatchewan-born trumpeter had travelled to Los Angeles in 1958 to work with Paul Bley at the Hillcrest club. Unknown to the outside world, Coleman and trumpeter

232

Don Cherry were rehearsing Coleman's compositions in the same city. Both musicians hung out at the Hillcrest, where they eventually succeeded Spanier in Bley's band. Spanier struck up a friendship with Coleman, and the two discussed Coleman's music; Spanier, who has a reputation for hyperbole, later claimed to have helped the saxophonist with his composing.[1] Whatever the validity of that claim, in 1959 Spanier was back in Montreal, talking up the ideas he had been exposed to in Los Angeles.

Coleman's early compositions quickly found other conduits to Montreal. Cisco Normand generated considerable excitement when he arrived from Detroit during the summer of 1960 and immediately began performing some of Coleman's tunes on vibraphone.[2] A few months later Nelson Symonds and tenor saxophonist Dougie Richardson returned to Montreal from Milwaukee, where they had learned some of Coleman's compositions while working in a band with American saxophonist Roland Kirk. René Thomas was another early admirer of Coleman's music, which he probably first heard on one of his trips to New York City, where Coleman had begun working in late 1959. Although Thomas remained committed to bebop, praise from such a highly respected member of the Montreal jazz community undoubtedly ensured that Coleman's music received a sympathetic listening locally.

Though none of these musicians followed Coleman's lead into free jazz, a few Montreal musicians did experiment privately with unstructured improvisation during the early 1960s. Cisco Normand, pianist Norm Zubis, and drummer Pierre Béluse jammed together a few times, but after listening to private tapes of the music they had made, the three musicians concluded free improvisation was interesting to play but tiresome to listen to. What attracted the Montreal beboppers most to Coleman's music was the melodic beauty of his early compositions, which remained quite traditional in their harmonies, rhythm, and structure; where the local musicians were reluctant to follow, however, was into the uncharted wilderness of Coleman's improvisations, in which he frequently ignored the structures of his own compositions.

Firsthand contact with American experimentalists was not long in coming to Montreal. In 1960 a booking agent convinced a Montreal nightclub to bring in a large band from the United States. The agent promised a dazzling rock spectacle, complete with costumes and lighting effects. When the band opened in Montreal near the end of the year, however, the club owner discovered that he had hired, not a progressive rock band, but a self-styled prophet and keyboard wizard who called himself Sun Ra and his musicians the Arkestra. This was modern jazz's most colourful and adventurous big band—a group of dedicated experimentalists who had been living in obscurity in Chicago for more than a decade, playing a strange and highly personalized brand of riffs and bebop that was already battering at the gates of freedom by the time the band arrived in Montreal. Among them was the tenor saxophonist John Gilmore,[3] an early free jazz model for John Coltrane.

Once the club owner realized Sun Ra had no intention of playing rock, he cancelled the engagement, leaving the band without sufficient money to return to Chicago. For the next four months—through the winter of 1960-61—Sun Ra and his Arkestra subsisted in Montreal. They performed at The Place coffee-house and, apparently, in a Laurentian resort town. Sun Ra cut a colourful figure in the city. He attended a prize fight at the Forum dressed in one of his outlandish, glittery stage costumes. He was interviewed on television. Finally, Canadian immigration authorities refused to renew the musicians' work permits, on the grounds that the Arkestra was disturbing public order. The band moved on to New, York City, where it took up residence.[4]

Among the musicians who sat in with Sun Ra in Montreal was Sonny Greenwich. The self-taught, Ontario-born guitarist was visiting Montreal for the first time, working with a rhythm and blues band out of Toronto. Over the next few years, Greenwich would become strongly influenced by Coltrane's music and persona. In 1963 Greenwich began residing intermittently in Montreal, finally taking up permanent residence in the city in 1966-67.[5] Coltrane himself performed in Montreal in 1963 and 1964. On the latter occasion he visited The Black Bottom; though he declined to sit in with the house trio, his influential drummer Elvin Jones did.

There were other early opportunities for Montreal musicians to expose themselves to free jazz. Paul Bley returned briefly to Montreal in 1962 for an engagement at La Tête de l'Art, during which he performed some Ornette Coleman compositions. A year or two later the flautist Prince Lasha, a former bandmate of Ornette Coleman who was exploring free jazz, and Mike White, one of the first jazz violinists to play in the new style, both moved to Montreal. The two musicians lived concurrently in the city for about one year, probably in 1963 or 1964. Both were highly active on the local scene, playing—frequently together—at The Black Bottom and the Penthouse. On one occasion Lasha performed in concert at Loyola College.

Despite this influx of new ideas and repertoire into Montreal during the early 1960s, the jazz community did not abandon its allegiance to a music based on clear harmonic and rhythmic structures. The local musicians did absorb some post-bop ideas—improvising over one or two modes, rather than over a chord progression, for example, and even briefly venturing outside the harmonic structure of a tune during a solo —but the rhythmic liberties offered by free jazz were not generally embraced. How much of this reluctance was due to conservatism among individual local musicians is debatable. Clearly, however, the social significance attributed to free jazz in the United States affected the way the new music was perceived and eventually performed in Montreal.

In the United States, the celebration of freedom within jazz—the rhythmic freedom, certainly, but also the freedom of individual musicians to express nakedly their anger and their joy—came to be identified with the struggle of the black population against white oppression and social injustice. All but a handful of the early free jazz players in the United States were black, and some were advocates of a black revolution. The raw emotion of their music seemed to speak for the pain and the aspirations of black America, and in particular for the militant black youth. Free jazz became, for some, freedom music.

This social climate—which gave so much immediacy and intensity to American free jazz, and which also gave, to some players, a purpose—was alien to Montreal and its musicians. The city's black community was relatively free of the desperation and militancy that had engulfed the black ghettoes south of the border; the city's black musicians had not attained the status of oracles within the community that their colleagues in the United States enjoyed among black youth. Moreover, many of the pace-setting jazz players in Montreal were white, and almost all were anglophone: as a group they were neither oppressed nor enraged.

And yet, free jazz did find a sympathetic audience in Quebec, in some quarters precisely because of its social and political overtones. Agitation for fundamental political and economic change increased rapidly after the election of Jean Lesage as premier in 1960. The nationalism unleashed by the Quiet Revolution quickly spawned a movement aimed at making Quebec an independent, francophone nation. This separatist movement gained momentum and strength as the decade progressed, posing an increasingly serious challenge to Canadian federalism; a decade later it would bring to power in Quebec a new political party committed to achieving independence through the parliamentary process. There were, however, some Québécois who believed that revolution was necessary to achieve fundamental social and economic change in Quebec, and genuine independence. In 1963 the Front de libération du Québec (FLQ) began a campaign of political violence in Montreal, bombing radio towers, Canadian Legion offices, and mailboxes. Through these and other actions, the FLQ hoped to incite a popular insurrection. The FLQ and other radical political groups in Quebec drew some of their inspiration and rhetoric from the Black Power movement in the United States: one widely discussed book published in Quebec in 1968 described the francophone working class as "the white niggers of America."[6] In this way, free jazz was touted in some circles in Quebec

—just as it was in the United States—as a music of freedom and revolution. Not suprisingly, then, the first musicians in Montreal to embrace free jazz wholeheartedly were four politicized Québécois.

The story of the group they formed, Le Jazz libre du Québec, is told in detail in the Epilogue which follows.[7] Their music, unstructured often to the point of anarchy, defied understanding in the traditional terms of jazz still current in Montreal; not suprisingly, the band was dismissed with derision and contempt by many of the city's mainstream players and fans. Moreover, Jazz libre's insistence on attaching a political message to its music only deepened its isolation and left it open to charges of musical charlatanism. Undaunted, the group pursued its musical and social ideals through seven of the most turbulent years in Quebec's history.

Within a year of Jazz libre's birth, however, another experimental, free jazz group had taken shape in Montreal. This was a trio led by Ontario-born Brian Barley, a young symphony clarinetist who had moved to Montreal in 1966 and immediately abandoned a promising career as a classical musician to devote himself to jazz and the tenor saxophone. In contrast with the music of Jazz libre, the music of Barley's trio was carefully structured; nevertheless, it provided a broad canvas for free improvisation and a driving rhythmic interplay among Barley, drummer Claude Ranger, and the trio's bassist—first Michel Donato, then Daniel Lessard. The trio, which eventually adopted the name Aquarius Rising, rehearsed regularly but performed rarely. It worked mainly in Quebec City, where Lessard had grown up and knew some of the club owners personally.

Barley's outstanding musicianship, and the fact that each member of the trio had worked in other jazz contexts (Barley was a soloist in Vogel's big band), ensured the group a sympathetic hearing among Montreal's more conservative players. But the city did not rush to embrace Aquarius Rising any more than it did Jazz libre. Moreover, though the two pioneering bands existed in Montreal at the same time and took their lead from the same free jazz movement in the United States, they never met to exchange ideas or to improvise together. Aquarius Rising's influence on the development of free jazz in Montreal was thus minimal. Its greatest legacy is an album it recorded in 1970, entitled *The Brian Barley Trio*. Soon afterward, Lessard left the trio and, discouraged by the lack of work in Montreal, returned to live in Quebec City. Barley set off in the other direction, to Toronto, where Donato had already settled. Ranger joined them there, and Aquarius Rising was revived for three nights. Less than a year later, Barley died, aged twenty-eight. In contrast, Jazz libre's influence was more enduring. The style of free collective improvisation which it pioneered in Montreal was carried on in the 1970s by such groups as Atelier de musique expérimentale and

Aquarius Rising poster. *Courtesy of Daniel Lessard.*

Ensemble de musique improvisée de Montreal; Jazz libre's last drummer, Mathieu Léger, was a founding member of the latter ensemble.

Yet jazz during the 1970s would be dominated neither by free improvisation nor by the mainstream. A third, hybrid stream—still in gestation as the 1960s ended—would speak for the new decade. Musicians in the United States and Europe had been toying with the idea of combining jazz and rock since 1967. Younger musicians who had been raised on rock were looking to jazz for new ideas and colours; older jazz musicians were adding electric instruments and rock rhythms to their music in an attempt to hold younger audiences. It wasn't until the spring of 1970, however, when Miles Davis recorded an album entitled *Bitches Brew*, that "jazz-rock," or "fusion," emerged as an identifiable new style of music with its own name.[8]

In Montreal, the beginnings of this stream can be traced back to 1967. In that pivotal year in Montreal's history, saxophonist Walter Boudreau and poet Raoul Duguay began a series of musical and performance experiments which led to the formation of a large, mixed-media ensemble called L'Infonie. The story of this ensemble, which worked with Jazz libre for a year until their differences became irreconcilable, is also told in the Epilogue. In their own ways, both groups exploded the traditional boundaries—musical and social—of jazz in Montreal. Boudreau did not think of L'Infonie as a fusion group, even after the word came into vogue; and in the strictest sense of the term—a fusion of jazz and rock and nothing more—it wasn't. Other styles of music, as well as other art forms, flavoured L'Infonie's brew. Nevertheless, L'Infonie was the first meeting place of jazz and rock in Montreal, and as such, it was the first step on the path to the 1970s. Other bands would follow. The 1970s would prove to be an unsettling, contradictory decade for jazz: heady for those practitioners of the new jazz-rock fusion who achieved popularity and commercial success, but deeply troubling for those who rejected rock's intrusion into jazz and wondered where jazz was headed.

EPILOGUE

The Birth of Free Jazz and Fusion

"First of all, we discovered psychedelic drugs."[1] Walter Boudreau, jazz musician turned contemporary music composer, was reflecting on the birth of L'Infonie, his late-1960s "orchestra of the infinite" which—for the first time in Quebec—fused jazz with a cosmos of other musics, from rock to classical.

> Whatever negative aspects psychedelic drugs had, they had a very positive aspect of opening up our minds. I personally opened up to all kinds of music—Mozart, Coltrane, Stockhausen, Palestrina, Monteverdi. I could see the relationship between the styles. I said, "I want to play *music*. I want to play jazz. I want to play a little bit of Bach. I want to play rock. I want to play contemporary music. I want the musicians to talk. I want us to dress crazy. I want the whole scene to look like a party, because playing music *is* a party!"
>
> We didn't sit down beforehand and say we're gonna do this. It was just intuitive. It was a basic movement of getting out there and opening up. L'Infonie was *la représentation exacte* of what was going through *les Québécois* then—discovering the world. We had nothing to do, in a way, with how it came to be. It just happened. We were a product of our time. In retrospect, one could equate this, socially, with Expo 67. The world's fair was the event that opened up Montreal to the world. This is what made Montreal an international city. This is what made *me* a cosmopolitan being.

Boudreau was nineteen years old when he stepped onto that world stage. Five or six nights a week, all season, the saxophonist led a jazz quartet in concert at the Youth Pavilion. During the afternoons, he frequently led other jazz groups at the Expo Theatre, accompanying poetry readings. It was at one of these jazz-and-poetry performances that Boudreau encountered someone who shared his hunger to embrace all musics and arts. Raoul Duguay, eight years Boudreau's senior, had taught himself to play the trumpet, completed a doctorate in philosophy, and worked as a music critic for CBC radio before stepping onto the stage at Expo Theatre to read his poetry and improvise texts with Boudreau's band. In that afternoon, the germ of L'Infonie was born.

"The philosophy of L'Infonie was total acceptance—acceptance of all forms of expression within one ensemble," Duguay said.[2] In the year following the close of Expo 67, the two young men came together on a number of occasions to explore that common vision. Duguay would organize a loosely structured, multimedia event to celebrate love and art and to protest the Vietnam War—and he'd invite Boudreau's jazz band along to play. Boudreau's quartet would be hired to play a jazz concert—and he'd bring along "three bass clarinets, three string basses, four drummers, two trumpets, a trombone, tapes, and Duguay." "That was my 'jazz group,'" Boudreau said, "which was not a jazz group any more, but it was not called L'Infonie yet."

These experiments in multimedia performance—"happenings" in the parlance of the late-1960s—crystallized into a large, organized ensemble called L'Infonie during the winter of 1968-69. Boudreau led the ensemble, writing all of the music and directing its performance on stage. Duguay manned the microphone, reading his poetry and improvising monologues. There were fifteen to twenty-two musicians under Boudreau's command, grouped into sections of trumpets, trombones, and saxophones like a conventional jazz orchestra. The similarity ended there. The rhythm section looked more like a progressive rock band, with electric bass and guitars, a piano and synthesizer, one or two drum sets, and an assortment of gongs, bells, automobile horns, conga drums, and other percussion instruments. But L'Infonie's repertoire of effects extended even further. While the music unfolded, artists on stage might paint abstract canvases which were projected onto large screens behind the band. Someone else might sit at a table, pounding out poems and tracts on a typewriter, then rushing to the microphone to read them. Skits were improvised. The piano player sold carrot juice to the audience from a blender whirring on stage. Someone might intone the Catholic catechism.

And then there were the costumes: Duguay dressed as a giant frog, or as a Santa Claus under a scorching midsummer sun. Hats made out of toilet seats or deer antlers. Cardboard crowns. Indian headdresses. Monks' robes. Hockey uniforms. A ballerina's tutu. Badges bearing L'Infonie's maxim: *beauté, bonté, paix*—"beauty, goodness, peace."

Duguay summed up the impact:

> The public saw L'Infonie as something bizarre, naturally, but also as something which was breaking down the taboos. We broke down all the cultural taboos. Our shows were huge. They attracted huge crowds. They were crazy. L'Infonie was like a tidal wave. We

L'Infonie in concert.

embraced everything. We did rock, jazz, classical, contemporary—we even did western! We did theatre, poetry, art, everything!

For almost three years, this LSD-fueled tribe of *infoniaques* enchanted
youthful audiences throughout Quebec. They performed at colleges and
universities, pop festivals, all-night poetry readings, theatres, nightclubs,
and even at Place des Arts, Montreal's concert hall. They ventured outside the province only twice, to perform at the National Arts Centre in
Ottawa and at the University of Toronto. They made LPs and 45s. They
were the subject of a documentary film.[3] And they seduced the media
with outrageous antics and quotes: they gave interviews standing on
their heads in yoga postures, or dripping wet after strolling through a
car wash; Boudreau prophesied to one reporter that L'Infonie would
grow to 333,333,333 members in thirty-three years—at which time they'd
perform in a huge crater in the Nevada desert. They published a hun-
dred-page "manifesto" assembled by Duguay, which contained mystical
incantations based on the number three, psychedelic drawings, a list of
the musicians' cherished colours (*"le bluet d'abitibi et du lac st-jean qui
pousse dans les tartes d'été"*—"the blueberries of Abitibi and Lake St. Jean
which grow in the pies of summer"), a eulogy on the beauty of all art

241

("*L'Art Est un Laboratoire Où L'Ordre Remplit le Chaos*"—"art is a laboratory where order fills chaos"), recipes ("*La Soupe Pizzicato à l'Aquarium Symphonique*"), lyrics to such original songs as "*Ma coeur est un Car Washshsh*" ("My heart is a car wash"), and the 333 "commandments" of L'Infonie ("*88. Puisse La Culture Aider le Savoir*"—"May culture aid knowledge").[4]

At the core of this cosmic parody ("God has a sense of humour. So do we"—Boudreau[5]) was the music. Boudreau took it very seriously. L'Infonie's repertoire ranged from lush orchestrations of Bach concertos and Beatles songs to original compositions incorporating metre changes and elements of rock, jazz, contemporary classical music, vocal chants, and synthesized electronic music. Prerecorded tapes of European classical music and the random sounds produced by spinning the dial on a radio were woven into the texture of the music. Boudreau:

> I composed the music deliberately to disturb the audience. I was using L'Infonie to open their ears to music that is less conventional. There was room for everything, if it was done with taste. Everything we did was written down. We'd do a few jazz charts so the musicians could improvise, and there were a few solos here and there, but they were all part of a bigger machine.

L'Infonie was not a jazz orchestra, but neither was it any other kind of orchestra then known to Quebec. Into its cauldron went all of the sounds and ideas that were buffeting the restless province; out of it poured a heady brew that defied definition but that worked magic on young audiences. Jazz was a minor, yet vital, ingredient of this musical brew: it expanded the emotional and expressive range of L'Infonie's strongly rock-based music with bursts of swing and moments of freely improvised caterwauling. In retrospect, what is significant historically about L'Infonie is not the quality of the jazz played by the band—to judge by the recordings, it was often crude—but the fact that in L'Infonie's repertoire, jazz mingled freely with rock and other styles of music. In this respect, L'Infonie attests to the impact which youth culture of the 1960s had upon an aspiring jazz musician growing up in Quebec during that decade.

Boudreau grew up in Sorel, a small ship-building city seventy kilometres downstream from Montreal, where as a child he studied piano with the nuns at a local Catholic girls school. He turned thirteen as the Quiet Revolution was beginning; that year he also took up the alto saxophone. At fourteen he began hitchhiking to Montreal on Saturdays for private saxophone lessons, a routine he maintained year-round for three years. In the meantime, Boudreau had also formed a small rock band in Sorel to play the latest pop hits and a few old standards and Latin dance tunes

Pianist Pierre Leduc's quartet at the Jazztek, 1968. Left to right: Ron Proby (trumpet, alto horn), Leduc, Walter Boudreau (soprano and alto saxophones); bottom: Richard Provencal (drums). *Photo by Maxine Pierre-Ayotte, courtesy of Pierre Leduc. John Gilmore Jazz History Collection, Concordia University Archives.*

for weddings and community events. The drummer in the band introduced Boudreau to bebop. Then, when he was fifteen, an older musician took him to hear John Coltrane perform at La Tête de l'Art. Overwhelmed by the experience, Boudreau immediately took up the soprano saxophone, in imitation of Coltrane. At seventeen he felt ready to call himself a jazz musician and organized his first jazz quartet.

After graduating from high school, Boudreau moved to Montreal to study science at university, but he soon dropped out and resolved to become a professional musician. A booking agent he met by chance found occasional jobs for his Sorel jazz quartet in Montreal coffeehouses. A few months later Boudreau was signing a contract to lead a jazz quartet at the world's fair. It was Boudreau's Sorel quartet that worked nightly at Expo's Youth Pavilion, with one significant exception—at the piano was Pierre Leduc, six years Boudreau's senior and already a central figure on the Montreal jazz scene.

Expo 67 exposed Boudreau to music of diverse cultures and styles, including jazz and experimental rock from the United States. He heard a new instrument called the synthesizer for the first time. When the world's fair closed, Boudreau moved rapidly into the local jazz community, subbing into bands and playing at The Black Bottom. The following year he joined Leduc's jazz quartet. Leduc in turn joined Boudreau's reassembled Youth Pavilion quartet to record an album of original compositions by both men.

It was Boudreau's enthusiasm for composition which led him beyond jazz. A self-taught composer, he looked for ideas and inspiration in whatever music he encountered. Rock had surrounded him from infancy, and modern jazz was a passion, but an unrestrained curiosity led him also to explore the music and techniques of contemporary classical music, including serial composition. He quickly obtained commissions for compositions from a film-maker and the CBC. In 1968 Boudreau began studying analysis and composition part-time with established contemporary music composers in Montreal.

All this was happening while Boudreau was working with Leduc's jazz quartet, playing a range of styles from boogie-woogie to loosely structured, free improvisation. Leduc, too, was listening to contemporary classical music and had begun composing. The two men, however, felt far removed from the controversial style of jazz called "free" or "avante-garde" that was being played by young black musicians in the United States. Increasingly, they looked to contemporary music for ideas to incorporate into their jazz. Eventually, they would come to define the free jazz they were experimenting with as an improvised approach to contemporary music. Leduc:

> The free jazz we were playing didn't have anything to do with free jazz in the United States, and the black issue there. The free jazz we were playing was connected to contemporary classical music. It expressed abstract emotions, personal emotions, the anguish about life in this century, but it wasn't connected to either politics or racial problems. It was purely a means of personal expression, though very intense. It was a mixture of jazz and the techniques of contemporary music. I didn't know Cecil Taylor's music, then. My playing came out of contemporary music—Xenakis, Stockhausen—mixed with my background in jazz.[6]

"Yes, I play free jazz...," Boudreau told a newspaper in late 1967:

> To be logical with oneself today, one must play free jazz. Only free jazz allows us enough space not to become stuck in an aesthetic which will one day be seen to have been reactionary. But I'm not interested in politics. I play free jazz for aesthetic reasons and for sentimental reasons.[7]

In 1968, after six months with Leduc's quartet, Boudreau resigned to

244

pursue composition. He detested working in nightclubs and could not understand why older musicians mourned the passing of an era when nightclub work had been plentiful. He rankled at the fact that many musicians had to earn their living playing for dancers and entertainers rather than be the focus of attention themselves. He rebelled against identification with any one style of music and scorned what he perceived as a narrow-mindedness among many local jazz musicians when it came to exploring other styles of music. In December 1968 he told a newspaper: "I refuse all labels: what I want to do must go beyond the limits of jazz, of serial music, of classical music, etc. I want to detach myself from all these concepts so that I can invent a new music, *my* music."[8]

On the north shore of Lake of Two Mountains, just beyond the suburbs of Montreal, lie several small towns. During the summer of 1967, Pointe Calumet was little more than a collection of summer cottages, sandy lots, hot-dog stands, and a roadside hotel. More than an hour's drive away, Walter Boudreau and Raoul Duguay were mixing jazz and poetry at the world's fair, but in the lounge of the Pointe Calumet hotel the entertainment was more conventional. Jean Préfontaine and his quartet were playing dance music. It was hardly the stuff dreams are made of, but it was a job.

Préfontaine was forty, the oldest musician in the band. His friends called him "Doc" because he had once studied medicine and psychology; only the previous year, he had been serving an internship in psychology at a hospital for war veterans near Montreal. Still, he preferred to think of himself as a musician. For more than a dozen years, he had been picking up occasional work playing saxophone in small clubs and outlying hotels. For eight of those years he had been a soldier, playing bassoon in a Canadian army band. Classical music had surrounded him from birth: his father, a biologist, played the piano; his mother sang opera; an aunt was a concert pianist and harpist. As a boy, Jean Préfontaine had been sent to a residential Catholic seminary school; there he had received formal musical training and learned to play clarinet and flute. Later he picked up the saxophone, and made the tenor his voice.

Through the summer of 1967, Préfontaine and his musicians—drummer Guy Thouin, bassist Maurice Richard, and electric guitarist Richard Chiasson—escaped into Montreal whenever they could. They frequently ended up at a basement coffee-house on Mountain Street called The Barrel, where an aspiring trumpet player named Mike Armstrong was booking jazz. Armstrong had begun presenting jazz concerts the previous year at Moose Hall, better known during the late 1950s as the meeting place of the Traditional Jazz Club of Montreal, a group of fans and part-time musicians devoted to Dixieland and New Orleans-style jazz. Armstrong called his presentations the Jazz Workshop, though they bore no relation to the Montreal musicians' organization of the 1950s which had first used that name. After a few concerts at Moose Hall, Armstrong moved to The Barrel, a poorly heated room under what was then the Legion hall. The room served as a folk and blues coffee-house during the evenings, but at midnight on Friday and Saturday nights Armstrong's Jazz Workshop took over. He began by hiring local musicians, favouring modernists such as Sonny Greenwich, trumpeter Ron Proby, and Sadik Hakim, the American pianist who had recently returned to Montreal to live.

By the early summer of 1967, Armstrong had expanded to a nightly jazz policy and begun importing free jazz musicians from the United States. Many of the most committed free players were heard late at night at The Barrel over the next six months: drummers Sunny Murray and Rashied Ali, trombonists Roswell Rudd and Grachan Moncur, tenor saxophonists Archie Shepp and Albert Ayler, and pianist Paul Bley. On one occasion Armstrong brought in a quartet of American musicians, led by alto saxophonist Marion Brown and including Rashied Ali, to play nightly for three weeks. Local drummer Dennis Brown, who was finding his way to free jazz after more than a decade of working in Montreal show bands, was among those who revelled in this sustained exposure to Ali and other American free players; however, it wasn't until Brown left Montreal for southern Ontario three years later that he began performing free jazz professionally.

Firsthand exposure to the intensity of free jazz, and discussions with some of the American players at The Barrel, inspired Préfontaine and his musicians to experiment with the idiom. They began improvising collectively on stage at the Pointe Calumet hotel on Sunday afternoons. When the engagement ended, Chiasson left the band. The other three musicians invited Yves Charbonneau, a Québécois trumpet player they had met at The Barrel, to join them in forming a cooperative free jazz quartet. Like the other musicians, Charbonneau had been playing mainly commercial music in club and hotel bands but was excited by the expressive possibilities of free collective improvisation. He was also deeply committed to the revolutionary ideology of Quebec's radical left.

The four musicians decided to live together communally. They saw the process of forming a free jazz group as an experiment in personal and collective self-knowledge as much as they considered it a problem of developing a common musical vocabulary. Thouin had an apartment at 1660 Papineau Street in east-end Montreal, at the foot of the Jacques Cartier Bridge. In the late summer of 1967 the musicians soundproofed the basement and moved in. They immediately began improvising music together for hours at a stretch, day and night. Thouin, who had abandoned a career as an optometrist to return to his childhood passion, the drums, remembered the intensity of that initial exploration:

> We began from zero. We weren't really jazzmen. We hadn't played much jazz. We didn't come from the culture of jazz. But we played, we expressed ourselves. We were searching—profoundly.[9]

After a few weeks of rehearsing, the quartet began playing in public at a small nightclub where the regular entertainment was a Spanish flamenco guitarist and dancer. Casa Espagnole, the informal name of the Association Espagnole on Sherbrooke Street West near Park, had become popular with artists, poets, and intellectuals who drew comfort from its bohemian atmosphere and modest prices. The quartet struck a deal with the owner of the place and began performing nightly in a dimly lit room above the flamenco show, three flights up from the sidewalk. When the flamenco music stopped, the quartet began improvising above them, collecting a little money at the door from the people who carried their glasses of wine and beer upstairs to listen. When the flamenco performers were ready to resume, the quartet ground to a halt and the crowds descended again.

The Barrel, meanwhile, had abandoned its costly policy of importing musicians from the United States and was hiring local players again. After a brief stay at Casa Espagnole, Préfontaine, Charbonneau, Thouin, and Richard moved to The Barrel. They still had not decided on a name for the band, so Armstrong hung a sign outside the door, in English, proclaiming a "New Canadian Free Jazz Quartet." The musicians objected to both the language of the sign and the Canadian label, and hastily decided on an alternative: Le Quatuor du nouveau jazz libre du Québec. The name stuck. *Nouveau* was dropped once the quartet became known, and a couple of years later the name was shortened further to Le Jazz libre du Québec, in part because the group was sometimes augmented to five or six musicians. Followers, however, referred to the band simply as Jazz libre—literally, free jazz.

The quartet performed regularly at The Barrel until mid-January 1968, then returned to Casa Espagnole. Shortly afterward, The Barrel closed, leaving Casa Espagnole as the sole home for free collective improvisation in Montreal. Jazz libre was quickly making a name for itself, in part through Préfontaine's salesmanship, but also because of the band's association with the separatist movement and radical politics. During its four-month residency at Casa Espagnole, the group frequently played one-night events elsewhere: they gave concerts at universities and col-

Le Quatuor de jazz libre du Québec, circa 1968: Yves Charbonneau (trumpet), Jean "Doc" Préfontaine (tenor saxophone), Guy Thouin (drums), Maurice Richard (bass). *Photo courtesy of* La Presse.

leges in Montreal, Sherbrooke, and other cities; they participated in multimedia happenings; and they collaborated in jazz and poetry performances with Raoul Duguay and Walter Boudreau.

While at Casa Espagnole, the four musicians also ended their experiment in communal living. Commitment to the group remained strong, but conflicts were arising about the nature of the music and its relationship to politics. Charbonneau was advocating revolution; Préfontaine considered himself a democratic socialist. Both men believed the political implications of their music were at least as important as the music itself. A year later Charbonneau would state his position bluntly to journalist Jacques Larue-Langlois: "Before being a musician, I am a revolutionary. Instead of carrying a machine-gun, I have a trumpet. I preach freedom by saying—play free."[10] Richard's politics are not known, though according to Thouin all four members of Jazz libre were politicized to some degree. Thouin, however, increasingly felt at odds with the politicization of the group's music. He was committed to playing free jazz but wanted the improvisations to be based on predetermined structures of some kind—a melodic motif, perhaps, or a rhythmic pattern, or even an abstract form or idea or mood that would serve to shape the music. Charbonneau, at the other extreme, equated structure with oppression: to impose any structure on the music would be to restrict the freedom of the musicians; and to consent to that would be to symbolically accept limitations on Quebec's demands for political and economic independence. The ideology of total revolution demanded totally free music.

In this spirit, the musicians would arrive on stage with no preconceived idea of what they were going to play. One musician would start playing and the others would join in; each would try to relate to what the others were playing while simultaneously making a personal statement. A single improvisation might last twenty minutes or longer. When it ended, the musicians would discuss what they had played, arguing among themselves and drawing the audience into the debate over the music and its political implications. Thouin:

> When we finished playing, often I wasn't happy with what had happened. It was too long; there was no structure. I was listening to the American groups at that time, and they had *some* structure. Even Cecil Taylor had themes, compositions. But we had nothing. I would argue with the other musicians on a philosophical level, saying that in the universe things didn't just happen without some structure—a rose is not a tulip, and there must be a structure there somewhere. But we had no structure: it was total nihilism. The discussions we had were very heated, even on stage. Often I would get furious. And there was a kind of forum with the audience. People would ask us what we were doing, and we talked about our music. It became a philosophical debate, a very profound, internal question—almost a spiritual search.

At the Casa Espagnole and other places where Jazz libre performed, people were talking of separatism, of socialism, of revolution, and of the Front de libération du Québec (FLQ). Thouin continued:

> The journalists began identifying us with the movement: we were like the representative of *Québec libre*. People within the movement, too, identified Jazz libre with *Québec libre*. It was the same thing as what was happening in the United States, with the black groups playing free jazz. It wasn't just music, it meant something more: it was a vehicle for a culture.
>
> You can't put the blame on the media, or on any one person. It was the context. If there was one group of people who said, "We are the white niggers of America," then the people jumped on the occasion to say that Jazz libre was a movement to liberate us from all the structures. There was something positive in it at the beginning, but it became stagnant. It went around in circles. The music didn't go anywhere. It was blocked at the political level: if we didn't play free, we were no longer political musicians. So we rejected all structure; for the others, that was a political statement, a movement for the liberation of Quebec. But where was it going?

> Because we were rejecting, we weren't constructing anything. You destroy, destroy, destroy—and you arrive at the bottom. Then where do you go? It was upsetting. It was real anguish. And it produced anxiety: it was anxious music.

In the spring of 1968, Jazz libre left Casa Espagnole to collaborate in two musical revues with some of the rising young stars of Quebec's cultural renaissance, including the singers Robert Charlebois and Louise Forestier. The second of these revues, called *L'Osstidcho*,[11] toured Quebec, won enthusiastic popular acclaim, and marked a turning point in the *chansonnier* tradition of the province. The young poet-singers were abandoning their acoustic guitars and solitary performances, and surrounding themselves with rock bands. Charlebois, then twenty-three and inspired by the hippie culture of California, was a leader in this new direction. In a daring embrace of modernity, he invited Jazz libre to continue performing with him after *L'Osstidcho* closed. Thouin:

> I don't know if you can understand the conflict that working with Charlebois presented for us. To leave free jazz and accompany a song by Charlebois was like putting us in a cement box and closing the lid. We accepted because it was a challenge. In the beginning there were no arrangements: he sang his songs and we played free. But it became necessary to structure our playing—to play the same beat for two minutes, or for the trumpet to play a certain thing. It was very difficult for the guys in Jazz libre; there was something in them that refused to accept it. Me, I played rock on the drums. But the other guys didn't accept it, because they were into the revolution. So we'd play the structure of Charlebois's songs, but when there were places to blow, it became free.

Through the remainder of 1968, Jazz libre accompanied Charlebois in concerts and nightclubs, and on television. They also played on four tracks of an album he recorded with Louise Forestier—including the hit title song, "Lindbergh." The music was clearly in the rock camp, however, and little jazz of any kind escaped the tight arrangements.

Meanwhile, Jazz libre was continuing to perform free jazz on its own. Charlebois's pianist, Pierre Nadeau, played with the group whenever he was free and a piano was available on stage. In December 1968, Jazz libre recorded their first and only album under their own name, using Nadeau on three of the five tracks. The music ranged from the unstructured free improvisation typical of the band's live performances to fairly conventional jazz compositions—all of them original—employing eight-bar phrases, swing rhythm, and consecutive solos. Jazz libre's compromise with structure had reached into the group's own repertoire.

A month later Jazz libre collaborated in another musical revue, this one called L'*Osstidchomeurt*, then set off to Europe with Charlebois and Louise Forestier for a concert tour. A riotous performance at the Olympia in Paris forced cancellation of the remainder of the tour but generated enormous publicity for Charlebois at home. The singer's star was rising fast, and the marriage with Jazz libre was becoming strained. After a series of summer concerts and television shows, Charlebois and Jazz libre parted company.

Jazz libre's year-long collaboration with Charlebois coincided with the gestation and birth of L'Infonie. The quartet participated in many of the happenings and experimental groupings led by Walter Boudreau and Raoul Duguay which led eventually to the formal creation of L'Infonie. In this way, two different conceptions of free jazz—Boudreau's, the more structured, and Jazz libre's, the more spontaneous—came together to conduct even more daring experiments in music and performance. The musicians of Jazz libre were steady members of L'Infonie from its birth. At the same time, they continued to perform regularly as an independent unit. Concerts frequently featured a set of music by Jazz libre followed by a performance of L'Infonie.

Boudreau welcomed other jazz musicians into his orchestra besides Jazz libre. Bassist Jacques Valois, from Boudreau's original Sorel jazz quartet, became a member, as did drummer Réjean Emond, another Sorel native, who had worked in Pierre Leduc's trio at Le Jazz Hot; initially, almost half of the members of L'Infonie were from Sorel. Only two anglophone musicians ever worked with L'Infonie: Sayyd Abdul Al-Khabyyr and Jack Rider. Both were bebop-schooled jazz saxophonists, and both recorded with the orchestra. Abdul Al-Khabyyr, a native of Harlem who had settled in Montreal during the 1950s, later spent much of the 1970s playing free jazz in his own coffee-house in Montreal. Rider, an immigrant from England, regarded the year he spent with L'Infonie as a kind of sabbatical from the personal problems and dearth of fulfilling work that was plaguing his life at the time:

> I was revolting in my own way against all of the shit going on around me. I dressed like a monk all the time in L'Infonie—dark spectacles, black robe, and a priest gave me one of those specially blessed ropes for a belt because he didn't like the piece of string I was using. We didn't make any money, but I had some put on one side and I just went through to the end, till I had two cents left in the bank, then I said, "I gotta leave the group now."

The personnel of L'Infonie fluctuated during its lifetime, but many players remained with the orchestra for long stretches. Among them was

Jazz libre. Unlike that of the other core members, however, the quartet's continued presence became a source of mounting friction within the orchestra. Jazz libre's gravity and musical destructiveness clashed with L'Infonie's joyous embrace of all musics from Bach to rock. Tensions frequently erupted into verbal battles. Jazz libre criticized Boudreau's music for being too structured, and Boudreau himself for imposing his vision of L'Infonie on the rest of the band. Boudreau criticized Jazz libre for lacking discipline and musicianship. The quartet, with the exception of Thouin who was himself tiring of the unrelenting confrontational attitude of his bandmates, became isolated within the larger ensemble. Thouin:

> Some of the guys in Jazz libre refused to accept a leader. They didn't want anyone telling them what to do. They wanted everyone in the band equal. But equality, communism, made no sense in a large ensemble like that.

Duguay did his best to mediate, but found the gulf widening:

> It was a conflict between a political and a cosmic philosophy, between proletarian realism and spirituality. Jazz libre was guerilla music, nihilist, against the system, but L'Infonie was based on the idea that ... it's the personal revolution that brings the social revolution, and not the opposite. So L'Infonie worked on the internal dimension. That was our political response to society.

Despite their common rebellion against the traditions of jazz, Boudreau's and Jazz libre's musical and social philosophies were irreconcilable. In 1970, after a year of conflict, the partnership fell apart. First, Thouin quit Jazz libre in exasperation, then Jazz libre left L'Infonie, to throw itself into direct social and political action. It's experiment with compromise was over. Thouin remained as L'Infonie's drummer for several months, then left to pursue formal music studies at McGill University. A year later he moved to India, joined an ashram, and became of a student of yoga and classical Indian tabla drumming.

Boudreau's problems with L'Infonie did not end with the departure of Jazz libre. The sheer size of the orchestra posed organizational and financial difficulties as well. The logistics of transporting musicians, instruments, costumes, props, sound equipment, lighting, and technical crews to and from an engagement were daunting. Despite L'Infonie's popularity, the cost of hiring such a large ensemble—twelve hundred dollars a night—limited the opportunities for work. That meant the orchestra members could not earn their living from the ensemble and were forced to seek work elsewhere, which in turn presented organizational problems in scheduling rehearsals and out-of-town engagements. L'Infonie requested financial support from the Quebec government to alleviate some of these problems but was turned down.

To pass the time while crews unloaded equipment and prepared the stage for an out-of-town engagement, some of the saxophonists in L'Infonie began rehearsing classical quartet repertoire in the dressing room. Boudreau took up the baritone saxophone for this rehearsal group and eventually began writing for the quartet. During the winter of 1971-72, he decided to reduce L'Infonie to eight musicians—the saxophone quartet plus a four-piece rock rhythm section. Duguay remained with the new formation, which retained the costumes and some of the antics of the previous large ensemble. But the music became more focused and disciplined, and demonstrated Boudreau's growing interest and skill in the contemporary music idiom.

The smaller L'Infonie gave its first major concert in Montreal in April 1972, at a sports arena at the University of Montreal. After it was over, Boudreau and Duguay decided to end their five-year partnership. Duguay, who had begun singing with L'Infonie, wanted to build on the following and experience he had gained with the orchestra and develop a career as a singer and performer. Boudreau remained committed to performing mainly instrumental music. That summer, L'Infonie did not perform at all while Boudreau travelled to West Germany on a Canada Council grant to study with Karlheinz Stockhausen, Iannis Xenakis, and other contemporary music composers. Returning to Montreal in the fall, he reformed the octet L'Infonie. The following spring it recorded—a fifty-minute performance of Boudreau's composition "Paix" ("peace"), integrating elements of contemporary music, rock, and jazz—and then made a lengthy summer tour of Quebec, subsidized by the federal government.

Boudreau was moving fast. When the tour ended, he disbanded the octet and set off for Europe again, to spend the fall and winter of 1973-74 in France studying with Xenakis. Returning to Montreal in the spring, Boudreau decided not to resurrect L'Infonie. Instead, he brought only the saxophonists together to form Le Quatuor de saxophones de L'Infonie. Rock, jazz, and theatrics were dropped, leaving an unaccompanied saxophone quartet to perform classical and contemporary music repertoire and original compositions by Boudreau.[12] Boudreau's metamorphosis from jazz musician to classical baritone saxophonist and contemporary music composer was complete.

Jazz libre left L'Infonie in the same year that political violence in Quebec reached a peak. In October 1970 different cells of the FLQ kidnapped first the senior British trade commissioner in Montreal and then the Quebec labour minister. The federal government responded by invoking the War Measures Act, sending in the military to conduct house-to-house searches, and detaining more than four hundred and fifty Quebec nationalists, political activists, intellectuals, and artists for their pro-separatist views; only two were ultimately convicted of offenses against public order. One cell of the underground organization executed the Quebec minister, Pierre Laporte, but the trade commissioner, James Cross, was released after two months in captivity when his kidnappers were allowed to leave for Cuba.

It was against this dramatic backdrop that Jazz libre entered a new phase of political and social engagement. In the spring before the kidnappings, the quartet began organizing a summer colony near the Laurentian town of Val David. A campsite was built where low-income people, youth, and artists could spend their vacation and participate in art workshops. Jazz libre performed at the colony during the summer, conducted music workshops, and helped stage a three-day pop festival on the grounds. When the colony disbanded in the fall, Jazz libre decided to establish another one on a permanent basis.

Late that year, while soldiers were searching Montreal for the FLQ kidnappers, Jazz libre rented a farm at Ste. Anne de la Rochelle in the Eastern Townships, about one hundred kilometres east of Montreal. The sympathetic owner set the rent at only one dollar a year, with an option to buy, but the tenants were responsible for paying the taxes and an overdue installment on the mortgage. Jazz libre overcame the initial financial crisis by launching a fund-raising appeal in January 1971, and performing a benefit concert at the Bibliothèque nationale du Québec in Montreal.[13] It then set about transforming the farm into Le Petit Québec libre ("the little free Quebec")—a communal base for political activists and artists committed to Quebec independence and radical social change. A printing press was installed at the 143-acre farm, allowing the commune to publish its own newsletter and a manifesto. The barn was converted into a rustic performance space. Jazz libre and other musicians performed there regularly, drawing audiences from as far away as Montreal. And through the summer of 1971, people came to camp at the farm, to attend the concerts, and to participate in theatre, craft, and music workshops.

The police also came. Authorities suspected the commune was linked to the FLQ and kept it under close surveillance. The Royal Canadian Mounted Police believed the farm was being used for secret meetings between the FLQ and radical groups from the United States, including the Black Panthers. On the night of 8 May 1972, four RCMP officers acting under orders crept onto the farm and set fire to the barn, burning it

MANIFESTE

DU

"PETIT

QUÉBEC

LIBRE"

Fils et filles de travailleurs québécois,
NOUS VOULONS, à partir d'une expérience communautaire, contribuer à la libération individuelle et collective des Québécois

NOUS VOULONS informer nous-mêmes nos compatriotes de nos buts et des moyens que la ferme du PETIT QUEBEC LIBRE met à la disposition de tous pour encourager l'expression de la créativité de chacun.

NOUS CROYONS que tout en donnant à notre projet une certaine publicité, les média d'information ont censuré grossièrement tout son contenu idéologique, comme ils censurent toute critique qui préconise un changement du système actuel.

NOUS VOULONS répondre à un besoin urgent que tout le monde ressent après la crise que nous venons de traverser, de trouver ensemble des terrains d'entente, des sentiments communs.

NOUS CROYONS que la méfiance, la délation, la culpabilité collective, entretenues par les média d'information, l' incompréhension et les luttes mesquines entre les groupes doivent disparaître rapidement pour céder la place à la solidarité.

NOUS VOULONS, par nos propres moyens et avec l'aide des patriotes, que le PETIT QUEBEC LIBRE soit l' affaire de tous les travailleurs québécois, leur propriété et leur réalisation collective.

NOUS CROYONS que chaque travailleur québécois doit participer activement à l'organisation de sa propre libération économique, politique, culturelle et sociale.

NOUS VOULONS vivre la démocratie au PETIT QUEBEC LIBRE: tous participent à l'organisation, aux décisions et aux réalisations.

NOUS CROYONS que leur "democracy" c'est une farce tragique, avec leurs élections truquées à tous les quatre ans, et leur parade de tristes bouffons-vedettes.

NOUS VOULONS la libération de tous les prisonniers politiques détenus injustement pour avoir osé dénoncer la clique de l'Establishment. Comme tous les peuples colonisés et exploités, le peuple québécois commence à relever la tête et à crier bien haut son besoin de liberté et de justice.

NOUS CROYONS que la loi sur les Mesures de guerre est une agression contre la liberté du peuple québécois tout entier et une preuve de plus de la lâcheté de ceux qui se disent ses représentants.

NOUS PROCLAMONS notre solidarité avec tous les peuples opprimés dans leur lutte de libération nationale.

NOUS CROYONS que par l'oppression, l'exploitation et les guerres qui écrasent les deux tiers de l'humanité, les 19 grands monopoles de l' impérialisme américain ne visent que leurs profits voraces et leurs intérêts inhumains au détriment de la survie de la race humaine et de l'existence même de notre planète.

Le "PETIT QUEBEC LIBRE" et sa portée sociale réside dans le fait que tout sera gratuit, c'est à dire que les gens donneront ce qu'ils voudront (si besoin est), et ceci dans le but de ne pas limiter la participation des gens à des questions d'argent ou de classes sociales (chômeurs, travailleurs, étudiants, assistés sociaux, etc.)

C'est l'OPERATION FUCK LA PIASSE! ET VIVE LES QUEBECOIS!

LE POUVOIR AU PEUPLE

Page from the manifesto of Le Petit Québec libre—a communal farm near Ste. Anne de la Rochelle in the Eastern Townships, established by Le Quatuor de jazz libre du Québec. *Jean Préfontaine Collection, Concordia University Archives.*

to the ground.[14]

Jazz libre returned to Montreal. That fall, with the help of a federal government make-work grant, they opened a coffee-house on St. Paul Street in Old Montreal, calling it L'Amorce. For a year and a half they performed free jazz at L'Amorce five or six nights a week, sharing the billing on weekends with other bands and artists. They installed a four-track tape recorder and recorded all their performances while simultaneously providing quadraphonic sound to the audience. Between sets they played jazz records and sold coffee, soft drinks, and cold pizza to the audience, which ranged from a handful on some weekday nights to sixty or more on weekends. And they continued to extol radical politics, hanging a picture of FLQ member Paul Rose in the front window and playing the "Internationale" at the end of their performances.

Jazz libre remained committed to free collective improvisation to the end. After Thouin's departure in 1970, the quartet went through several drummers and bassists, but Charbonneau and Préfontaine kept it firmly in the politicized free camp. With a drummer named Jean-Guy Poirier, the group travelled to Italy in the late summer of 1973 to perform at a music festival. Soon after its return, however, Poirier quit, making room for the group's final drummer, a young Ontario-born francophone named Mathieu Léger. A young American cellist named Tristan Honsinger also performed regularly with Jazz libre at L'Amorce. Honsinger had fled to Montreal to avoid military conscription during the Vietnam War; later he would move to Europe and develop a career as a performer of free improvised music.

L'Amorce came to an end shortly after midnight on 25 June 1974, while Old Montreal was engulfed in rioting. City police had been called in to nearby Jacques Cartier square to clear the area of rowdy crowds celebrating St. Jean Baptiste Day, the national holiday of Quebec. For the third night in a row, the celebrations had turned violent: windows had been smashed and shops damaged. The police attack on the night of 24 June—St. John Baptiste Day—was particularly vicious. People were clubbed and thrown into police wagons; motorcycles chased citizens down sidewalks; reporters were roughed up and their cameras smashed. People in the crowd fought back with stones and fists, injuring several police officers and overturning and burning police cars. The city's police and citizens fought running battles over a ten-square-block area of Old Montreal for much of the night.[15]

At twenty-two minutes after midnight, flames were spotted at a four-storey building on the corner of St. Jean Baptiste Street and St. Paul, four blocks from the square. The building housed L'Amorce. Firemen took three hours to extinguish the general-alarm blaze. When it was over, the coffee-house was in ruins. Fire department investigators determined the fire had been deliberately set and turned the case over to the city police. The police investigated. No arrests were made. The case was never solved.[16] That summer, Le Jazz libre du Québec broke up.

NOTES

Chapter One

1. Willie (William) Eckstein was occasionally called Billy Eckstein in Montreal, not to be confused with the American singer Billy Eckstine, whose real name was Eckstein.

2. The sequence of Thomas's journeys and recordings is based upon recording dates, some of them approximate, given in Jack Litchfield, *The Canadian Jazz Discography: 1916-1980* (Toronto: University of Toronto Press, 1982), 41-42, 722. Thomas recorded three test recordings of "Delirious Rag" and "A Classical Spasm" for Victor in New York on 20 November 1916, but these were not issued. On 4 December, Thomas again recorded the same tunes for Victor in New York, an unknown number of times; the fourth takes of both tunes from this second session were issued. It is not known how many, if any, unissued piano rolls were made at Thomas's 1916 sessions in Chicago and New York, or whether he made more than one trip to each city to produce these rolls.

3. Ragtime was a formally composed piano music whose origins lay in the attempt by black American musicians trained in the European system of music to replicate in their compositions something of the polyrhythms of African and early black American folk musics. Originally intended as dance music, ragtime contained no improvisation and was printed as sheet music and sold all over North America and Europe. It was thus the first black music of the United States to achieve wide commercial popularity, introducing the white middle class to black folk styles and conceptions of music. Early jazz was based heavily in ragtime, but with the added crucial ingredient of the blues. See William Schafer and Johannes Riedel, *The Art of Ragtime* (New York: Da Capo, 1977).

4. James Lincoln Collier, *The Making of Jazz: A Comprehensive History* (1978; reprint, New York: Delta, 1979), 72.

5. Collier, 72.

6. The ODJB first recorded on 30 January 1917 for Columbia, but the Columbia record was not issued until after Victor's, which is regarded by historians as the first jazz record. The band issued about a dozen records before falling apart in the mid-1920s. "Jass" was an early spelling of "jazz."

7. It wasn't until after 1920 that whites began to develop a jazz tradition of their own. On the influence of the ODJB and the spread of white jazz, see Collier, *Making of Jazz*, 72-77; and Ben Sidran, *Black Talk* (1971; reprint, New York: Da Capo, 1981), 51.

8. Robin W. Winks, *The Blacks in Canada: A History* (Montreal: McGill-Queen's University Press, 1971), 300.

9. Sidran, *Black Talk*, 62.

10. My sources on black history in Canada are: William Lewis Edmonds, "The Coloured Race in Canada," *Saturday Night*, 13 July 1929, 4-5; *Encyclopedia of Music in Canada*, s.v. "black musicians"; and Winks, *Blacks in Canada*. *Encyclopedia of Music in Canada* states that the earliest documentation of a black musician in Canada is found in the *Quebec Gazette* of 30 November 1775, which refers to a runaway slave named Lowcanes who spoke French and played the violin. During the American Revolution, the British used black musicians in their army as buglers.

11. On the life of Canadian black railway porters, see McKenzie Porter, "Three Thousand Nights on Wheels," *Maclean's*, 15 March 1949.

12. In fact, by 1928 there may have been five black nightlife establishments in the St. Antoine district. The first of these was the Recreation Key Club, which opened on St. James Street in 1897. It changed its name to the Utopia Club, moved to 22 St. Antoine Street in 1911, then in 1912 moved to its final location on St. Antoine Street somewhere between Windsor and Mountain. In 1914, the Standard Club opened at 80 St. Antoine Street and five years later moved to the corner of St. Antoine and Desrivières. The Nemderoloc Club opened in 1922 at 180a St. Antoine. These three clubs were primarily social clubs offering gambling, billiards, and beer to private members and their guests. However, it is likely that live music, and especially piano, was occasionally performed there. According to Wilfred Emmerson Israel, two additional establishments, which he calls cabarets, had opened by 1928 and did offer live music for dancing. These were located at 1256 and 1323 St. Antoine Street. See Interlude 1 for details. Street numbering in Montreal changed several times during these years, therefore the numbers given above may not correspond to present-day addresses. Wilfred Emmerson Israel, "The Montreal Negro Community," Master's thesis, McGill University, Montreal, 1928, 183-85, 189-90.

13. Winks, *Blacks in Canada*, 333.

14. The earliest known ragtime composers in Canada were W. H. Hodgins and

G. A. Adams, both of whom published music in 1899. While ragtime is a black music, Montreal was not unique in having white ragtime composers and performers. One of the most celebrated ragtime composers was Joseph Lamb, an American-born white musician who lived in Kitchener, Ontario, after 1901. Ragtime enjoyed a major revival in the 1950s, but in Canada this was centred in Toronto. *Encyclopedia of Music in Canada*, s.v. "ragtime."

15. While Guilaroff was the first woman in Canada to record ragtime, numerous women in Canada recorded earlier than her, playing mostly French Canadian music. Nor was Guilaroff the only woman to work as a theatre pianist in Montreal: one Miss Leo Claude was pianist at the Rex theatre in 1920, and Marion Burns also substituted for Eckstein at the Strand. Two women who are believed to have played popular music, possibly including some jazz or ragtime, on piano in Montreal during the 1920s remain undocumented: Vera Millington and Olga Spencer.

16. For a history of vaudeville in Quebec, see Chantal Hébert, *Le Burlesque au Québec: Un divertissement populaire* (Ville LaSalle, Que.: Hurtubise HMH, 1981). Hébert distinguishes between vaudeville and burlesque: the former did not include a chorus line while the latter did, at least until the 1930s when burlesque in Quebec evolved into a theatrical form which enjoyed great popularity until 1950, and was still alive in the 1980s. However, early newspaper advertisements frequently referred to all live stage shows in Montreal as vaudeville, and I use the term here in this general sense.

17. The Six Brown Brothers performed with faces and hands painted white or black, a common theatrical device at the time. This could have been used to conceal White's race from audiences if he did perform publicly with the band, whose other members are believed to have been white. The personnel of the group changed through its fifteen years of existence and has never been established conclusively, but White is listed as the composer of at least one tune recorded by the band in 1916. Though the original band members were Canadians, and the band began recording five years before Harry Thomas, it was resident in the United States. *Encyclopedia of Music in Canada*, s.v. "Six Brown Brothers"; and Litchfield, *Discography*, 697.

18. My sources on Prohibition in Canada are: Graeme Decarie, Department of History, Concordia University, telephone interview with author, 2 December 1983; and J. Castell Hopkins, *The Canadian Annual Review of Public Affairs* (Toronto: Canadian Annual Review), 1918, 1919, 1920, 1921.

19. Advertisement, *Montreal Star*, January 1918 (exact date unknown). Most band names and engagements mentioned in this chapter are from Montreal newspaper advertisements.

20. Newspaper advertisements show that Prevoa's Singing Coloured Band, which also appears to have worked in Montreal under the name Prevoa's

Mammoth Coloured Jazz Band, appeared in the city during January and February 1921. (The name is sometimes spelled Prevon in advertisements.) On 15 March 1921, George Wright and his eight-piece band from Chicago, billed as the Original Darkey Jazz Band, opened Montreal's Roseland Ballroom; the group included violinist Willie Tyler, who had previously recorded with W. C. Handy's orchestra. On the same bill at the Roseland opening was a group of unknown origin called the Captivating Ragtime Band. Wright remained in Montreal for seven months, leading bands at dance halls under such names as Wright's Jazz Band and the Kings of Syncopation. In October 1921 he apparently sailed to Europe from Montreal with his band.

21. Rudi Blesh and Harriet Janis, *They All Played Ragtime*, 4th ed. (New York: Oak, 1971), 154.

22. White was not the only black composer versed in ragtime to reside in Canada. Others included Shelton Brooks, Nathaniel Dett, and Lou Hooper. *Encyclopedia of Music in Canada*, s.v. "ragtime."

23. Yerkes bands known to have worked in Montreal were: Yerkes's Famous Band, which played at the Blue Bird Café from the venue's official opening on 29 May 1920 to early August 1920; Yerkes's Novelty Entertainers, which played at the Dansant de Luxe from the hall's official opening on 16 October 1920 to early November 1920; and Yerkes's Flotilla Orchestra, a ten-piece band led by Dick Barton which played on vaudeville at the Princess theatre during the week of 6 October 1923. Yerkes recorded seven issued titles in Montreal in 1920, in addition to numerous American recordings.

24. Cornetist Nat Natoli worked with the Original Memphis Five during its Montreal engagement, though he was not a regular member of the band. A leading hot player of the day, Natoli went on to work with Jean Goldkette and Paul Whiteman.

25. Gershwin returned to New York City before the Whiteman tour arrived in Montreal, leaving the Montreal première of "Rhapsody in Blue" in the hands of a substitute pianist, Milton Rettenburg. In 1982 the Smithsonian Institute in the United States released a double-LP recreation of the 1924 Whiteman tour program called *Paul Whiteman at Aeolian Hall* (Smithsonian Collection R028). John S. Wilson, reviewing the recordings for the *New York Times* on 25 April 1982, wrote that "Whiteman's program gave no evidence that he had ever heard of" Jelly Roll Morton, Sidney Bechet, or Louis Armstrong, the leading black jazz musicians of the day. Jazz pretensions aside, Whiteman was a major figure in the history of North American popular music whose work is still being assessed by scholars.

26. One example of this cooperative spirit between white and black musicians in Montreal occurred in 1923. Millard Thomas and his Famous Chicago Novelty Orchestra joined forces with Andy Tipaldi's Melody Kings and Simon Martucci's

orchestra to perform a benefit dance and cabaret, held at the Mount Royal hotel, for the National Vaudeville Artists Sick Fund. Advertisement, *Montreal Daily Star*, 6 April 1923, 6.

27. "Jazz's Day Is Done and White People Will Come to Their Senses," *Herald* (Montreal), 17 June 1922.

28. Anne Shaw Faulkner, "Where Does Jazz Lead?" *Maclean's*, October 1921, 27. The full version of the article was originally published as "Does Jazz Put the Sin in Syncopation," *Ladies' Home Journal*, August 1921, 16, 34. Faulkner was the pen-name of Mrs. Marx E. Oberndorfer, national music chairperson of the General Federation of Women's Clubs.

29. Edward E. Moogk, *Roll Back the Years: History of Canadian Recorded Sound and Its Legacy, Genesis to 1930* (Ottawa: National Library, 1975). Researchers Jim Kidd, Jack Litchfield, and Alex Robertson provided additional information on early Montreal recording history for this chapter. See also *Encyclopedia of Music in Canada*, s.v. "Berliner," "Compo," "RCA Limited," and "recorded sound."

30. According to Alex Robertson, who interviewed Herbert Berliner before his death, Emile Berliner bought the Foisy Frères chain of music stores. At least two of these stores were on St. Catherine Street.

31. Race labels existed in the United States in 1920, but it wasn't until 1923—the same year Compo launched Ajax—that the race market boomed. Collier, *Making of Jazz*, 90, writes: "1923 was the year in which jazz finally came to be widely recorded. The record companies had little idea of what jazz was, but they were discovering that there was a large market among blacks for their own music. Totally without system, they recorded whatever they could find. Now musicians, both black and white, had a stock of examples before them, and very quickly began to study them." See also Sidran, *Black Talk*, 65-67, on the impact of recording on jazz.

32. My source on sales in Montreal and the West Indies is Jim Kidd, letter to author, 19 October 1985, John Gilmore Jazz History Collection, Concordia University Archives, Montreal.

33. Gennett issued one or two recordings by each of a handful of black singers and minor jazz bands but did not bother to issue its recordings of King Oliver and Jelly Roll Morton in Canada. Mamie Smith records were available on Okeh and Phonola. Okeh also issued recordings by King Oliver, Clarence Williams, James P. Johnson, and several other race artists, though researchers have still not established conclusively whether Okeh's recordings of Louis Armstrong and his Hot Five were issued in Canada; a few have been found in Winnipeg. Whether Victor released any race records in Canada is not known.

34. As far as discographers have been able to establish, Compo took the initiative

to record black musicians for issue on a Compo label only once after the death of Ajax. This was in 1938, when Compo recorded American trumpeter Jabbo Jenkins in Montreal, where he was playing an engagement. The record was released under the name Arthur Williams Swing Trio on the Decca label, oddly enough in the 26000 series, which contained Herbert Berliner's personal favorites. However, after the death of Ajax, Compo did issue recordings of black musicians on some of the American labels it was franchised to press and release in Canada.

35. These were XWA (later CFCF) and CKAC. So-called "phantom" radio stations also existed. These bought air time on CFCF or CKAC's transmitters, used their own call numbers, and scheduled regular broadcasts. For example, Canadian National Railways ran a station called CNRM. But it wasn't until 1932 that a third station with its own frequency, CHLP, went on the air in Montreal. On early radio in Canada, see Roger Baulu, *CKAC: Une histoire d'amour* (Montreal: Stanké, 1982); Bill McNeil and Morris Wolfe, *Signing On: The Birth of Radio in Canada* (Toronto: Doubleday, 1982); and Sandy Stewart, *A Pictorial History of Radio in Canada* (Toronto: Gage, 1975).

36. The program of the Famous Chicago Novelty Orchestra's broadcast was published in *La Presse* (Montreal), 14 June 1923: "(1) Overture - Medley - Light Cavalry Crooning; (2) Running Wild - Fox Trot; (3) Trio - Humereska - Dvorak - Violin, M. Holiday, Saxophone, M. Harris, piano, M. Thomas; (4) Romany Love - Fox Trot; (5) Solo de saxophone—Teddy Trombone—M. Cassamore; (6) Fuzzy Wuzzy Bird - Fox Trot; (7) Solo de violin - Cavatina - M. Holiday; (8) Yes! We Have No Bananas! - Fox Trot; (9) Solo de saxophone - Eli Eli—Harris; (10) I'll Be Here When You Come Back - Fox Trot; (11) Wearied Blues - Fox Trot" [sic]. The broadcast also presented a classical concert by pianist Phillip Kool, and singers John Cahill and Gordon Provencher. It is possible that Thomas and other local black musicians broadcast on local radio on other occasions, but no evidence has been found.

37. CFCF became the Montreal outlet for programs of the NBC network in the United States, while CKAC became the local outlet for the CBS network. Both Montreal stations broadcast local programs in both English and French during the 1920s.

Chapter Two

1. Later renamed Kahnawake.

2. Probable instrumentation of the Shorter Brothers Band upon arrival in Montreal: Jimmy Jones (trumpet), Frank Johnson (trombone, vocals), Henry Johnson (tenor saxophone, clarinet), Andy Shorter (saxophone), Bill Shorter (piano and/or saxophone), Benny Johnson (guitar), Arnold Shorter (bass and/or trumpet), Johnson Sr. (drums).

3. Robert Langlois, letter to author, December 1982, Langlois file, John Gilmore Jazz History Collection, Concordia University Archives, Montreal. My translation.

4. "The Blackbirds Review Is Syncopation Incarnate and Feathered Febrility," *Montreal Star*, 13 May 1929.

5. "Racket Boys in Montreal's Chinatown," *Weekender*, 3 June 1939, 3. The Chinese Paradise Grill abandoned black shows in the spring of 1938.

6. Personnel of the Harlem Dukes of Rhythm for the summer 1935 tour: Jimmy Jones (trumpet), Herbert Augustus Johnson (alto saxophone, violin), Bill Kersey (tenor saxophone), Herb Johnson (tenor saxophone), Frank Johnson (trombone), Benny Johnson (guitar), Arthur Davis (piano, arranger), Willie Wade (drums).

7. Leo W. Bertley, *Montreal's Oldest Black Congregation* (Pierrefonds, Que.: Bilongo, 1976), 7, states that approximately eighty percent of blacks in Montreal were unemployed during the Depression, while the remainder were underemployed and underpaid. Source is not given.

8. Montreal's white musicians had their meeting places, too, during the Depression. Girard remembered that white musicians jammed at a basement room on McGill Street and hung out after work at Bowen's Café on Peel Street.

9. Samuel B. Charters and Leonard Kunstadt, *Jazz: A History of the New York Scene* (New York: Da Capo, 1981), 26.

10. Ben Sidran, *Black Talk* (1971; reprint, New York: Da Capo, 1981), 81, argues that the increase in racial discrimination felt across North America during the Depression "strengthened lower-class Negro culture by defining it as the sole territory for black expression." The Depression, Sidran notes, also witnessed the emergence of the blues as the dominant idiom in jazz (even as whites were hailing the late 1930s as the Swing Era) and the birth of the Black Muslims organization in the United States, which later attracted many musicians.

11. On rare occasions—for example, the appearance of Millard Thomas and his Famous Chicago Novelty Orchestra at the Mount Royal hotel in 1922—black musicians were hired to perform on uptown stages as vaudeville acts.

12. "Contracts," clause 15, Bylaws of Local 11 of the Canadian Federation of Musicians, undated, Clyde Duncan Collection, Concordia University Archives, Montreal. It is not known whether these bylaws were formally adopted by Local 11. An original typescript of the complete bylaws was found among the private papers of deceased member Clyde Duncan in 1982. (Duncan served as vice-president of Local 11 from 1935 until early 1938.) However, there is no indication on the typescript that the bylaws were adopted by the local, nor are any bylaws contained in the unpublished papers of Local 11 held by Public Archives

Canada. Nevertheless, the formality of the language used in the typescript, and its preservation by an officer of the local, suggest the bylaws reflect the official position of the local, even if they were not formally adopted.

13. "Importation," Bylaws of Local 11 of the Canadian Federation of Musicians.

14. Jack Hirschberg, "Montreal Local Absorbs Canadian Musicos Guild: Fines Cancelled as 30 Men Change Over in Deal Expected to Raise Music Fees," *Metronome*, November 1939.

15. Newsletter, Local 406 of the American Federation of Musicians, Musicians' Guild of Montreal, 27 November 1939.

Chapter Three

1. All quotations from Myron Sutton are from an interview with the author, Niagara Falls, Ont., 15 December 1981.

2. Albert McCarthy, *Big Band Jazz* (London: Putnam, 1974), 159, states briefly that Sutton (misspelled Mylon Sutton) worked with Primus in Buffalo in 1921 and was still with the band in 1926. This is clearly inaccurate. It is possible that Sutton subbed into the Primus band on some occasion in 1921, but he was only eighteen at the time and still attending high school. Furthermore, during my interview with Sutton, he recalled working with Joe Stewart from 1924 to 1926, and working with Primus only from 1926 to about early 1927.

3. Clyde Duncan apparently did not work with Sutton's band right away; possibly the Gatineau Country Club had told Sutton it would hire only a piano and drums for the rhythm section. However, Duncan was working with the band by the time it made a brief return engagement to the Gatineau Country Club in early 1934. The saxophonist from Windsor is unknown, but apparently he did not remain with the band for long.

4. Sutton identified the trombonist in a photograph of the Royal Ambassadors as a man named Burroughs, but it is not known whether he was any relation to the trumpeter Sutton brought to Canada.

5. Smitty was Elmer Smith; Boston Herbie was Herbert Augustus Johnson.

6. Two other Canadian black dance bands are known to have been active during the 1930s, both of them in Toronto, but more research is needed to establish their birth dates and histories. The first of these was apparently led by Harry Lucas, a pianist from Chatham, Ontario, with whom three band names are linked: the Harlem Aces, the Rhythm Aces, and the Rhythm Knights. A second black orchestra was led by pianist Cy McLean, who arrived in Toronto from Sidney, Nova Scotia, probably about 1933-34. On both leaders, see *Encyclopedia of Music*

in Canada, s.v. "black music"; and Norman Richmond, "The Uphill Struggle of Our Black Musicians," *Toronto Star,* 14 April 1979. On McLean, see Jack Batten, "The Jazz Pianist Toronto Ignored," *Toronto Star,* 28 June 1969; and Ralph Thomas, "For Him Day Starts at Night," *Toronto Star,* 20 October 1962.

7. A photograph of the Canadian Ambassadors was published in *Down Beat,* November 1937. Sutton placed a display advertisement in *Down Beat,* July 1938, offering the Ambassadors' congratulations to the magazine on the occasion of its fourth anniversary issue. News of the band appeared in the October and December 1937 issues of *Metronome,* and in the *Chicago Defender,* 30 October 1937.

8. The contents of the unidentified, undated clipping suggest it was published circa 1934, possibly in a company newsletter. Sutton scrapbook, Myron Sutton Collection, Concordia University Archives, Montreal.

9. Vivian M. Robbins, *Musical Buxton* (Buxton, Ont.: privately printed, [1969?]).

10. My source on American and Canadian laws affecting the importation of musicians is Robert David Leiter's history of the American Federation of Musicians, *The Musicians and Petrillo* (New York: Octagon, 1974), 32-36. The relevant Canadian orders in council are P.C. 1413 (7 August 1929) and P.C. 1329 (11 April 1947).

11. Sutton claimed that he never worked at Rockhead's Paradise. According to Sutton, Rufus Rockhead wanted to hire the Canadian Ambassadors but refused to pay the unspecified salary which Sutton demanded for the band.

12. Undated program notes for concert at Victoria Hall, Westmount, Sutton scrapbook, Sutton Collection. Personnel: Sutton (alto sax), George Sealey (tenor sax), Ted Brock (trumpet), Hymie Montgomery (trumpet), Steep Wade (piano), Leon Jacobs (bass), Willie Wade (drums), Willy Girard (violin, guest artist); Buddy Bowser (master of ceremonies, vocalist). Concerts were scheduled for 19 April, 3 May, and 17 May 1941, though only the first two are confirmed to have taken place.

13. Jim Hewlett, "Swing Wins: Imported Group Triumphs before Canadian Audience, Critics," *Chicago Defender,* 21 June 1941, 12; "Musicians to Present Next Concert Soon," unidentified, undated newspaper clipping, Sutton scrapbook, Sutton Collection. See also contract for concert series, Sutton scrapbook.

14. The Canadian Press obituary carried a Montreal dateline because it was filed from the news agency's Montreal bureau, extracted from John Gilmore, "Montreal Jazz Great Sutton Dies—and an Era Ends," *Gazette* (Montreal), 22 June 1982, sec. C, p. 1.

1. Pacifique Plante, *Montréal sous le règne de la pègre* (Montreal: Aux Editions de l'Action nationale, 1950), 61-62.

2. Jim Coleman, "Night Club," *Maclean's*, 15 October 1944.

3. The big bands should not be confused with the so-called "society orchestras," which also played dance music, though usually in hotels and expensive restaurants. Big bands typically comprised a reed section (saxophones, sometimes doubling clarinets and flutes), a brass section (trumpets and trombones, sometimes regarded as separate sections), and a rhythm section (drums, bass, and piano and/or guitar). In contrast, society orchestras generally used several violins, fewer brass than reeds, and a rhythm section. Both types of orchestra employed one or two featured vocalists. The music played by society orchestras was not big-band jazz: it didn't swing, it had no connection to black American music, and the musicians didn't improvise solos. For a professional musician devoted to jazz, the principal incentive to accepting work in a society orchestra was monetary: the society orchestras in Montreal paid, on average, twice as much as nightclub bands. Not suprisingly, society work in Montreal remained the exclusive domain of white musicians long after racial barriers were officially dismantled in the city. It was common practice for hotels to import a foreign bandleader, who would then assemble a society orchestra of local musicians to play the leader's repertoire. The Mount Royal hotel provided lengthy engagements for a series of foreign leaders, beginning in the 1920s: Joseph C. Smith, Jack Denny, Charlie Dornberger (formerly of the Paul Whiteman orchestra), Lloyd Huntley, and Don Turner were all from the United States, while Rex Battle came to the hotel from Britain. The Montreal-born pianist Max Chamitov led a society orchestra at the Mount Royal from 1948 to 1955.

4. Pianists Oscar Peterson and Steep Wade, and saxophonists Herb Johnson and Hugh Sealey.

5. Professional big bands were led by Bix Belair (trumpet), Frank Costi (tenor sax), Roland David (tenor sax), Maynard Ferguson (trumpet), Hal Hartley (saxophone), and Stan Wood (bass).

6. Among the part-time, semiprofessional big bands active in Montreal during the 1940s were the Escorts (cooperative, led by Ron Rutherford), the Esquires (cooperative, later the Johnny Holmes Orchestra), the Modernaires (led by Archie Etienne), the Westernaires (cooperative, led by Jim Ware and later Roy Dohn), the Blue Serenaders (cooperative), and bands led by Johnny Holmes (trumpet), Blake Sewell (saxophone), Harrison Jones (piano), and Jack Bain (alto sax).

7. The instrumentation of the Johnny Holmes Orchestra was five saxophones, three trombones, four trumpets (including Holmes), piano, bass, and drums.

8. Quoted in Harold Dingman, "Oscar Peterson," *Liberty*, 12 January 1946, 19.

9. Peterson's account, "Words and Music: Oscar Peterson," CBC-TV documentary, premiered 16 February 1983.

10. Quoted in Leonard Feather, *From Satchmo to Miles* (New York: Stein and Day, 1972), 190.

11. Gene Lees, "Oscar Peterson: The Early Years," *Jazzletter* (P.O. Box 240, Ojai, CA 93023, U.S.A.), November 1984, 6. Lees' biography of Peterson is forthcoming by Lester & Orpen Dennys, Toronto.

12. Quoted in Lees, 6.

13. Dingman, "Oscar Peterson," 19.

14. Gene Lees, "The Trouble with Jazz Piano: The Viewpoint of Oscar Peterson," *Down Beat*, 29 October 1959, 23.

15. G. K., "Negro Jazz Pianist in Impressive Debut," *Herald* (Montreal), 16 February 1946, 10.

16. Lou Hooper, Jr., interview with author, Montreal, 1 September 1982.

17. Quoted in Feather, *Satchmo to Miles*, 190-91.

18. Lees, "Oscar Peterson: The Early Years," 8. See also Gene Lees, letter to author, 2 November 1985, Peterson file, John Gilmore Jazz History Collection, Concordia University Archives, Montreal.

19. "Words and Music: Oscar Peterson," CBC-TV.

20. Quoted in Lees, "The Trouble with Jazz Piano," 22.

21. Maynard Ferguson, "My Early Days in Music," *Coda*, July 1959, 20.

22. Ferguson, 20. In fact, Ferguson's big band was together less than three years, from summer 1945 to fall or winter 1947-48.

Chapter Five

1. This account is taken from William Brown-Forbes, "New Canadian Mixed Ork Wows Hot Jazz Fans," *Down Beat*, 21 May 1947, 12, which lists the personnel of the band Metcalf was planning to bring from New York City to Canada as: Dickie Wells (trombone), Happy Caldwell (tenor sax), Walter Bishop (piano), Jimmy Butts (bass), George Thompson (drums), and Metcalf (trumpet).

However, Metcalf's oral history, told in Leonard Kunstadt, "The Story of Louie Metcalf," *Record Research*, No. 46, October 1962, 3-9 (which proves unreliable concerning the reasons for the demise of Metcalf's Montreal band) states that he disbanded in New York City due to a shortage of work. This account does not mention a planned Canadian tour, nor does it explain why Metcalf went to Montreal. It lists the same personnel for Metcalf's New York band, except for Jimmy Reynolds (piano).

2. James Lincoln Collier, *The Making of Jazz: A Comprehensive History* (1978; reprint, New York: Delta, 1979), 360.

3. Kunstadt, "The Story of Louie Metcalf," 10. The first significant vave of public enthusiasm in Canada for Dixieland and New Orleans style jazz coincided with the rise of bebop, according to Mark Miller, *Jazz in Canada: Fourteen Lives* (Toronto: University of Toronto Press, 1982), 10. However, New Orleans or Dixieland style jazz has never been as popular in Montreal as it has been elsewhere in Canada, especially Toronto.

4. Girard never lost the knack. Pianist Keith White recalled: "I played a job with him one time and he started playing square-dance tunes because someone requested it. And he had everybody in the place stomping on the floor. He was swinging the shit out of square dances—and he knew them cold! Everybody was flipping."

5. All quotations from Willy Girard are my translations from an interview conducted in French.

6. Metcalf probably gained Canadian immigration clearance to work in Montreal by applying in the category of "outstanding soloist." Indeed, it would have been hard to claim that a Canadian trumpet player of equal talent, experience, and drawing power could have been found to take his place. In any event, Canadian immigration barriers against American musicians were lifted in 1947.

7. Ken Johnstone, "Mixed Band: Famed Jazz Musician Builds Unique Band," *Standard* (Montreal), 15 May 1946, 16-17. Photographs by Louis Jaques.

8. Brown-Forbes, "New Canadian Mixed Ork," 12.

9. All quotations from May Oliver are from an interview with the author, Montreal, 17 February 1982.

10. Leonard Feather, *Inside Jazz* (New York: Da Capo, 1977), 35-36.

11. The Metcalf band's book of arrangements has not been found. Copies of Macdonald's scores for the band are in the John Gilmore Jazz History Collection, Concordia University Archives, Montreal.

12. Louis Metcalf's names were sometimes misspelled Louie and/or Metcalfe in Montreal. The first reflects the French pronunciation; the second corresponds to that of a street in uptown Montreal.

13. Jack Long, tape-recorded letter to the author, March 1983, Gilmore Collection.

14. Brown-Forbes, "New Canadian Mixed Ork," 12.

15. The musicians in Metcalf's band apparently received lower salaries individually than other nightclub musicians in Montreal. The most likely explanation is that the Café St. Michel was only willing to pay for the services of six or fewer musicians: if so, Metcalf would have divided the band's total salary among the seven men, with each receiving lower than union scale. Another possible explanation is that Metcalf demanded a higher fee in recognition of his status, but that the club insisted he supplement his leader's scale (generally twice that of a sideman) by paying his sidemen less.

16. "Metcalf Band Scores with Jazz Concert," *Standard* (Montreal), 15 May 1949, 16. Wilkinson believed Metcalf lost money on the production. Other concerts may have been held at McGill University.

17. Quoted in Kunstadt, "The Story of Louie Metcalf," 10-11. The three-year penalty imposed by U.S. Immigration is not explained; the Canadian musicians may have been told they couldn't apply for entry to the United States again for another three years.

18. Meredith's band worked at the Café St. Michel from September 1949 to May 1950.

19. A letter from Billy Graham to the author, 7 March 1983, reveals the state of the Metcalf band at the time:

> I had been doing concerts and one-nighters with the band after it left the St. Michel [in August 1949]. Sadik and I replaced Steep and Wilkie during that period, and we were both with the band when it was about to go back into the St. Michel. At the rehearsal in the afternoon of the evening we were to start back at the St. Michel, Louis and I had a small row over my paying a fine for being late for that rehearsal, and I quit on the spot as I didn't think it was justified. (Impulsive youth!) Al Jennings replaced me.... On the band's week off, six weeks later, they all drove to Ottawa to visit Louis Armstrong (who was a friend of Metcalf's) and that is when they got busted. Quitting the band as I did probably saved me from the same fate, as I'm sure I would have been in the same car.... So, for about four or six months prior to that, Sadik and I were in the band.... I was with the band up to six weeks before they got busted... that is the only date I'm sure of.

Based on this account, the personnel of the Metcalf band at the time of the arrests was most likely: Metcalf, Winestone, Watanabe, King, Hakim, and Jennings. Billy Graham file, Gilmore Collection.

20. "Four 'Reefer' Smokers Jailed for Six Months," *Herald* (Montreal), 25 November 1950. See also William Wardwell, "Musicians' Bail Readjusted in 'Reefer' Possession Case," *Herald*, 22 November 1950; and Henry Whiston, "Trumpeter Metcalf Jailed: Marijuana," *Down Beat*, 29 December 1950. Records of the court proceedings are available at Service des dossiers, Palais de Justice, Montreal, under the following file numbers: Hakim - 10385; Winestone - 10386; King - 10387; Metcalfe [sic] - 10388.

21. Authorities at Parthenais detention centre and Bordeaux prison in Montreal, where the musicians were probably incarcerated, say prison records of the four have been destroyed. Access to files of Canadian deportations is restricted by federal legislation protecting privacy.

22. Several fans of the International Band, including pianist Keith White, recalled that Metcalf's technical limitations on the trumpet restricted his ability to play fast bebop lines. However, he apparently scat sang bebop with great fluency on stage at the Café St. Michel.

23. Collier, *Making of Jazz*, 354.

24. Quoted in Brown-Forbes, "New Canadian Mixed Ork," 12.

25. Monogram 156 features Wilk Wilkinson and his Boptet playing "Wilk's Bop," an original composition by Butch Watanabe, and "All The Things You Are," arranged by Montreal saxophonist Nick Ayoub. The exact date and place of the recording are unknown, but based on the chronology of the Metcalf band given here and the personal testimony of some of the participants, it must have been made in Montreal in 1950, not in Toronto in 1949 as given in Jack Litchfield, *The Canadian Jazz Discography: 1916-1980* (Toronto: University of Toronto Press, 1982), 757. Some sources believe the record was recorded in the Café St. Michel. While this was the first recording of bebop in Canada, it was not the first bebop recording made by Canadian musicians. Toronto alto saxophonist Moe Koffman's Main Stemmers recorded four bebop titles in Buffalo, New York, in 1948 for the Main Stem label. See Litchfield, *Discography*, 388.

Chapter Six

1. The story is a composite created by the author from numerous anecdotes heard in the course of researching this book.

2. For a discography of Wade's piano recordings, see John Gilmore, "Harold 'Steep' Wade: Canadian Jazz Legend," *Names and Numbers* (Amsterdam), No. 6

(January 1987), 20-21. No recordings have been found of Wade playing saxophone.

3. Quoted in Mark Miller, *Jazz in Canada: Fourteen Lives* (Toronto: University of Toronto Press, 1982), 127.

4. Miller, 127.

5. The extent of Steep Wade's formal musical training is not known. Thryphenia Collins (telephone interview with author, 15 September 1983), a neighbour of the Wades, remembered Steep going for lessons at the Iverly Community Centre when he was about five years old. However, Winnie Sealey (interview with author, Montreal, 21 August 1982), sister of Hugh and George Sealey, claimed Steep didn't begin taking piano lessons until after he had started playing in nightclubs as a teenager, and then only on the advice of older musicians. Daisy (Peterson) Sweeney (telephone interview with author, 15 September 1983) taught music to many Montreal jazz musicians but not to Steep; she believed he may have taken lessons with a Professor Smite on St. Catherine Street.

6. Harold Wade's school records, Personnel Department, Protestant School Board of Greater Montreal.

7. Minutes, 20 June 1950, Local 406 of the American Federation of Musicians, Musicians' Guild of Montreal.

8. "Embraceable You," performed by Parker, Wade, Hal Gaylor (bass), and Bobby Malloy (drums), was one of five tunes recorded by Parker in Montreal (three taken from the TV broadcast, two at the Chez Paree) that have been issued on *Bird on the Road* (Jazz Showcase 5003). See Jack Litchfield, *The Canadian Jazz Discography: 1916-1980* (Toronto: University of Toronto Press, 1982), 367-69, for details. Kinescopes of the TV broadcast were apparently made but have never been found and are presumed destroyed.

9. Report of coroner's investigation into the death (6 December 1953) of Harold Wade, Gouvernement du Québec, Ministère de la justice, Direction générales des affaires criminelles, Bureau du coroner, Montreal.

Interlude Two

1. A popular dice game. See below, chapter 8, note 5.

Chapter Seven

1. Ken Johnstone, "Montreal's Bargain Night Out," *Maclean's*, 15 November 1951, 16-17, 61-63. The Bellevue Casino opened in the late 1940s on the site of a large

nightclub/dance hall called the Auditorium, on Ontario Street West near the corner of Bleury. It closed in September 1962 when the city expropriated part of the site to widen Ontario Street.

2. Kenny Rockhead, interview with author, Montreal, 4 May 1983.

3. During the mid-1940s, white tenor saxophonist and entertainer Irving Pall led a mixed band at Rockhead's, and white drummer Wilkie Wilkinson worked briefly in a mixed show band at the same club.

4. Discrimination in the entertainment, hotel, and music industries is difficult to document. Nevertheless, to the oral testimonies of resident Montreal blacks which await systematic gathering can be added the evidence of historian Robin W. Winks, *The Blacks in Canada: A History* (Montreal: McGill-Queen's University Press, 1971), 420-21. According to Winks, only one hotel in Montreal could be depended upon *not* to turn away blacks in 1941. A decade later, according to Winks, the 1951 edition of *The Negro Motorist Green Book*, published in New York, listed only two hotels in Montreal which accepted blacks.

5. The El Morocco where Kaye worked was the third club by that name in Montreal. The original was on Mansfield Street, on the site of numerous other clubs including the Embassy. The second was on the northwest corner of St. Catherine Street and Metcalfe, on the site of the Washington Club and others; it was demolished to make way for a bank. The third, on Closse Street, later became Norm Silver's Moustache club.

6. May Oliver, interview with author, Montreal, 17 February 1982.

7. Jack Long, tape-recorded letter to author, March 1983, John Gilmore Jazz History Collection, Concordia University Archives, Montreal.

8. The rooming-house has been immortalized in a jazz composition by Montreal pianist Jerry de Villiers entitled "1476 Crescent." It was recorded by de Villiers' quartet in 1963 (Trans-Canada TC-A-81).

9. White's analysis of the options open to him as a young pianist during the 1950s is revealing:

> I quickly realized that if I wanted to become a professional musician: one, I was going to have to read, so that I could read wallpaper; two, I was going to have to learn to play commercial music—and play it well—because otherwise I wasn't going to make a decent living out of music; or, three, I could become an arranger. And I didn't want to do any of these things. I wanted to just play jazz. And I could quickly see that the only way you're going to be a top jazz musician, or make really good money, is if you're a virtuoso pianist to begin with, like Peterson or George Shearing. And I wasn't that either.

1. Frank Kennedy, "Hoodlum Squads Run Wild in Roughest Election Yet," *Herald* (Montreal), 26 October 1954, 3.

2. Wilfred Emmerson Israel, "The Montreal Negro Community," Master's thesis, McGill University, 1928.

3. My sources on crime, vice, and corruption in Montreal are: Ken Johnstone, "How Plante and Drapeau Licked the Montreal Underworld," *Maclean's*, 1 December 1954, 12-13, 102-14; Pax Plante, with David MacDonald, "The Shame of My City: Crime in Montreal," illustrated five-part series, *Star Weekly* (magazine supplement to the *Montreal Star*), 24 June 1961, 2-6; 1 July, 6-11; 8 July, 10-13; 15 July, 14-17; 22 July, 15-17; and Alain Stanké and Jean-Louis Morgan, *Pax, lutte à finir avec le pègre* (Montreal: Les Editions La Presse, 1972). Statistics on profits and employment are from Plante and MacDonald, 1 July, 8.

4. The addresses of some famous Montreal brothels have become part of the folklore of the city: 312 Ontario East, 401 Mayer, and 209 Mountain.

5. Barbotte, or barboothe as it was also called, first appeared in Montreal in the 1920s. The most popular gambling game, it also yielded the highest profit for the house. Players competed against one another, with the house taking a percentage of the winner's earnings. The house's percentage ranged from five cents on a dollar to seventy-five cents on a hundred dollars: the smaller the winning, the higher the house's percentage. Thus, while some tables handled bets as high as several thousand dollars, it was to the house's advantage to encourage smaller bets, which took less time to play and yielded faster profits. In this way, barbotte became popular with lower-income people. Games were organized in residential buildings holding an average of three tables each; because the only equipment required was dice and a table, the games frequently "floated" from address to address to avoid detection.

6. Jazz and vice have walked hand in hand in more places than Montreal. However, as Leroy Ostransky shows in *Jazz City: The Impact of Our Cities on the Development of Jazz* (Englewood Cliffs, N.J.: Prentice-Hall, 1978), this has been due to socioeconomic factors rather than any inherent proclivity of jazz musicians for vice. The cities where jazz has thrived in the United States (Ostransky examines New Orleans, Chicago, Kansas City, and New York City) were each, during their jazz heyday, major transportation centres with a cosmopolitan culture. The transportation industries attracted transient workers, which in turn attracted a vice industry to exploit the needs of large numbers of single men with wages to spend. Vice in turn stimulated nightlife, to which musicians in search of work were drawn. Moreover, the black neighbourhoods where jazz thrived were usually adjacent to, or part of, the vice districts of these cities, both because blacks lacked the political and economic power to oppose vice and because city authorities often encouraged vice in black neighbourhoods.

Montreal clearly fits this model, though on a smaller scale than the cities examined by Ostransky. Montreal is a major transportation centre with a highly cosmopolitan population. Its railway industry has attracted black workers from the United States; its port has supplied a steady stream of sailors with money to spend; and its black neighbourhood both fostered an indigenous vice industry and was adjacent to the city's thriving uptown nightlife centre. As well, the principal black nightclubs outside of the St. Antoine district were situated at the heart of the city's most notorious vice centre, lower St. Lawrence Blvd. around the corner of St. Catherine Street.

7. Israel Sealy, president of the Canadian Clef Club (Local 11 of the Canadian Federation of Musicians), letter to Norman S. Dowd, secretary-treasurer of the All-Canadian Congress of Labour, 11 June 1941; and unpublished report from Sealy to Dowd, 14 July 1941. Public Archives Canada (Ottawa), unpublished papers of CFM Local 11, Manuscript Division, Labour Collections: Canadian Labour Congress Defunct Local Series, vol. 104, file 14.

8. Pacifique Plante, *Montréal sous le règne de la pègre* (Montreal: Aux Editions de l'Action nationale, 1950). The articles in *Le Devoir* (Montreal) ran from 28 November 1949 to 18 February 1950.

9. Johnstone, "How Plante and Drapeau Licked the Montreal Underworld," 12. This lengthy article summarizes the Caron inquiry which ran from September 1950 to April 1953, and the events leading up to it. The complete text of Caron's judgement was published in the *Montreal Star*, 9 October 1954, 8-19, and *Le Devoir* (Montreal), 9 October 1954, 1-8. See also the forty-page supplement, *Document complet sur l'Enquette Caron*, published by *Le Devoir*, 16 October 1954.

10. Al Palmer, "10-Month Battle between Musicians, Actors Ends," *Herald* (Montreal), 16 November 1954, 2; Al Palmer, "Chorines Given New Lift with AFM-AGVA Armistice," *Herald*, 17 November 1954, 14.

11. "Drapeau Goes in on a Landslide: 'Clean Up City Hall' Campaign Swamps All 8 Rivals," *Gazette* (Montreal), 26 October 1954, 1.

12. Al Palmer, "Cabarets Aid in Clean-Up Drive," *Herald* (Montreal), 12 November 1954, 3.

13. "City Hall Stops Gratuities Paid Annually to Reporters," *Herald* (Montreal), 20 December 1954, 7.

14. "Mayor Puts Ban on Lotteries, Even for Charitable Causes," *Herald* (Montreal), 22 December 1954, 3.

15. Al Palmer, "Gambling Czars Give Up," *Herald* (Montreal), 6 January 1955, 2. Pinball machines were driven out of Montreal by May 1955. See "Pinball Ban Approved, Effective Date Left Open," *Herald* (Montreal), 15 February 1955, 7; Bill

Bantley, "Pinballs Head for Scrapheap as Council Sets May 1 Deadline," *Herald*, 23 March 1955, 2.

16. "Liquor, Morality Squad Combine: 108 Arrested in 4 Raids," *Herald* (Montreal), 24 January 1955, 1.

17. "East-End Clubs Feeling Pinch of 'Vice Crusade'," *Herald* (Montreal), 12 February 1955, 7. The article reports west-end clubs were also suffering.

18. "Hired Killers Reported in City as Frank Petrulla Still at Liberty," *Herald* (Montreal), 23 July 1955, 3, 6.

19. Quoted in Robert Stewart, "Rockhead's Paradise," *Canadian Magazine*, 21 July 1973, 22.

20. Accounts of the closing of Rockhead's Paradise—both those provided orally by musicians,and those published in sources cited in notes 19, 21, 25, and 26 to this chapter—are not consistent on the year; 1951 and 1952 have also been mentioned. All things considered, 1953 seems the most likely year. Advertisements for the club stopped appearing in the *Herald* (Montreal) in April 1953. The provincial government authority responsible for issuing liquor permits has destroyed whatever files it had on Rockhead's Paradise, according to Pierre Lafrenière, Le directeur des permis et contrôles d'exploitation, Régis des permis d'alcool du Québec, letter to author, 3 September 1985, Rockhead's Paradise file, John Gilmore Jazz History Collection, Concordia University Archives, Montreal.

21. Quoted in Stewart, "Rockhead's Paradise," 22. Wayne Clark, "Welcome to Paradise," *Weekend Magazine*, 7 February 1976, 12-14, repeats Rockhead's version of the payoff demand.

22. Kenny Rockhead, interview with author, Montreal, 4 May 1983.

23. The Union nationale incumbent in Montreal-Saint-Henri, Joseph-Hormisdas Delisle, had previously served as a Montreal city councillor and member of the city's executive committee. He lost his seat in the Quebec national assembly to the Liberal's Philippe Lalonde by more than five thousand votes. Bibliothèque de la législature, Service de documentation politique, *Répertoire des parlementaires québécois, 1867-1978* (Quebec City: Bibliothèque de la legislature, Service de documentation politique, 1980).

24. Quoted in Stewart, "'Rockhead's Paradise," 22.

25. Brenda Zosky Proulx, "'Paradise' Is Faded but It's Not All Lost: Rockhead's Used to Jump and So Did Rising Sun but Now It's a Battle to Save Two City Institutions," *Gazette* (Montreal), 22 May 1982, sec. D, p. 1.

26. Ian Mayer, "Club Owner Rufus Rockhead Dies," *Gazette* (Montreal), 24

September 1981.

27. Statistics of the Radio-Television Manufacturers Association showed 281,958 TV sets in Quebec at the end of September 1954, with reported sales of 29,062 sets in September. Close to one million sets were reported across Canada. "On and Off the Record," *Gazette* (Montreal), 17 November 1954, 4.

28. Chantal Hébert, *Le Burlesque au Québec: Un divertissement populaire* (Ville LaSalle, Quebec: Hurtubise HMH, 1981), 84.

29. Hébert, 77, 82. Hébert attributes part of the blame for the demise of Radio-Cité and Quebec vaudeville in general to the nightclubs, in particular the higher salaries offered by clubs to performers. According to Hébert, some vaudeville theatres tried to hold their top performers by allowing them to leave the theatre early and perform at a nightclub later the same night. However, it should be remembered that vaudeville and the nightclub industry had coexisted for more than two decades in Montreal prior to the arrival of television. Furthermore, as I indicate below, television was a leading contributor to the higher salary demands of performers, which had a detrimental effect on the nightclubs as well as vaudeville.

30. For a woman's viewpoint on the change in nightclub entertainment, see the anonymous account of a Montreal barmaid, "Ce que je pense de nos cabarets," *Le magazine Maclean*, November 1961, 14, 51-52.

Chapter Nine

1. My source on organized crime and Drapeau's renewed cleanup campaign is Pax Plante, with David MacDonald, "The Shame of My City: Crime in Montreal," illustrated five-part series, *Star Weekly* (magazine supplement to the *Montreal Star*), 24 June 1961, 2-6; 1 July, 6-11; 8 July, 10-13; 15 July, 14-17; 22 July, 15-17.

2. Ironically, while *café* is French for "coffee," many nightclubs in Montreal have been called cafés (e.g., Café St. Michel), while most coffee-houses of the 1960s did not use the word *café* as part of their names.

3. See "Student jazz societies" in Appendix 1.

4. Len Dobbin, "Montreal Modern," *Coda*, April 1961, 5.

5. Nightclubs in Trois Rivières, 125 kilometres downstream from Montreal, provided steady work for Montreal jazz musicians during the early 1960s. Stan Patrick, Cisco Normand, and others worked there regularly, driving back to Montreal after work to jam at Le Mas.

6. These included Pierre Béluse, Michel Donato, Richard Ferland, Don Habib,

Buddy Hampton, Stu Loseby, Cisco Normand, Al Penfold, Claude Resther, Jack Rider, and Bob Rollins. Normand abandoned a lucrative career as a studio drummer and vibraphonist after three years, preferring a drastically reduced income and a return to the insecurity of club work to the stress and musical compromises of the studio world.

7. Mark Miller, *Jazz in Canada: Fourteen Lives* (Toronto: University of Toronto Press, 1982), 12.

8. Miller, 100.

9. While most of the demands of this market were met by the jazz nightclubs, occasional jazz concerts continued. The most significant development in this domain was a series of jazz concerts held every summer from 1961 to 1965, in effect Montreal's first jazz festival. The jazz concerts, possibly organized by the Montreal Festivals and/or the Canadian Broadcasting Corporation as part of a larger arts festival in the city, ran six nights at La Comédie Canadienne theatre (formerly the Gayety and Radio-Cité) in 1961 and 1962. International jazz stars and local players performed. In 1963 seven nights of concerts were held at the Loew's theatre. In 1964 and 1965, the venue moved to Place des Arts, the city's new concert hall; however, fewer jazz concerts were presented and local musicians were excluded. For details of the concerts, see Len Dobbin's reports in *Coda*: October 1961, 28-29; October 1962, 23-25; September 1963, 20-21; October-November 1964, 12; October-November 1965, 19.

10. Quoted in Leonard Feather, liner notes to *Sonny Rollins: Brass and Trio* (Verve UMV 2555), reissue of *Sonny Rollins and the Big Brass* (Metrojazz (E) S1002), recorded in New York City, 11 July 1958.

11. On one occasion, Quebec *chansonnier* Claude Gauthier, accompanying himself on acoustic guitar, shared a billing at Le Jazz Hot with the jazz quartet of American vibraphonist Terry Gibbs. This unusual combination was not typical of the club's policy: Cobetto had taken a personal interest in Gauthier's career and booked him for two nights at Le Jazz Hot to expose him to a wider audience.

12. Black Bottom was the name of a dance popular among blacks during the 1920s; the term appears in such tune titles of the day as Jelly Roll Morton's "Black Bottom Stomp." Pianist Lou Hooper, in his unpublished autobiography "That Happy Road," National Library, Ottawa, 1972, 54, refers to the area of the St. Antoine district around Mountain and St. Antoine as "Blackbottom." However, no interviewees or other sources used this term in connection with the district.

13. Miller, *Jazz in Canada*, 163.

14. Among the musicians who worked in Symonds' trios at The Black Bottom

278

were: bassists Charlie Biddle, Roland Haynes, and Fred McHugh; drummers Chico Hawkins, Clayton Johnson, Billy McCant, Bernie Primeau, Jerry Taylor, and Norm Villeneuve; and organist Buddy Jones. For a review of Symonds at The Black Bottom, see Alan Offstein, "Nelson Symonds at the Black Bottom, Montreal," *Coda*, June-July 1966, 34.

15. Montreal Bylaw 3416 ("Behaviour of certain employees in establishments dispensing alcoholic beverages"), enacted by city council on 9 March 1967.

16. For an outsider's appraisal of the Montreal jazz scene during the summer of 1967, see John Norris, "Montreal's Jazz Underground," *Coda*, August-September 1967, 37-38. Another, less tangible symptom of the decline of jazz in Montreal after Expo 67 may be the disappearance, apparently after only one issue in late 1968, of a new magazine in Montreal called *Cinéjazz*, published by Emmanuel Cocke. As its title suggests, the French-language magazine was devoted equally to cinema and jazz, with an emphasis in both cases on the modern. The first issue contained brief articles on Le Quatuor du nouveau jazz libre du Québec and Walter Boudreau.

Chapter 10

1. Mark Miller, *Jazz in Canada: Fourteen Lives* (Toronto: University of Toronto Press, 1982), 99.

2. Len Dobbin, "Montreal Modern," *Coda*, October 1960, 6.

3. No relation to the author of this book.

4. Sun Ra's sojourn in Montreal is discussed briefly in John Litweiler, *The Freedom Principle: Jazz after 1958* (New York: William Morrow, 1984), 143-44; and Valerie Wilmer, *As Serious as Your Life: The Story of the New Jazz* (Westport, Conn.: Lawrence Hill, 1980), 89.

5. Miller, *Jazz in Canada*, 194-98.

6. "The liberation struggle launched by the American blacks ... arouses growing interest among the French-Canadian population, for the workers of Quebec are aware of their condition as niggers, exploited men, second-class citizens." Pierre Vallières, *White Niggers of America*, trans. Joan Pinkham (Toronto: McClelland and Stewart, 1971), 21. Originally published in French as *Nègres blancs d'Amérique: Autobiographie précoce d'un "terroriste" québécois* (Montreal: Editions Parti pris, 1968).

7. While Le Jazz libre du Québec was the first band in Montreal to play free jazz, it was not the first in Canada to do so. In 1962, musicians in Toronto formed the Artists' Jazz Band. In 1966, pianist/bassist Stuart Broomer formed a free jazz

band in Toronto, and pianist Al Neil turned from bebop to the new music in Vancouver. See *Encyclopedia of Music in Canada*, s.v. "Artists' Jazz Band" and "Jazz: avante garde."

8. James Lincoln Collier, *The Making of Jazz: A Comprehensive History* (1978; reprint, New York: Delta, 1979), 435. Among the early explorers of this style mentioned by Collier are vibraphonist Gary Burton, guitarist Larry Coryell, flautist Jeremy Steig, and the British group Soft Machine. See also Collier, 495.

Epilogue

1. Unless otherwise noted, all quotations from Walter Boudreau are my translations (where necessary) from an interview conducted in French and English.

2. Unless otherwise noted, all quotations from Raoul Duguay are my translations from an interview conducted in French.

3. Roger Frappier, *L'Infonie Inachevée*, 1973.

4. Raoul Duguay, *Manifeste de l'Infonie: Le Toutartbel* (Montreal: Editions du jour, 1970). My translation.

5. Undated clipping, *Sept Jours*, Walter Boudreau Collection, Concordia University Archives, Montreal. My translation.

6. My translation from an interview conducted in French.

7. Gilles Ouellet, "Walter Boudreau au premier rang," *La Presse* (Montreal), 18 November 1967, 24. My translation.

8. "Qui est Walter Boudreau?" undated clipping, *L'Echo* (Sorel), December 1968. Boudreau Collection. My translation.

9. All quotations from Guy Thouin are my translations from interviews conducted in French.

10. Quoted in Jacques Larue-Langlois, "Une Musique jaille de l'âme québécoise," *Perspectives* (*La Presse*), 10 May 1969. My translation.

11. The title is a phonetic spelling of *l'hostie de show*, Québécois slang combining blasphemy of the Catholic communion host with the English word *show*. The later *L'Osstidchomeurt* means roughly "the death of *L'Osstidcho*."

12. In the early 1980s, when L'Infonie had faded in the public's memory, the quartet's name was changed to Le Quatuor de saxophones de Montréal. It was

still active at the time of publication.

13. "Un S.O.S. du Jazz libre du Québec," *Le Devoir* (Montreal), 12 January 1971, 10; Jean Basile, "$1,000 pour organiser 'Le P'tit Québec Libre': Une initiative du Jazz libre du Québec," *Le Devoir*, 28 January 1971, 10.

14. Jean F. Keable, *Rapport de la commission d'enquête sur les opérations policiers en territoire québécois* (Gouvernement du Québec: Ministère de la justice, 1981), 321-32.

15. George-Hébert Germain, "L'Escoude anti-émeute vide encore le Vieux Montréal," *La Presse* (Montreal), 25 June 1974, 1; Lewis Harris and Steve Hendler, "St. Jean Baptiste Day in Old Montreal: Police, Celebrants Battle in Streets," *Montreal Star*, 25 June 1974, 1, 3.

16. Jean-Pierre Lemay, analyst, Section d'incendies criminels, Montreal Urban Community police, telephone interview with author, 4 April 1986. Lemay said the file on the police investigation has been destroyed as a matter of routine procedure but that other police records confirm the details given here. The fire was first reported at 21 St. Paul Street West, and therefore both police and fire department records catalogue the blaze at that address; L'Amorce was at number 25. See also the photograph headlined "Incendie dans le Vieux Montreal," *La Presse* (Montreal), 25 June 1974, 3.
In speculating about the cause of the fire, several theories suggest themselves. In the wake of the RCMP arson at Le Petit Québec libre, the police or other authorities are suspect. However, precisely because of this fact, it is conceivable that the radical left itself decided to burn L'Amorce as a tactical move aimed at heightening antagonism against the police, or generating more public sympathy for the left, or influencing political developments in Quebec in some other way. But it is also possible that the fire was not deliberately set at all. A few hours after the fire was extinguished, Montreal firemen began an unofficial work-to-rule action to protest the city's refusal to negotiate a cost-of-living increase. It is conceivable that the fire department's investigation of the blaze was influenced by this action, or even that the fire department labelled the fire an arson as a means of transferring responsibility for follow-up work to the police department. According to Lemay, police records do not state that police investigators concluded it was arson, only that they carried out an investigation after receiving the fire department's report.

APPENDIX ONE

Organizations

Following are all known organizations—including unions, musicians' organizations, jazz societies, and record collectors' groups—which were active in Montreal prior to 1970 and which either had a direct influence on the making of jazz in the city or which reflect public interest in jazz. Names of organizations followed by an asterisk (*) have a separate entry.

American Federation of Musicians, Local 406
1905 -

The largest and most powerful musicians' union in Montreal. The American Federation of Musicians (AFM) was founded in the United States in 1896 and chartered by the American Federation of Labor. Musicians' associations in Toronto and Vancouver were the first in Canada to join the AFM, in 1901; in the same year, the AFM expanded its name to the American Federation of Musicians of the U.S. and Canada. In 1905, the Fédération des musiciens de Montréal (formerly Association protectrice des musiciens de Montréal, founded in 1898) joined the AFM, becoming Local 406. The name of the local was changed to Musicians' Guild of Montreal/Guilde des musiciens de Montréal in October 1938. A year later it absorbed the membership of Local 10 of the Canadian Federation of Musicians,* a rival, all-Canadian union. Until this point, Local 406 had refused to admit blacks as members, and through an unwritten understanding with employers had prevented black musicians from working in hotels and most of the nightclubs in the west-central "uptown" area of the city. By 1940 Local 406 was admitting black musicians, most of them defectors from the all-black Local 11 of the Canadian Federation of Musicians, also known as the Canadian Clef Club.* The latter organization disappeared at the end of 1943. Thereafter, Local 406 was the only union for instrumentalists in Montreal until 1978, when dissident members formed the Syndicat de la musique

282

du Québec.

Bibliography: For a history of the AFM prior to 1953, see Robert David Leiter, *The Musicians and Petrillo* (New York: Octagon, 1974). On the AFM and other musicians' unions (but not the Canadian Federation of Musicians) in Canada, see *Encyclopedia of Music in Canada*, s.v. "unions."

Canadian Clef Club
1928 -1943

A self-help organization for black musicians in Montreal which became Local 11 of the Canadian Federation of Musicians. Originally called the Canadian Coloured Clef Club, it later dropped the word Coloured from its name, though it continued to offer membership only to black musicians, who were barred from joining either the American Federation of Musicians Local 406* or the Canadian Federation of Musicians Local 10.* All of the Canadian Clef Club's known activities were confined to Montreal. Many of its members played jazz.

The Canadian Coloured Clef Club was founded in 1928 by violinist Arthur Provost. It was likely patterned after the all-black Clef Club in New York City, founded by bandleader James Reese Europe in 1910. (The Clef Club Jazz Band from New York played at the Palais de Danse in Montreal in 1918.) The Montreal club had a charter and at least twenty members at its birth. Members presented classical music concerts at a room near St. Lawrence Blvd., possibly on St. Urbain Street. The club faded from view at the beginning of the Depression and probably was inactive for several years. Then, at an unknown date after 1932, it was revived and reorganized by clarinetist Sydney Flood. An unidentified, undated newspaper clipping in bassist Clyde Duncan's papers reports twenty-three musicians belonged to the Canadian Coloured Clef Club at the time of this revival. They included the leading black jazz musicians in Montreal: Clyde Duncan; Lloyd Duncan; Lou Hooper (who had played with the Clef Club orchestra in New York City while resident there during the 1920s); Terry Hooper; Benny Johnson; Brad[ley] Moxley; George Sealey; Hugh Sealey; Andy Shorter; Bill Shorter; Elmer Smith; Myron Sutton; Harold Wade; and Randolph Whinfield. (Other members were: Ernie Baker; J. A. Brown; A. B. Crawford; L. D. [possibly Lou] Fletcher; Sydney Flood; Herman Jones; E. M. Packwood; Benny Starks; and Blaine Woodward.) The headquarters of the club was on St. Antoine Street West near Mountain Street.

On 22 July 1935, twenty-one members of the Canadian Clef Club applied for a charter from the All-Canadian Congress of Labour (later the Canadian Congress of Labour). The charter was granted on 26 July, and the Canadian Clef Club became Local 11 of the Canadian Federation of Musicians. (The original charter members of Local 11 were: A. Brown; Nina Brown; Mario Carmagno; Clyde Duncan; Bob Everleigh; Sydney Flood; Art Jones; Jimmy Jones; Norman Jones; A. Dudley Nurse; Eddie Perkins; Hugh Sealey; E. [possibly Eddie] Simms; Bill Shorter; Elmer Smith; Myron Sutton; Harold Wade; Gertrude Waters; Randolph Whinfield; Eugene Williams; and Blaine Woodward.) As a union, the Canadian Clef Club attempted to standardize contracts and terms of employment for its members, boycott employers who failed to respect its regulations, and regulate the importation of American musicians by Montreal bandleaders and employers. As a club, unofficially known as "the musicians' club," it hosted regular jam sessions at its meeting room, inviting touring American musicians and white Montreal musicians to participate.

The local was plagued with high unemployment and underemployment among its members. The principal reason for this was an unwritten understanding between the American Federation of Musicians (AFM) Local 406 and employers in Montreal which barred black musicians from working in hotels and most of the nightclubs in the west-central "uptown" area of the city; the blacks were confined to the "downtown" St. Antoine district and the "east end" around St. Catherine Street and St. Lawrence Blvd. The economic impact of this discrimination was exacerbated by a general slump in the nightclub industry resulting from the Depression and new, restrictive provincial liquor laws. Members of Local 11 lost confidence in the ability of the union to protect their livelihood, and membership fluctuated as musicians withdrew during periods of unemployment and returned once they found work. Membership peaked at twenty-five in February 1939, varying to sixteen in April 1940; twenty-four in June 1940; fourteen in August 1941; and eleven in February 1942. Membership was further eroded as musicians left to enlist in army bands after the outbreak of the Second World War.

The role of the AFM in the demise of the Canadian Clef Club is not known; no written records have been found which document the date and circumstances of the AFM's decision to admit black musicians from Montreal into the union. However, unconfirmed oral accounts suggest that AFM Local 406 began admitting blacks at about the same time that it absorbed the all-white Local 10 of the Canadian Federation of Musicians, in October 1939. Allusions to "east-end" musicians turning to the AFM are made in a newsletter published by AFM Local 406 in November 1939, and Local 406 records show that membership was being granted to black musicians in Montreal by 1940. Blacks admitted to Local 406 obtained access, in theory at least, to jobs that had previously been guarded by the AFM for its exclusively white membership. In this way, the colour barrier in Montreal began to fall, further undermining the Canadian Clef Club's *raison d'être* in the city.

The Canadian Clef Club, as Local 11, continued to exist for several more years. On 3 February 1942, according to records of Local 11, it held a joint board meeting with AFM Local 406 to discuss working conditions, wages, and an unspecified "working agreement which has been in operation for some time." There is no mention of the meeting in Local 406 records, and no other details are known. By the summer of 1942, Local 11's membership had dropped so low that it did not send a delegate to a meeting of the All-Canadian Congress of Labour. In September 1943 it wrote to the Congress saying it could no longer survive and asking that its few remaining members be kept in abeyance until after the war, or until more members could be recruited. The Congress replied that the local could remain intact with as few as five dues-paying members, but there is no trace of Local 11 after its final letter to the Congress in November 1943 inquiring what dues the five members would be required to pay; a Congress reply six months later was apparently too late to save Local 11 from extinction. The Canadian Clef Club's social and musical activities are believed to have stopped soon after its demise as a union. The Canadian Federation of Musicians itself later disappeared, leaving the AFM as the sole union in Canada.

Officers of Local 11: Presidents—Sydney Flood (July 1935-August 1940); Israel Sealy (possibly spelt Sealey or Seely) (August 1940-September 1943). Vice-presidents—Bill Shorter and Clyde Duncan (1935-early 1938); Lou Hooper (1938); Gertrude Waters (1939); Herb Johnson (November 1939-?). Treasurers—Israel Sealy (1935-1940); Arthur Davis (August 1940-November 1943).

Bibliography: For records of the Canadian Clef Club after it became a union, see unpublished papers of CFM Local 11, Public Archives Canada (Ottawa), Manuscript Division, Labour Collection: Canadian Labour Congress, Chartered Local Series, vol. 67, files 9 and 10; Canadian Labour Congress, Defunct Local Series, vol. 104, file 14. For undated bylaws of the Canadian Clef Club, see Clyde Duncan Collection, Concordia University Archives. On the Clef Club in New York City, see Samuel B. Charters and Leonard Kunstadt, *Jazz: A History of the New York Scene* (New York: Doubleday, 1962), 23-41.

Canadian Federation of Musicians, Local 10
1934 - 1939

One of two Montreal locals of the Canadian Federation of Musicians

(CFM), a now-defunct union chartered by the All-Canadian Congress of Labour (later the Canadian Labour Congress). Local 10, also called the Montreal Association of Musicians, did not admit blacks as members; the city's black musicians belonged to CFM Local 11, also called the Canadian Clef Club.* No known jazz musicians belonged to Local 10; its members worked mainly in dance and theatre orchestras, and occasionally in radio.

Local 10 was formed in 1934 during a dispute between the American Federation of Musicians* (AFM) and the Canadian Broadcasting Corporation (CBC). The AFM wanted to establish a closed shop at the CBC, thereby preventing musicians belonging to a rival Canadian union, the National Musicians' Union of Canada, from working in CBC radio stations; the AFM had already established firm control over private radio stations in Canada and over American radio networks. An AFM strike against the CBC, in support of its demand for a closed shop and a salary increase at the CBC, began in Montreal and quickly spread across Canada. Many AFM members resigned during the strike. In Montreal, these defectors established Local 10 of the National Musicians' Union of Canada, which changed its name in mid-1935 to the Canadian Federation of Musicians.

Despite its appeal to nationalist sentiments, the CFM never posed a strong threat to the AFM in Canada. It had established locals in only seven cities by 1938; by February 1939 only two locals remained, in Montreal and London, Ontario. Nor did Local 10 ever seriously threaten the AFM's dominance in Montreal. Though the CBC refused to grant the AFM a closed shop, forcing the union to abandon its strike on 11 July 1934, most of the instrumental work at the CBC continued to go to AFM members. The CFM protested that the CBC was not recognizing Local 10 as a legitimate union and was not allocating work to the CFM and AFM locals in proportion to the size of their memberships, but these appeals had little impact, and Local 10 members obtained minimal work at the CBC. Nor was Local 10 able to place an orchestra composed of its members in the Mount Royal hotel or either of the hotels operated by Canada's two national railways in Montreal; these were all AFM domains. This inability of the CFM to help its Montreal members break into such lucrative markets led to its downfall. Disenchantment due to high unemployment among Local 10 members made the union susceptible to defections and raiding by the AFM.

Local 10's membership reached a peak of 144 in November 1935. It dropped to a low of forty-nine in December 1936 after the local's president, Albert Bray (died 1942), defected to the rival Federation of Canadian Labour, from where he apparently wooed other members of Local 10. Over the next two-and-a-half years Local 10 slowly built its membership up to seventy-four, only to be crippled by a second presidential defection. In early October 1939 it was discovered that Bray's successor, Lieut. Howard F. Fogg (born 27 April 1889), had secretly gone over to AFM Local 406 and was urging Local 10 members to follow him. Fogg had previously belonged to the AFM, but had defected to the CFM to avoid paying a one-hundred-dollar fine; the AFM apparently enticed him back to the fold by cancelling the fine. This tactic of cancelling outstanding fines was used to lure most of Local 10's membership back to the AFM. About fifteen loyal members of Local 10 elected new officers, including Louis Goudriot as president, in a desperate attempt to keep the local alive. As a union, however, they had become powerless and could find little work for themselves. On 14 October 1939, Local 10 officially ceased to exist: its remaining members terminated their affiliation with the All-Canadian Congress of Labour and joined AFM Local 406.

Bibliography: For records, see unpublished papers of CFM Local 10, Public Archives Canada (Ottawa), Manuscript Division, Labour Collection: Canadian Labour Congress Defunct Local Series, vol. 104, files 12 and 13. On the takeover by AFM Local 406, see Jack Hirshberg. "Montreal Local Absorbs Canadian Musicos Guild," *Metronome*, November 1939; and Musicians' Guild of Montreal (AFM Local 406), Minutes of general meeting, 2 October 1939; and Newsletter, Musicians' Guild of Montreal, 27 November 1939.

Canadian Federation of Musicians, Local 11. *See* Canadian Clef Club

Clef Club. *See* Canadian Clef Club

Emanon Jazz Society
late 1951 - ca. 1957

A group of jazz fans which organized jazz performances, supported the Jazz Workshop,* and actively encouraged public interest in, and support for, jazz in Montreal. Formed in fall 1951 on the ruins of the New Jazz Society* and the Oscar Peterson Fan Club,* the Emanon Jazz Society took its name from the title ("no name" spelt backwards) of a composition by American trumpeter Dizzy Gillespie. In October 1952 the society adopted a constitution which outlined the duties of the board of directors and three officers, stipulated a twenty-five-cent fine for members missing more than two consecutive meetings, and set annual dues at two dollars. Members were entitled to discounts at record stores and free

EMANON JAZZ SOCIETY

PRESENTS

REPEAT PERFORMANCE

BY POPULAR DEMAND

CONCERT

IN MODERN MUSIC

CANADIAN LEGION AUDITORIUM
1191 MONTAIN STREET

THURSDAY NIGHT, JUNE 9th 8.45 P.M.

STEVE GARRICK

AND HIS 18 PIECE ORCHESTRA

MAURY KAYE	BILLY GRAHAM
OCTETTE	QUINTETTE

ORIGINAL COMPOSITIONS AND ARRANGEMENTS BY:

STEVE GARRICK	HAL GAYLOR
MAURY KAYE	WALLY DUNBAR
ROGER HUFFORD	SHORTY ROGERS

ADMISSION :   BALCONY $ 1.00
ORCHESTRA $ 1.25

ASTOR PRINTING LTD., TA. 3788

Flyer for jazz concert organized by Emanon Jazz Society. *Courtesy of Billy Graham. John Gilmore Jazz History Collection, Concordia University Archives.*

American bandleader Stan Kenton (far left) meets some members of the Emanon Jazz Society at the Seville theatre where Kenton's orchestra was appearing, circa 1952. Standing left to right: Harold Smith, Peter Tidemann, Abby Smollen, Len Dobbin; seated: Pat Sorrentino. *Photo by Dal of Montreal, courtesy of John Lymberger. John Gilmore Jazz History Collection, Concordia University Archives.*

admission to Emanon meetings; guests were charged admission. The society granted honourary memberships to musicians to enable them to participate in Emanon jam sessions without running foul of the American Federation of Musicians,* which apparently prohibited free jamming by musicians except at private clubs of which they were members.

Meetings of the Emanon Jazz Society were held on Saturday afternoons at various locations, including: the former YMCA building at Stanley and Dorchester; the subsequent YMCA on Drummond; the CFCF radio station building on Côte des Neiges; the Casino Français on St. Lawrence Blvd., and other clubs; briefly in a room above the Video Café at 1352 Dorchester Blvd. West, which was subsequently used by the Jazz Workshop; the Sheraton-Mt. Royal hotel at 1455 Peel; and the Canadian Legion hall on Mountain. The meetings featured record presentations, lectures by members about the influence of important jazz artists, lecture/demonstrations by local musicians, and jam sessions. Musicians visiting the city were invited to talk and perform. On at least two occasions, American bandleader Stan Kenton addressed the society; his 28 June 1952 appearance is documented on a short film by Associated Screen News called *Canadian Cameo Series: Spotlight #5*, released in 1953.

In addition to regular meetings, Emanon members also: hosted record sessions at their homes; wrote letters to Montreal radio stations requesting more air time for jazz; published a newsletter in 1952, which included news about the society and the Jazz Workshop, excerpts from other publications pertaining to jazz, profiles of musicians, and listings of local jazz events and radio broadcasts; and organized jazz concerts. Among the concerts were a benefit for bassist Hal Gaylor, injured in an accident (March 1952), and a Thursday night concert at the Legion hall featuring the Steve Garrick big band, Maury Kaye quintet, and Billy Graham quintet, with overlapping personnel (June 1955). At the peak of its popularity, the Emanon Jazz Society was drawing up to 350 people to some of its events.

The society's first president was pianist Alfie Wade; a subsequent president was John Lymburner. Members included Len Dobbin, who became Montreal correspondent to *Coda* magazine in 1959; Harold Smith, then employed by Decca; and Abby Smollen, a record distributor.

Bibliography: For newsletters, see Emanon Jazz Society file, John Gilmore Jazz History Collection, Concordia University Archives.

Féderation des musiciens de Montréal. *See* American Federation of Musicians, Local 406

Guilde des musiciens de Montréal. *See* American Federation of Musicians, Local 406

Hot Club of Montreal
ca. early 1945 - ?

A club for record collectors founded by Arnold Maggs and others. Its core membership of about seven was interested mainly in bebop and the music of Stan Kenton, and held meetings at members' homes. No musicians belonged to the club and it did not promote live jazz.

Hot Jazz Society
late 1944 - late 1945 or 1946

A club for record collectors and jazz fans founded by George Karpinsky and Dorothy Vaughn. Membership never exceeded ten and did not include musicians. Meetings were held irregularly in the evenings at the Music Bar record store, 5177 Decarie Blvd. The owners of the store, Eddie and Abe Crelinsten, consulted members of the Hot Jazz Society on which American musicians to import for a series of jazz concerts they produced at His Majesty's theatre.

Jazz Appreciation Society
ca. 1953 - ca. 1954

A group of record collectors and jazz fans which held meetings to play and discuss records at a branch of the YMCA.

Jazz Unlimited
1952

An organization of unknown nature headed by Micky Katz and Mark Shafer. It apparently produced Saturday afternoon concerts and jam sessions at the Legion hall, featuring bands drawn from local nightclubs. The only confirmed concerts, in September and October 1952, used bands led by Al Cowans, Maury Kaye, and Milt Sealey.

Jazz Workshop
1952 - ca. 1954

A registered nonprofit organization founded in mid-1952 by Paul Bley, Keith White, and other Montreal musicians. Bley became president; White became treasurer. Membership cost twenty-five dollars a year and was restricted to musicians. The primary goals of the organization were to rent a space where musicians could meet, rehearse, and jam, and to bring American jazz artists to Montreal to play with Workshop members. Secondary goals, which were never effectively realized, included attracting student musicians in search of instrumental teachers and the creation of a library of jazz music.

To raise funds for rental of a space, the Workshop immediately began organizing occasional Saturday afternoon jazz concerts at the Chez

Paree. The musicians performed without pay, the Workshop collected money at the door, and the nightclub retained the bar receipts. About six of these concerts featured American musicians imported by the Workshop, including guitarist Chuck Wayne, trombonist Kai Winding, alto saxophonist Charlie Parker, and singer Peggy Lee. The American musicians were recruited and brought to Montreal by Bley, who was studying music in New York City and travelling regularly between the cities. By October 1952, after three concerts, the Workshop had raised enough money to rent a room above the Video Café, 1352 Dorchester Blvd. West, previously used for meetings of the Emanon Jazz Society.* The Workshop used the room for jamming, including private sessions with the American musicians it imported. The Emanon Jazz Society continued to use the room occasionally for meetings and helped publicize Workshop events through its network of members and its newsletter.

On 11 December 1952, CBFT-TV, the bilingual Montreal station of the Canadian Broadcasting Corporation, launched a half-hour, Thursday night television program called *Jazz Workshop*. It featured members of the Workshop in concert. The first program featured the Three G's (Steve Garrick, Hal Gaylor, and Billy Graham), Nick Ayoub, Larry McManus, Max Chamitov, and Tony Romandini. On 5 February 1953, Charlie Parker, who had been brought to Montreal by the Workshop for a concert at the Chez Paree, appeared on the program playing with Bley, Neil Michaud, drummer Ted Paskert, and American visitors guitarist Dick Garcia and tenor saxophonist Brew Moore. At some point, the CBC apparently began using non-Workshop members on its program, and the musicians' organization severed its ties with the CBC.

The Workshop had produced about a dozen concerts at the Chez Paree when the nightclub came under new management and cancelled its agreement with the musicians. White resigned as treasurer in a dispute over finances, leaving Bley with full control over the Workshop. He began hiring American musicians to play for a week at a time at the Workshop's room and charging admission at the door. The guests, including saxophonists Sonny Rollins, Jackie McLean, and Allen Eager, were usually accompanied by Bley and Michaud. At some point, Workshop members joined Steve Garrick in organizing a cooperative big band; whoever showed up at rehearsal with an arrangement led the band through that particular number. Garrick was the most prolific writer, and as members became accustomed to his leadership the band gradually ceased to be a cooperative effort and became known as the Steve Garrick Orchestra. It continued to rehearse and perform occasional concerts until about 1958. The Jazz Workshop itself fell apart in about 1954, for several reasons: internal disputes over finances and direction; regular surveillance of the Workshop room by police drug squads, which intimidated some members and guests and harassed the owners of the Video Café; Bley's increasing absence from Montreal and disillusionment with the Workshop; and White's withdrawal from the local jazz scene. During the 1970s, White resurrected the name Jazz Workshop for occasional jazz concerts which he produced in Montreal; the last was held at the Musée des Beaux Arts on 20 April 1980.

In 1966 and 1967 Mike Armstrong used the name Jazz Workshop (l'Atelier de Jazz) in connection with jazz concerts he produced at Moose Hall and subsequently with a jazz nightclub he ran called The Barrel. These activities had no connection with the Jazz Workshop organization or its registered name.

For details and discography of Parker's concert and TV appearance, see Jack Litchfield, *The Canadian Jazz Discography: 1916-1980* (Toronto: University of Toronto Press, 1982), 367-69.

Montreal Association of Musicians. *See* Canadian Federation of Musicians, Local 10

Montreal Jazz Society
1958 - ca. 1965

A loosely knit group of musicians and jazz fans founded in April 1958 by John Cordell, a commercial artist and part-time bassist from the Netherlands. During its first four years, the society organized weekly jam sessions in various nightclubs by securing bookings for a local rhythm section trio and ensuring a large turnout. The first sessions were held on Monday nights at L'Echourie. When the gatherings outgrew that location, they were moved to Café St. Jacques in mid-1958; there René Thomas became leader of the rhythm sections, and guest artists occasionally appeared, including American tenor saxophonist Zoot Sims and Belgian guitarist/harmonica player Toots Thielemans. After a little more than a year at the Café St. Jacques, the society moved its sessions to El Cortijo, a converted garage on Sherbrooke Street East, for a couple of weeks, and then, on 17 November 1959, to Lutece (Chez Bozo) on Crescent Street, where sessions were held on Tuesday nights, still under Thomas. In April 1960 Keith White took over as leader of the rhythm sections. An unsigned editorial in the May 1960 issue of *Coda* magazine congratulated the Montreal Jazz Society on its second anniversary, celebrated in April, and added: "It has been largely due to the efforts of John Cordell and the musicians who have played at various sessions of the Montreal Jazz Society that there is modern jazz activity in Montreal."

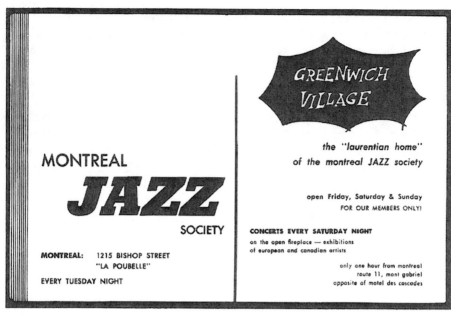

MONTREAL

JAZZ

SOCIETY

MONTREAL: 1215 BISHOP STREET
"LA POUBELLE"

EVERY TUESDAY NIGHT

GREENWICH VILLAGE

the "laurentian home"
of the montreal JAZZ society

open Friday, Saturday & Sunday
FOR OUR MEMBERS ONLY!

CONCERTS EVERY SATURDAY NIGHT
on the open fireplace — exhibitions
of european and canadian artists

only one hour from montreal
route 11, mont gabriel
opposite of motel des cascades

Table card. *Courtesy of Cisco Normand. John Gilmore Jazz History Collection, Concordia University Archives.*

After complaints from neighbours about noise, the society moved its sessions to La Poubelle on Bishop Street in June 1960. Cordell left the society, apparently amid complaints from musicians about his leadership. By October 1961, Hans (possibly Johan) Kunst was leading the society (*Coda*, October 1961, 6), and Cisco Normand was leading the rhythm sections. Sessions continued at La Poubelle for an unknown period. As well, the society began organizing other jazz sessions: on Thursday and Friday nights at the Penthouse; during weekends at Greenwich Village, a musicians-only house in Mont Gabriel, a mountain resort town seventy-five kilometres north of Montreal; and on Sunday evenings at the Mountain Playhouse. The latter venue was short-lived, and Greenwich Village closed in spring 1962 due to financial losses.

By summer 1962, the Montreal Jazz Society had moved its sessions to La Tête de l'Art, where it met on Wednesday nights. The society underwent a fundamental transformation at this location. Kunst and Guy Lachapelle began managing La Tête de l'Art and booking American jazz musicians to perform at the club for week-long engagements, accompanied by Montreal rhythm sections. The name Montreal Jazz Society was used as a banner for the club's jazz policy, though conventional nightclub bookings of American jazz artists replaced open jam sessions for Montreal musicians. On 15 September 1962, American trumpeter Ted Curson recorded an LP entitled *Ted Curson Quintet Live at La Tête de l'Art*

(Trans World TWJ7000), using local musicians Al Doctor (alto sax); Maury Kaye (piano); Charlie Biddle (bass); and Charlie Duncan (drums); the LP was intended to help promote the club's jazz policy, but apparently sold poorly. By fall 1962, Kunst and Lachapelle were also booking jazz acts at the Penthouse. By spring 1963 they had stopped using local rhythm sections to accompany American guests and were instead booking complete American bands; leaders included: Sonny Stitt, Wynton Kelly, Roy Haynes, J. J. Johnson, Clifford Jordan, Donald Byrd, and Pepper Adams. This policy caused La Tête de l'Art financial problems, and it closed from 23 March to 9 May 1963. Soon after it reopened, Kunst was relegated to booking only, and a new manager was installed (*Coda*, July 1963, 7). The club resumed booking complete American bands, including: John Coltrane quartet, Clark Terry quintet; the Newport Festival All-Stars; Slide Hampton; and Jackie McLean. How long this policy continued at La Tête de l'Art, and how long the name Montreal Jazz Society was used in connection with the policy, is not known; however, in summer 1963 Kunst was still involved in producing jazz shows at the club. In September 1963 Kunst launched a jazz policy, using the name Montreal Jazz Society, at the Metropole, where Bob Rollins was manager. After three money-losing bookings (Paul Winter septet; Slide Hampton big band; and Woody Herman big band), the jazz policy was abandoned. La Tête de l'Art eventually closed; Kunst left Montreal; the name Montreal Jazz Society disappeared in about 1965; and Lachapelle abandoned jazz.

Bibliography: Gerald Welsh, "The Ups and Downs of Jazz in Montreal," *Montrealer*, July 1960. For details of weekly activities of the Montreal Jazz Society, see Len Dobbin's regular columns in *Coda* during this period.

Montreal Vintage Music Society
1966 -

A group of record collectors and discographical researchers specializing in early jazz and related musics. The society was formed by about six collectors at the instigation of Jim Kidd, then a broadcaster at CFCF. They met informally in private homes about a dozen times from January 1964 to late 1966. On 6 December 1966, they held their first official meeting as the Montreal Vintage Music Society, at Dick Bourcier's home in Laval, Quebec. Thereafter, meetings were held about once a month, attracting a core membership of about fifteen to twenty. Most members have been residents of the Montreal area, but a few have travelled from southeastern Ontario.

Meetings have typically lasted at least four hours and involved presentations by members or guests on some aspect of jazz, discographical research, or collecting recordings, sheet music, and books about music. As well, members have auctioned collectibles, tested one another on aural recognition of recordings and musicians, and shown films featuring music performances. Professional musicians who have attended meetings as guests include: Al Baculis, Art Blakey, Cozy Cole, Vic Dickenson, Bobby Hackett, Johnny Holmes, and Jonah Jones. A social event has usually followed the meetings.

The Montreal Vintage Music Society, and especially member Hank Fleischman, was responsible for bringing pianist Lou Hooper to the attention of the jazz world again in the 1960s. Fleischman "discovered" Hooper, then in his sixties, at a bar in the Laurentians north of Montreal, where he was working as a cocktail pianist. Hooper, who had virtually abandoned jazz, joined the society, was interviewed extensively by members, and, with the society's encouragement, resumed playing jazz. He subsequently recorded a solo LP in 1973 (CBC RCI380).

In December 1968 the society began publishing a newsletter containing discographical research and news. In 1972 the Montreal Vintage Music Society and the West Mississauga Jazz Muddies, a similar group formed in 1971 in the Toronto area, began holding joint annual meetings as the Canadian Collectors Convention (sometimes Congress). These conventions have served to exchange research, honour Canadian musicians (including Hooper in 1977), sell collectibles, and hear guest speakers; the conventions have alternated between Montreal and Toronto, though one was held in Ottawa in 1982. The Montreal Vintage Music Society has also organized an annual dinner and dance. It was still active as this book went to press.

Members of the society have included: Jack Litchfield, author of *The Canadian Jazz Discography: 1916-1980* and *This Is Jazz*, a privately published discography of the 1947 American radio program of the same name; Edward Moogk, author of *Roll Back the Years*; Peter Johnston, coauthor (with Charles Garrod) of a multivolume discography of Harry James and his Orchestra; Hank Fleischman, author of an unpublished label listing of Compo and other record companies (donated to the National Library, Ottawa); Trevor Tolley, record reviewer and writer for *Coda* magazine; Jerry Valburn, owner of the American record company Jazz Archives; Marv Ekers, owner of the Montreal record company Jazz Guild; and radio broadcasters George Karpinsky, Jim Kidd, Ron Sweètman, and Len Dobbin, the latter also Montreal correspondent for *Coda* magazine (1959-ca. 1971) and jazz columnist for the *Gazette* (Montreal) (5 March 1981 -).

Musicians' Club, The. *See* Canadian Clef Club

Musicians' Guild of Montreal. *See* American Federation of Musicians, Local 406

National Musicians' Union of Canada. *See* Canadian Federation of Musicians, Local 10.

New Jazz Society
ca. 1950

An organization for jazz fans formed by *Metronome* magazine in the United States, with chapters in many cities. The Montreal chapter was short-lived. It was formed by members of the waning Oscar Peterson Fan Club.* As the New Jazz Society, these fans held weekly meetings, frequently at the YWCA, at which they listened to records and organized jam sessions. When the members tired of sending dues to the parent organization in the United States, they abandoned the society and formed the Emanon Jazz Society.*

Oscar Peterson Fan Club
ca. 1949

A loose organization of jazz fans who rallied around a common enthusiasm for Oscar Peterson but who were interested in modern jazz in general and who wanted to form a jazz society. Members held weekly Saturday afternoon meetings to listen to records. They also organized jam sessions for local and visiting musicians. Peterson performed at the first meeting, held at the Chez Paree, but apparently did not attend subsequent meetings, held at a variety of locations including the YWCA, the Legion hall, Moose Hall, and various nightclubs. After about one year, the club's core members became a chapter of the New Jazz Society* and the Oscar Peterson Fan Club ceased to exist.

Student jazz societies

From the late-1950s through the mid-1960s, students at colleges and universities in Montreal organized jazz societies. The society at Sir George Williams College (University from 18 December 1959) had the greatest impact on the Montreal jazz community. Meetings were held regularly on Saturday afternoons at the school's Norris building on Drummond Street. They featured jam sessions and occasional lectures by musicians about jazz or music theory. The Sir George Williams society served as a focal point for many of the city's young jazz musicians, including: bassist Errol Chatham, saxophonist Wimp Henstridge, trumpeter Al Penfold, and pianists Stan Patrick, Billy Georgette and Joe Sealy. Members also participated in jam sessions at the Little Vienna restaurant on Stanley Street opposite the Norris building, which began a jazz policy in November 1958 with the encouragement of the society's members. The society brought American pianist Thelonious Monk to Montreal for a concert at Plateau Hall. In 1966 the society organized a concert by the Pierre Leduc trio which was recorded live (Elysee ELM.2003 and ELS.5003).

Jazz societies at Loyola College (which merged with Sir George Williams University in 1974 to become Concordia University), McGill University, and Université de Montréal presented jazz concerts, occasionally featuring American musicians.

Traditional Jazz Club of Montreal
1956 - 1960

An organization of record collectors, researchers, and fans of early jazz and related musics which, through its social activities, encouraged the formation of semiprofessional bands to perform New Orleans-style jazz and Dixieland jazz. The club was founded in November 1956 by John Norris (an immigrant from Britain who moved to Toronto in June 1957 and launched *Coda* magazine) and Geoff Williams (who returned to England in April 1958). It was intended to promote interest in early jazz, the blues, spirituals, and gospel. Thirty-two people attended the first official meeting at the Westmount YMCA on 13 February 1957. Meetings were held every two weeks until 23 April 1959, then weekly thereafter. During its first year, the club served mainly as a record-appreciation and social club. Annual dues were $5.00 for members and $2.50 for members' wives; guests were charged thirty-five cents per meeting.

Soon after its formation, the club asked some friends who were semiprofessional musicians to form a band to play at a club party in

298

November 1957. The band decided to remain together, called itself the Mountain City Jazz Band, and subsequently played for dances at Moose Hall and elsewhere, frequently in tandem with a second band called the Applejack Skiffle Group. (The personnel of the Mountain City Jazz Band, from its formation to October 1959, was: Pat Kelly, trumpet; Erik Nielson, clarinet; Ron Vango, piano; Dan McCrae, banjo; and Leo Eurwin, drums. Subsequent personnel changes included Vango switching to trombone.) Apparently, the musicians were not members of the Traditional Jazz Club and there was no formal relationship between the Mountain City Jazz Band and the club; however, some club members helped organize dances at which the band played.

Meanwhile, the Traditional Jazz Club continued its regular meetings, featuring presentations of records and research. Blues singer Brother John Sellers attended one meeting as a guest. The club produced a newsletter written by Peter Evans, who also wrote a regular column on the activities of the club and the Mountain City Jazz Band for *Coda*, beginning in the first issue of the magazine in May 1958. By May 1959 the club was holding weekly dances; during the summer of 1959 it organized a riverboat cruise and dance which attracted three hundred people; and by March 1960 it had registered as a nonprofit organization. However, as interest grew in the club's social activities, usually involving the Mountain City Jazz Band, attendance at record and research presentation meetings dwindled to the point where, by 1960, these meetings were being held in members' homes. The last documented club meeting was held in September 1960, at which time Ted Comben was president and Sylvia Irwin was secretary.

In summer 1960 the Mountain City Jazz Band split into two groups at the climax of a lingering dispute over whether it should play the traditional New Orleans ensemble style of early jazz or the more popular but less authentic Dixieland style. Thereafter, Pat Kelly's Jazz Group played Dixieland style (Kelly, trumpet; John Winters, clarinet; Ron Vango, trombone; Pat Rich, piano; Dan McCrae, banjo; Vlad Rahr, bass; Tommy Thomson, drums), while Kid Martyn's Jazzmen played the traditional New Orleans style (Barry "Kid" Martyn, drums; Bob Wright, clarinet; Alex Bluck, trombone; Bill Furter, banjo; Les Walker, bass). Both groups played at weekly dances organized by veterans of the Traditional Jazz Club until summer 1968, when the dances were discontinued due to dwindling attendance.

Bibliography: For details of the club's meetings and social activities from spring 1958, see Peter Evans's regular columns in *Coda*.

APPENDIX TWO

Addresses

Following are addresses and/or approximate locations of some of the places where jazz was made and/or jazz musicians worked in Montreal prior to 1970. Street numbering in Montreal has changed several times: first during 1854-55, then again during 1865-66. In 1905 city streets were divided into east and west at St. Lawrence Blvd. Finally, between 1924 and 1931, all numbers were changed to their present state. Because the last change was made gradually over a period of seven years, it is not known whether the street numbers of those venues listed below which were open before 1931 correspond to present numbers.

Abbreviations: cr - corner; nr - near; W - west; E - east; x/y between x and y; St. - Saint (not Street); B - Boulevard.

Alberta Lounge	Osbourne, cr Windsor (present site of Chateau Champlain hotel)
Aldo's	1061 Mountain
Algiers	1061 Mountain
L'Amorce	25 St. Paul E
L'Anse	194 St. Paul W
Arcadia Ballroom	1223 Bleury
Association Espagnole	485 Sherbrooke W
Auditorium	375 Ontario W
Bamboo Cage	Stanley
Barrel, The	1191 Mountain, basement
Beacon Grill	1112 St. Antoine W
Belhumeur, Café	4145 Gouin E
Bellevue Casino	375 Ontario W

Belmar	1424 Peel
Belmont Park	riverside, Gouin at Berri
Belmont theatre	cr St. Lawrence B and Mt. Royal
Birdland	above Dunn's, 892 St. Catherine W
Bizarre, Café	2055 Bishop
Black Bottom, The	1350 St. Antoine W, cr Aqueduct; to 22 St. Paul E in late 1967
Black Magic Room	in Chez Paree, 1258 Stanley
Black Orchid	above Dunn's, 892 St. Catherine W
Blue Sky	St. Catherine W nr St. Lawrence B
Bohème, Café La	1418 Guy
Capital, Café	St. Catherine W nr University
Cartier Ballroom	1306 Amherst, cr St. Catherine E
Casa Espagnole	485 Sherbrooke W nr Park
Casa Loma	94 St. Catherine E
Casino Français	St. Lawrence B nr St. Catherine
Chabada Jazz Club	1430 Stanley
Chanteclair	Notre Dame E
Chez Maurice	1244 St. Catherine W
Chez Paree	1258 Stanley
Chinese Paradise Grill	57 Lagauchetière
Chorie	Pine
Circle A	904 St. Catherine W
Ciro's	St. Catherine W nr Bishop
Clan, Le	Bélanger
Clef Club room	1188 St. Antoine W and/or 1302 St. Antoine W
Commodore	984 St. Lawrence B
Connie's Inn	1417 St. Lawrence B, cr St. Catherine E
Copa Cabana	1112 St. Catherine W
Cosy Grill	322A St. Catherine W; 676 St. Catherine W
Cotton Grill	1281 Phillips Square
Downbeat	1424 Peel
Dunn's	892 St. Catherine W
El Mocambo	Iberville nr St. Catherine E

El Morocco	Mansfield; 1410 Metcalfe, cr St. Catherine W; 1445 Closse
El Patio	1224 St. Lawrence B
Embassy	Mansfield
L'Enfer	nr Bishop and Dorchester; to 229 Ontario W nr Bleury and/or 2137 Bleury
Esquire	1224 Stanley
L'Est, Café de	4558 Notre Dame E
L'Experience	Mountain
Faison Doré, Au	1147 St. Lawrence B
Folies Royal	Sherbrooke W, cr Old Orchard
42 Club	Notre Dame
400 Club	Dorchester, cr University
Frolics	1417 St. Lawrence B, cr St. Catherine E
Galerie	in Old Montreal
Gayety theatre	St. Catherine W, cr St. Urbain
Grenier, Le	1429 Crescent
Gumbo, The	Stanley, north of St. Catherine W
Hale Haikala	626 Notre Dame W
Harlem Paradise	772 Mountain
His/Her Majesty's theatre	Guy, St. Catherine W/Maisonneuve
Hollywood	92 St. Catherine E
Jardin de Danse	2200 St. Catherine E.
Jazz Gallery	Mountain
Jazz Hot, Le	94 St. Catherine E, above Casa Loma
Jazz Hut	1194 Peel
Jazztek	1418 Guy, above Café La Bohème
"Jazz Workshop" (The Barrel)	1191 Mountain, basement
Jazz Workshop room	above Video Café, 1352 Dorchester W
Kasavubu Jazz Club	Western, nr Minto (present site of Decarie Expressway nr Maisonneuve)
Kit-Kat Cabaret	1224 Stanley

Latin Quarter	Mountain
Lido, Café	1258 Stanley
Lindy's	Park, southwest cr St. Joseph B
Lion d'Or	1676 Ontario E
Little Vienna restaurant	Stanley, St. Catherine/Maisonneuve
Lutece/Chez Bozo	1208 Crescent
Mas, Le	3524 St. Dominique
Metropole	400 Sherbrooke W
Monte Carlo	1770 Mountain
Montmartre	59 St. Catherine W, cr Clark (1930s);
	1417 St. Lawrence B,
	cr. St. Catherine E (1950s)
Moonlight Gardens	St. Catherine E nr Amherst
Moose Hall	3485A Park
Mountain Playhouse	1250 Remembrance Rd,
	on Mount Royal
"Musicians' Workshop"	
(Kasavubu)	Western, nr Minto (present site of
	Decarie Expressway nr Maisonneuve)
Négapo, Le	St. Charles, in Longueuil
New Ideal Gardens	770 Mountain
New Orleans Café	188 Dorchester E
Op, Le	3545 Park
Palais d'Or	1224 Stanley
Paramount Grill	1290 St. Urbain
Penthouse	1194 Peel
Piccadilly	1459 St. Alexander
Place, The	Stanley
Poubelle, La	1215 Bishop
Press Club	1201 Phillips Square
Rand's	4551 St. Catherine E
Rendez-Vous	1224 St. Lawrence B
Rockhead's Paradise	1258 St. Antoine W

Roseland Ballroom	Phillips Square; 375 Ontario W
Roxy theatre	St. Lawrence B nr St. Catherine
Ruby Foo's	7815 Decarie
St. André's Ballroom	906 St. Catherine E nr St. André
St. Jacques, Café	St. Catherine E nr St. Denis
St. Michel, Café	770 Mountain, 2nd floor
Savoy	1457 St. Alexander
Seven Steps	1430 Stanley
Seville theatre	2155 St. Catherine W
Snake Pit, The	770 Mountain, street level
Shanghai, The	cr St. Catherine and St. Lawrence B
Sohmer Park	738 Notre Dame E
Soul City	770 Mountain, 2nd floor
Stadium Ballroom	cr Dorchester and De Lorimier
Starland theatre	1174 St. Lawrence B, Dorchester/St. Catherine
Swiss restaurant	1463 Metcalfe
Terminal	1114 St. Antoine W
Tête de l'Art, La	1451 Metcalfe
Tic-Toc	1258 Stanley
Val d'Or	1417 St. Lawrence B, cr St. Catherine E.
Venetian Gardens	1224 St. Catherine W
Verdun pavilion	nr Woodland and LaSalle
Vic's	St. Catherine W nr St. Lawrence B
Victoria Hall	4626 St. Catherine W
Vienna Grill	St. Catherine E nr Papineau
Vieux Moulin	Sherbrooke nr Bleury
Washington Club	1004 Mt. Royal Place; cr St. Catherine W and Metcalfe

APPENDIX THREE

Key to photo of Vic Vogel Big Band

Key to photograph on page 229:
1. Al Baculis (clarinet); 2. Alvin Pall (tenor saxophone); 3. Gerry Danovitch (alto saxophone); 4. Leo Perron (alto saxophone); 5. Nick Ayoub (tenor saxophone); 6. unidentified; 7. Herbie Spanier (trumpet); 8. Gerry Vaillancourt (trombone); 9. Bix Belair (trumpet); 10. Mike Lawson (trombone); 11. Gilles Laflamme (trumpet); 12. Al Penfold (trumpet); 13. Paul Lafortune (drums); 14. Jacques Dompierre (percussion); 15. Vic Vogel (trombone, piano).

BIBLIOGRAPHY

Books

Chilton, John. *Who's Who of Jazz: Storyville to Swing Street*. Philadelphia: Chilton Book Company, 1972.

Collier, James Lincoln. *The Making of Jazz: A Comprehensive History*. 1978. Reprint. New York: Delta, 1979.

Duguay, Raoul, comp. *Musiques du Kébèk*. Montreal: Editions du Jour, 1971.

Feather, Leonard. *The Encyclopedia of Jazz*. Second edition. New York: Bonanza, 1960.

Feather, Leonard. *The Encyclopedia of Jazz in the Sixties*. New York: Bonanza, 1966.

Feather, Leonard, and Ira Gitler. *The Encyclopedia of Jazz in the Seventies*. New York: Horizon, 1976.

Hébert, Chantal. *Le Burlesque au Québec: Un divertissement populaire*. Ville LaSalle, Québec: Hurtubise HMH, 1981.

Kallmann, Helmut, Gilles Potvin, and Kenneth Winters, eds. *Encyclopedia of Music in Canada*. Toronto: University of Toronto Press, 1981.

Leiter, Robert David. *The Musicians and Petrillo*. New York: Octagon, 1974.

Litchfield, Jack. *The Canadian Jazz Discography: 1916-1980*. Toronto: University of Toronto Press, 1982.

Miller, Mark. *Jazz in Canada: Fourteen Lives*. Toronto: University of Toronto Press, 1982.

Moogk, Edward E. *Roll Back the Years: History of Canadian Recorded Sound and Its Legacy, Genesis to 1930*. Ottawa: National Library, 1975.

Ostransky, Leroy. *Jazz City: The Impact of Our Cities on the Development of Jazz*. Englewood Cliffs, New Jersey: Prentice-Hall, Inc., 1978.

Rust, Brian. *Jazz Records 1897-1942*. Two volumes. London: Storyville Publications, 1970.

Sidran, Ben. *Black Talk*. 1971. Reprint. New York: Da Capo, 1981.

Winks, Robin W. *The Blacks in Canada: A History*. Montreal: McGill-Queen's University Press, 1971.

Theses

Israel, Wilfred Emmerson. "The Montreal Negro Community." Master's thesis, McGill University, Montreal, 1928.

Vigerhous, Gideon. "The Montreal Jazz Community: A Study of Class, Status, and Job Satisfaction." Master's thesis, Carleton University, Ottawa, 1972.

Articles, Booklets, and Periodicals

Bertley, Leo W. *Montreal's Oldest Black Congregation: Union Church*. Pierrefonds, Quebec: Bilongo, 1976.

Coda magazine. Volume 1, number 1 (May 1958) to volume 9, number 9 (September-October 1970), particularly monthly columns by Montreal correspondent Len Dobbin beginning June 1959. Toronto.

Johnstone, Ken. "How Plante and Drapeau Licked the Montreal Underworld." *Maclean's*, 1 December 1954, 12-13, 102-14.

Plante, Pax, and David MacDonald. "The Shame of My City: Crime in Montreal." *Star Weekly* (magazine supplement to the *Montreal Star*), 24 June 1961, 2-6; 1 July, 6-11; 8 July, 10-13; 15 July, 14-17; 22 July, 15-17.

Robbins, Vivian M. *Musical Buxton*. Buxton, Ontario: privately printed [1969?].

Collections

Walter Boudreau Collection, Concordia University Archives, Montreal. Contains documents of Boudreau's career, and documents and scores of L'Infonie.

Clyde Duncan Collection, Concordia University Archives, Montreal. Contains documents of Duncan's career and of the Canadian Clef Club.

John Gilmore Jazz History Collection, Concordia University Archives, Montreal. Contains jazz history documents, with special emphasis on Montreal history, including: tapes of interviews with Montreal musicians; memorabilia of Montreal musicians and bands; music scores; audio recordings; photographs; posters; clippings; manuscripts.

Johnny Holmes Collection, Concordia University Archives, Montreal. Contains photographs, scores, and audio recordings of Holmes's bands.

Labour collections, Manuscript Division, Public Archives Canada, Ottawa. Contains papers of the Canadian Federation of Musicians, Locals 10 and 11 (Montreal).

Jean Préfontaine Collection, Concordia University Archives, Montreal. Contains documents of Le Quatuor de jazz libre du Québec and related events.

Alex Robertson Collection, Concordia University Archives, Montreal. Contains original research; rare audio recordings and sheet music; periodicals and books; with special emphasis on early Canadian recording and music publishing.

Myron Sutton Collection, Concordia University Archives, Montreal. Contains scrapbook, private papers, photographs, and audio recordings documenting Sutton's career and the Canadian Ambassadors.

INDEX

Numbers in italics refer to illustrations

AFTERWORD*
to the Second Edition

In the more than twenty years since this book was first published by Véhicule Press, I have often been asked why the book ends where it does and why I haven't brought it up to date. The answers are entwined. When I began writing this book in 1981, no attempt had yet been made to tell the story of jazz in Montreal, or indeed in any other Canadian city. For the first couple of years, I was researching almost blindly, gathering stray facts and names, tracking musicians down across the continent, and making tenuous connections in the stories I was hearing. Gradually, a picture began to emerge of a world of jazz and nightlife that seemed at times fantastical to me. Listening to veteran Montreal musicians tell their stories, I sometimes felt like Roland Lavallée's son listening to his father with affectionate disbelief: "Oh, Dad, it couldn't have been like that. No place in the world could be like that!" But as Roland told his son, and as so many veteran musicians told me, it *was* like that. The contrast between the era I was writing about and the Montreal jazz scene of the 1980s could not have been more glaring.

It soon became clear to me that the era I was writing about – not only the music, but the musicians' workplace and sense of community – had disappeared forever. It's tempting to use phrases like "death of a community" but it wasn't that dramatic: musicians just began drifting away; new sounds were in the air. By 1970 it was all over. Montreal's nightclubs could no longer support a large and stable jazz community. Indeed, there was no longer a homogenous community to speak of. Jazz in Montreal did not die, when I looked around me in the 1980s I saw, not a single community of musicians with a common musical language, but smaller cliques. I heard styles of music, each claiming a jazz lineage, that were so different in conception and in the instrumental techniques required to play them that musicians from different cliques were ill at ease making music together. Divisions and antagonisms were palpable, even to a non-musician like

323

me. Mainstream musicians were competing with jazz-rock bands for scarce work in the nightclubs, while young, mostly francophone players were experimenting with free jazz and collective improvisation, developing what came to be called *musique actuelle*. Jazz education had moved from the informal classroom of the bandstand to degree programs at the city's two English universities, Concordia and McGill. And the rapidly expanding Montreal International Jazz Festival, launched in 1980, was having an impact, at the time still immeasurable, on the jazz scene in the city and on the public's perceptions of the music. It was all strikingly different from the world of Montreal jazz and nightlife that I was writing about, and yet this new era was only a little more than a decade old. The transformation of the city's jazz scene had been rapid and convulsive. But the new era was too young and still too much in flux, I concluded, for me to do anything more than document the new directions blazed by l'Infonie and Jazz Libre. The rest would have to wait.

Enough time has now passed for someone to write a comprehensive history of jazz in Montreal after 1970. The key musicians, events, and currents of the past 40 years have come into focus. So different is the new era that it deserves a book of its own – the next volume, if you will, in the ongoing story of jazz in Montreal. Whoever takes up the challenge will bring to it his or her own perspective, as they should. I will only say now that in the years since my book was first published it has become evident to me that the next volume can, and perhaps should, be a very different kind of book. The reason is simple: we can now hear the music of the past.

Jazz in Montreal was scarcely recorded during its first 50 years. The few commercial recordings that were made tell us very little about the jazz that was being played in public, night after night, prior to 1970. A few private recordings have been found, but they are rare, especially from the early years. Hopefully, more private recordings will be discovered, offering new insights, but at the time I was working on this book I could only imagine what most of the bands actually sounded like. This fact necessarily shaped the book you hold in your hands: I couldn't write a history of jazz *music* in Montreal, I could only write a history of the musicians who made it, and of the forces that shaped their lives.

The picture is much brighter now. The jazz made in Montreal since 1970, and especially since 1980, has been extensively recorded, both commercially and privately. As a result, the next volume in Montreal's jazz history can be about the music as much as about the musicians. The next writer can actually listen to the past, and not just imagine it. He or she can hear the instrumental voices of the musicians, trace the development of individual and regional styles, and hear the influence of one musician or band on another. But there is a caveat: the history cannot be written if the primary historical record is lost. Every effort should now be made, by individual researchers and by institutions, to gather and conserve in archives the raw materials of Montreal's post-1970 jazz history. Commercial recordings, newspaper files, and official documents are relatively safe in the national archives of Quebec and Canada. What we are in danger of losing are the life stories of the musicians, and their irreplaceable collections of private audio and video recordings, handwritten music scores, photographs, and other memorabilia. This is the raw stuff of history. It is perishable, easily damaged, and easily discarded. It would be an immeasurable loss to Quebec's social and cultural history, and indeed to future creative work in jazz and other art forms, if this rich store of primary material were allowed to slip through our collective hands.

John Gilmore

---

* First published, in slightly different form, in the French translation of this book, *Une histoire du jazz à Montréal* (Montreal: Lux Éditeur, 2009). See also: John Gilmore, "Jazz Research in Canada: Issues and Directions," in *Ethnomusicology in Canada,* edited by Robert Witmer. (Toronto: Institute of Canadian Music, 1990).

ADDITIONAL NOTES
Second Edition

Page 28   ... their names are lost to history.

The early history of jazz in Montreal is elusive, and any account must be somewhat conjectural. My account was written in the 1980s. Later research by Mark Miller supports my thesis that professional black American jazz musicians began arriving in Montreal soon after the onset of the jazz craze. However, Miller believes that Slap Rags White was not the first to take up residence. According to Miller, Charles Prevoa (instrument unknown), from Boston, led a black band at Stanley Hall, on Stanley Street below St. Catherine Street, for several months in 1917, and maintained an address listing in Montreal from 1917 to 1923. There may have been others before him. Miller also asserts that Millard Thomas arrived in Montreal before White, though Thomas may have spent only a short time in Montreal on his initial visit before moving to Quebec City. Furthermore, Miller and other researchers now reject the notion that White performed or recorded with the Six Brown Brothers, though Bruce Vermazen has identified three of White's compositions in the group's discography. See: Mark Miller, *Such Melodious Racket: The Lost History of Jazz in Canada, 1914-1949* (Toronto: The Mercury Press, 1997) and *Some Hustling This! – Taking Jazz To The World, 1914-1929* (Mercury, 2005); and Bruce Vermazen, *That Moaning Saxophone: The Six Brown Brothers and the Dawning of a Musical Craze* (New York: Oxford University Press, 2004).

Page 30   ... may have included black performers.

This now seems improbable. Sousa's large concert bands performed mostly marches, popular songs, and European classics. His bands are not known to have included black musicians, though it is possible that black performers or musicians appeared separately as part of the entertainment program at Dominion Park. Sousa was not a fan of jazz. Nevertheless, his band included some ragtime in its repertoire and, as jazz gained in popularity, Sousa sometimes featured sections of the band, such as the saxophones, playing popular tunes in a jazz style. See: Paul Edmund Bierley, *The Incredible Band of John Philip Sousa* (Champaign, IL: University of Illinois Press, 2006) for details of Sousa's 1918 tour, which included Montreal. According to Bierley, Sousa had previously performed in Montreal in November 1911.

Page 289   photo caption

Correct spelling: John Lymburner (not Lymberger).

Page 308   Collections

Concordia University Archives collections are now catalogued as follows:

Walter Boudreau fonds (P021)
Clyde Duncan fonds (P018)
John Gilmore fonds (P004)
Johnny Holmes fonds (P016)
Jean Préfontaine fonds (P020)
Alex Robertson collection (P023)
Myron Sutton fonds (P019)

Additional collections relating to jazz history have since been acquired by Concordia University Archives. See: http://archives3.concordia.ca/

Labour collections:

Files relating to the Canadian Federation of Musicians, locals 10 and 11, are catalogued at Library and Archives Canada, Ottawa, within the fonds of the Canadian Labour Congress (CLC) MG28-I103, as follows:

MG 28-I103, Series: National unions and chartered locals, financial reports, Volume 79, File 31: "Musicians, Canadian Federations of Local 11. Canadian Clef Club. Montreal, Quebec. Monthly Reports. July 1938-October 1939."

MG 28-I103, Series: Defunct local union files. Volume 104, File 12: "Musicians, Canadian Federation of Local 10. Montreal, Quebec. 1935-1940." (Part 1)

MG 28-I103, Series: Defunct local union files. Volume 104, File 13: "Musicians, Canadian Federation of Local 10. Montreal, Quebec. 1935-1940." (Part 2)

MG 28-I103, Series: Defunct local union files. Volume 104, File 14: "Musicians, Canadian Federation of Local 11. Montreal, Quebec. 1935-1944."

See: http://www.collectionscanada.gc.ca/

ACKNOWLEDGMENTS
Second Edition

I am grateful for further assistance in bringing out this second edition. Thanks to Andrew Homzy and Mark Miller, for invaluable feedback. To Simon Dardick, of Véhicule Press, for kind permission to reproduce the original cover and title page. To Nathalie Hodgson, Concordia University Archives, and Ilene McKenna, Library and Archives Canada, for providing updated cataloguing information. To Grace Gilmore and Charles Cutler, Stephen Orlov and Karen Kaderavek, Rod McNabb and Vlasta Ulovec, and Bill Harris, for hospitality. To Irving Lustigman, for technical assistance. And special thanks to Ken Edwards, of Reality Street, for generous help with print production and guidance through digital realms.

Also by John Gilmore

Nonfiction

Who's Who of Jazz in Montreal:
Ragtime to 1970

Fiction

Head of a Man